CONSOLIDATED BROADCASTING AND MEDIA LEGISLATION 1923–2005

AUSTRALIA
Law Book Co. Ltd
Sydney

CANADA AND THE USA
Carswell
Toronto

NEW ZEALAND
Brookers
Wellington

SINGAPORE AND MALAYSIA
Sweet and Maxwell
Singapore and Kuala Lumpur

Consolidated Broadcasting and Media Legislation 1923–2005

Kevin Gleeson

DUBLIN
THOMSON ROUND HALL
2005

Published in 2005 by
Thomson Round Hall
43 Fitzwilliam Place
Dublin 2
Ireland

Typeset by
Thomson Round Hall, Dublin

Printed by
MPG Books, Cornwall

ISBN 1-85800-422-5

A catalogue reference for this book is available from the British Library.

TABLE OF CONTENTS

INTRODUCTION

This publication is a consolidation of Irish legislation affecting radio, television and film. The Principal Acts associated with this consolidation are the Wireless Telegraphy Act 1926, the Broadcasting Authority Act 1960 and a variety of film-related legislation.

Irish legislation is often published in a manner that can make it difficult to interpret and determine the state of legislation in force at a particular moment in time. For certain bodies of legislation, this may involve gathering together the Principal Act and all subsequent legislation that affects the Principal Act and applying any amendments or repeals. This can be a complex and confusing activity and generally requires a significant amount of time and patience. In this publication, the laborious chore of applying all amendments and repeals to the Principal Acts has been completed, giving an up-to-date view of Irish broadcasting and media legislation in force as of the date of publication.

Section 1—Wireless Telegraphy Acts 1926–1988

The Principal Act is the Wireless Telegraphy Act 1926. Other Wireless Telegraphy-related Acts have been included as separate chapters.

Section 1 of this publication consolidates the five Wireless Telegraphy Acts, which are:

- Wireless Telegraphy Act 1926 (No. 45 of 1926).
- Wireless Telegraphy Act 1956 (No. 4 of 1956).
- Broadcasting (Offences) Act 1968 (No. 35 of 1968).
- Wireless Telegraphy Act 1972 (No. 5 of 1972).
- Broadcasting and Wireless Telegraphy Act 1988 (No. 19 of 1988).

There were four Wireless Telegraphy Acts enacted between 1926 and 1988, none of which have been repealed. The provisions of the Wireless Telegraphy Act 1956 have been fully incorporated into the text of the Principal Act.

The long title to the Wireless Telegraphy Act 1926 (the Principal Act) states:

> "AN ACT TO MAKE PROVISION FOR THE REGULATION AND CONTROL OF WIRELESS TELEGRAPHY ON LAND, AT SEA, AND IN THE AIR, AND FOR THE REGULATION AND CONTROL OF CERTAIN CLASSES OF VISUAL AND SOUND SIGNALLING STATIONS, AND FOR THE ESTABLISHMENT AND MAINTENANCE OF STATE BROADCASTING STATIONS, AND TO PROVIDE FOR OTHER MATTERS RELATING TO WIRELESS TELEGRAPHY, SIGNALLING, AND BROADCASTING RESPECTIVELY."

This Act came into operation on its passing on December 24, 1926.

Section 2—Broadcasting Authority Acts 1960–2003

Section 2 of this publication consolidates the 17 Broadcasting Acts enacted between 1960 and 2003, none of which have been repealed. The Principal Act in this section is the Broadcasting Authority Act 1960. The provisions of four Acts (the Broadcasting Authority (Amendment) Acts 1964, 1971, 1973 and 1974) have been fully incorporated in the text of the Principal Act.

- Broadcasting Authority Act 1960.
- Broadcasting Authority (Amendment) Act 1964.
- Broadcasting Authority (Amendment) Act 1966.
- Broadcasting Authority (Amendment) Act 1971.
- Broadcasting Authority (Amendment) Act 1973.
- Broadcasting Authority (Amendment) Act 1974.
- Broadcasting Authority (Amendment) Act 1976.
- Broadcasting Authority (Amendment) Act 1979.
- Radio and Television Act 1988.
- Broadcasting Act 1990.
- Broadcasting Authority (Amendment) Act 1993.
- Referendum Act 1998.
- Broadcasting (Major Events Television Coverage) Act 1999.
- Broadcasting Act 2001.
- Communications Regulation Act 2002.
- Broadcasting (Major Events Television Coverage) (Amendment) Act 2003.
- Broadcasting (Funding) Act 2003.

The long title to the Broadcasting Authority Act 1960 (the Principal Act) states:

> "AN ACT TO ENABLE AN AUTHORITY TO BE ESTABLISHED FOR THE PURPOSE OF PROVIDING A NATIONAL TELEVISION AND SOUND BROADCASTING SERVICE, TO AMEND AND EXTEND THE WIRELESS TELEGRAPHY ACTS, 1926 AND 1956, AND TO PROVIDE FOR MATTERS CONNECTED WITH THE MATTERS AFORESAID."

This Act came into operation on its passing on April 12, 1960.

Section 3—Irish film and media legislation

Section 3 presents a variety of Irish media legislation which primarily affects film censorship in the State, the Irish Film Board and video recordings. The Acts in this section include:

- Censorship of Films Act 1923.
- Censorship of Films (Amendment) Act 1925.
- Censorship of Films (Amendment) Act 1930.
- Censorship of Films (Amendment) Act 1970.
- Censorship of Films (Amendment) Act 1992.

- Irish Film Board Act 1980.
- Irish Film Board (Amendment) Act 1993.
- Irish Film Board (Amendment) Act 1997.
- Irish Film Board (Amendment) Act 2000.
- National Film Studios of Ireland Limited Act 1980.
- Video Recordings Act 1989.

Amending Acts are presented in separate chapters for each of the Acts. Where there is an amendment or a repeal to another Act, these changes are applied to the appropriate legislation and an amendment history note is inserted after the section affected noting that the amendment or repeal has been made. Notes are also made in the amending Act, so there is always a clear link between the amended section and the amending legislation.

Spent, repealed and surplus provisions

The amending provisions are removed from the text of the amending Acts and applied to the amended Act. This means that some of the amending Acts are shortened to a considerable extent. For example, the Broadcasting Authority (Amendment) Act 1976 originally contained 18 sections but is now reduced to two.

To avoid confusion, where a section is omitted, a note containing abbreviated details is included to indicate the reason, *e.g.* because it has been repealed or it is itself a repealing or an amending provision. If applicable, a note for a saving provision or repeal may also appear as appropriate.

Notes are provided throughout the text to explain or clarify certain affecting provisions. They are also used to highlight important commencement provisions and to provide information.

Kevin Gleeson

Table of Relevant Statutory Instruments

Regulations in regard to Wireless Receiving Licences 1927 (S.I. No.1 of 1927)
Broadcasting (Advisory Committee) Order 1927 (S.I. No.31 of 1927)
Regulations in regard to Wireless Receiving Licences (No.2) 1927 (S.I. No.54 of 1927)
Wireless Receiving Licences Regulations 1927 to 1934 (S.I. No.249 of 1934)
Wireless (Receiving Licences) Regulations 1937 (S.I. No.261 of 1937)
Wireless Telegraphy (Experimenter's Licence) Regulations 1937 (S.I. No.330 of 1937)
Wireless (Receiving Licences) (Amendment) (No. 1) Regulations 1940 (S.I. No.117 of 1940)
Wireless (Receiving Licences) (Amendment) (No. 2) Regulations 1949 (S.I. No.282 of 1949)
Wireless Telegraphy (Business Radio Licence) Regulations 1949 (S.I. No.320 of 1949)
Wireless Telegraphy (Experimenter's Licence) (Amendment) (No. 1) Regulations 1951 (S.I. No.232 of 1951)
Wireless (Receiving Licences) (Amendment) (No. 3) Regulations 1953 (S.I. No.55 of 1953)
Wireless Telegraphy (Business Radio Licence) Regulations 1956 (S.I. No.2 of 1956)
Wireless Telegraphy (Business Radio Licence) Regulations 1957 (S.I. No.181 of 1957)
Wireless (Receiving Licences) (Amendment) Regulations 1961 (S.I. No.174 of 1961)
Wireless Telegraphy (Control of Interference from Electric Motors) Regulations 1963 (S.I. No.108 of 1963)
Wireless Telegraphy (Control of Interference from Ignition Apparatus) Regulations 1963 (S.I. No.223 of 1963)
Wireless Telegraphy Act, 1926 (Section 3) (Exemption of Sound Broadcasting Receivers) Order 1972 (S.I. No.211 of 1972)
Wireless Telegraphy Act, 1972 (Period for the Purpose of Section 4) Order 1973 (S.I. No.34 of 1973)
Wireless Telegraphy Act, 1972 (Appointed Day) Order 1973 (S.I. No.35 of 1973)
Wireless Telegraphy Act, 1972. (Form of notice for the Purpose of Section 2) Regulations 1973 (S.I. No.36 of 1973)
Wireless Telegraphy (Wired Broadcast Relay Licence) Regulations 1974 (S.I. No.67 of 1974)
Wireless Telegraphy Act, 1926 (Section 3) (Exemption of Certain Wired Broadcast relay Stations) Order 1976 (S.I. No.200 of 1976)
Wireless Telegraphy (Business Radio Licence (Amendment) Regulations 1980 (S.I. No.193 of 1980)
Wireless Telegraphy (Experimenter's Licence)(Amendment) Regulations 1980 (S.I. No.194 of 1980)
Wireless Telegraphy (Business Radio Licence) (Amendment) Regulations 1981 (S.I. No.114 of 1981)
Wireless Telegraphy (Experimenter's Licence) (Amendment) Regulations 1981 (S.I. No.115 of 1981)

Wireless Telegraphy (Control of Sale, Letting on hire or Manufacture, and Importation of Radio Transceivers) Order 1981 (S.I. No.400 of 1981)

Wireless Telegraphy (Personal Radio Licence) Regulations 1982 (S.I. No.8 of 1982)

Wireless Telegraphy (Business Radio Licence) (Amendment) Regulations 1982 (S.I. No.73 of 1982)

Wireless Telegraphy (Experimenter's Licence) (Amendment) Regulations 1982 (S.I. No.74 of 1982)

Customs-Free Airport (Extensions of Law) (No. 2) Regulation 1983 (S.I. No.48 of 1983)

Wireless Telegraphy (Experimenter's Licence) (Amendment) Regulations 1983 (S.I. No.87 of 1983)

Wireless Telegraphy (Business Radio Licence) (Amendment) Regulations 1983 (S.I. No.88 of 1983)

Wireless Telegraphy (Business Radio Licence) (Amendment) Regulations 1985 (S.I. No.84 of 1985)

Wireless Telegraphy (Experimenter's Licence) (Amendment) Regulations 1985 (S.I. No.85 of 1985)

Wireless Telegraphy (Experimenter's Licence) (Amendment) Regulations 1986 (S.I. No.74 of 1986)

Wireless Telegraphy (Business Radio Licence) (Amendment) Regulations 1986 (S.I. No.75 of 1986)

Wireless Telegraphy (Wired Broadcast Relay Licence) (Amendment) Regulations 1988 (S.I. No.82 of 1988)

Wireless Telegraphy (Community Repeater Licence) Regulations 1988 (S.I. No.83 of 1988)

Wireless Telegraphy (Television Programme ReTransmission) Regulations 1989 (S.I. No.39 of 1989)

Wireless Telegraphy (Television Programme Retransmission and Relay) Regulations 1991 (S.I. No.252 of 1991)

Wireless Telegraphy (Business Radio Licence) (Amendment) Regulations 1992 (S.I. No.114 of 1992)

Wireless Telegraphy (Experimenter's Licence) (Amendment) Regulations 1992 (S.I. No.132 of 1992)

Wireless Telegraphy Act, 1926. Wireless Telegraphy (Radio Link Licence) Regulations 1992 (S.I. No.319 of 1992)

Broadcasting (Transfer of Departmental Administration and Ministerial Functions) Order 1993 (S.I. No.13 of 1993)

European Communities (Satellite Telecommunications Services) Regulations 1997 (S.I. No.372 of 1997)

Wireless Telegraphy Act, 1926 (Section 3) (Exemption of Mobile Telephones) Order 1997 (S.I. No.409 of 1997)

Wireless Telegraphy Act, 1926 (Section 3) (Exemption of Cordless Telephones) Order 1997 (S.I. No.410 of 1997)

Wireless Telegraphy Act, 1926 (Section 3) (Exemption of Short Range Business Radios) Order 1998 (S.I. No.93 of 1998)

European Communities (Telecommunications Licences) Regulations (S.I. No.96 of 1998)

Wireless Telegraphy Act, 1926 (Section 3) (Exemption of Satellite Earth Stations for Satellite Personnal Communication Services (S-PCS)) Order 1998 (S.I. No.214 of 1998)

Wireless Telegraphy Act, 1926 (Section 3) (Exemption of Citizens Band (CB) Radios) Order, 1998 (S.I. No.436 of 1998)

Wireless Telegraphy (Programme Services Distribution) Regulations 1999 (S.I. No.73 of 1999)

Wireless Telegraphy Act, 1926 (Section 3) (Exemption of INMARSAT-D Terminals For Land Mobile Applications) Order 1999 (S.I. No.100 of 1999)

Wireless Telegraphy Act, 1926 (Section 3) (Exemption of INMARSAT-C Terminals For Land Mobile Applications) Order 1999 (S.I. No.101 of 1999)

Wireless Telegraphy Act, 1926 (Section 3) (Exemption of INMARSAT-M Terminals For Land Mobile Applications) Order 1999 (S.I. No.102 of 1999)

Wireless Telegraphy Act, 1926 (Section 3) (Exemption of Omnitracs Terminals For The Euteltracs System) Order 1999 (S.I. No.103 of 1999)

Wireless Telegraphy Act, 1926 (Section 3) (Exemption of (I) Arcanet Suitcase Terminals) Order 1999 (S.I. No.104 of 1999)

Wireless Telegraphy Act, 1926 (Section 3) (Exemption of EMS-PRODAT Terminals For Land Mobile Applications) Order, 1999 (S.I. No.105 of 1999)

Wireless Telegraphy Act, 1926 (Section 3) (Exemption of EMS-MSSAT Terminals For Land Mobile Applications) Order 1999 (S.I. No.106 of 1999)

Wireless Telegraphy Act, 1926 (Section 3) (Exemption of DCS 1800 Mobile Terminals) Order 1999 (S.I. No.107 of 1999)

Wireless Telegraphy Act, 1926 (Section 3) (Exemption of Ermes Paging Receivers) Order 1999 (S.I. No.108 of 1999)

Wireless Telegraphy Act, 1926 (Section 3) (Exemption of Inmarsat Mini-M Terminals For Land Mobile Applications) Order 1999 (S.I. No.109 of 1999)

Wireless Telegraphy Act, 1926 (Section 3) (Exemption of (II) Arcanet Suitcase Terminals) Order 1999 (S.I. No.110 of 1999)

Wireless Telegraphy (Fixed Wireless Point To Multi-Point Access Licence) Regulations 1999 (S.I. No.287 of 1999)

Wireless Telegraphy (Carrigaline UHF Television Programme Retransmission) Regulations 1999 (S.I. No.347 of 1999)

Wireless Telegraphy (UHF Television Programme Retransmission) Regulations 1999 (S.I. No.348 of 1999)

Wireless Telegraphy (GSM and TACS Mobile Telephony Licence) Regulations 1999 (S.I. No.442 of 1999)

Wireless Telegraphy Act, 1926 (Section 3) (Exemption of Mobile Satellite Earth Stations for Satellite Personal Communication Systems operating in bands below 1 GHz (S-PCS<1 GHz) Order 2000 (S.I. No.173 of 2000)

Wireless Telegraphy (Fixed Satellite Earth Stations) Regulations 2000. (S.I. No.261 of 2000)

Wireless Telegraphy Act, 1926 (Section 3) (Exemption of Certain Fixed Satellite Receiving Earth Stations) Order, 2000 (S.I. No.273 of 2000)

Wireless Telegraphy (Teleport Facility) Regulations 2001 (S.I. No.18 of 2001)
Wireless Telegraphy (CarrigalineUHF Television Programme Retransmission) (Amendment) Regulations 2001 (S.I. No.189 of 2001)
Wireless Telegraphy (UHF Television Programme Retransmission) (Amendment) Regulations 2001 (S.I. No.190 of 2001)
European Communities (Radio Equipment and Telecommunications Terminal Equipment) Regulations 2001 (S.I. No.240 of 2001)
Wireless Telegraphy Act 1926 (Section 3) (Exemption of Certain Classes of Land Mobile Earth Stations) Order 2001 (S.I. No.398 of 2001)
Wireless Telegraphy (Third Generation and GSM Mobile Telephony Licence) Regulations 2002 (S.I. No.345 of 2002)
Wireless Telegraphy Act, 1926 (Section 3) (Exemption of Short Range Devices) Order 2002 (S.I. No.405 of 2002)
Wireless Telegraphy (Mobile Radio Systems) Regulations 2002 (S.I. No.435 of 2002)
Wireless Telegraphy (Experimenter's Licence) Regulations, 2002 (S.I. No.450 of 2002)
Wireless Telegraphy (Fixed Wireless Point to Multi-Point Access Licence) (Amendment) Regulations 2002 (S.I. No.467 of 2002)
Communications Regulation Act 2002 (Establishment Day) Order 2002 (S.I. No.510 of 2002)
Telecommunications (Miscellaneous Provisions) Act, 1996 (Section 6) Postal Levy No. 3 Order 2002 (S.I. No.549 of 2002)
Telecommunications Tariff Regulation Order 2003 (S.I. No.31 of 2003)
Wireless Telegraphy (Fixed Wireless Access Local Area Licence) Regulations 2003 (S.I. No.79 of 2003)
Wireless Telegraphy Act, 1926 (Section 3) (Exemption of Mobile Telephones) (Amendment) Order (S.I. No.158 of 2003)
Wireless Telegraphy (Fixed Wireless Point to Multi-point Access Licence) (Amendment) (No.2) Regulations (2003 S.I. No.338 of 2003)
Wireless Telegraphy (GSM Mobile Telephony Licence) (Amendment) Regulations, 2003 (S.I. No.339 of 2003)
Wireless Telegraphy (Third Generation and GSM Mobile Telephony Licence) (Amendment) Regulations 2003 (S.I. No.340 of 2003)
Communications Regulation Act 2002 (Section 30) Levy Order 2003 (S.I. No.346 of 2003)
Communications Regulation Act, 2002 (Section 30) (Amendment) Levy Order 2003 (S.I. No.392 of 2003)
Wireless Telegraphy Act, 1926 (Section 3) (Exemption of Certain Classes of Fixed Satellite Earth Stations) Order 2003 (S.I. No.505 of 2003)
Wireless Telegraphy (Carrigaline UHF Television Programme Retransmission) (Amendment) Regulations 2003 (S.I. No.506 of 2003)
Wireless Telegraphy (UHF Television Programme Retransmission)(Amendment) Regulations 2003 (S.I.No.507 of 2003)
Wireless Telegraphy (Multipoint Microwave Distribution System) Regultions 2003 (S.I. No. 529 of 2003

SECTION 1

WIRELESS TELEGRAPHY ACT 1926

(No. 45 of 1926)

ARRANGEMENT OF SECTIONS

AN ACT TO MAKE PROVISION FOR THE REGULATION AND CONTROL OF WIRELESS TELEGRAPHY ON LAND, AT SEA, AND IN THE AIR, AND FOR THE REGULATION AND CONTROL OF CERTAIN CLASSES OF VISUAL AND SOUND SIGNALLING STATIONS, AND FOR THE ESTABLISHMENT AND MAINTENANCE OF STATE BROADCASTING STATIONS, AND TO PROVIDE FOR OTHER MATTERS RELATING TO WIRELESS TELEGRAPHY, SIGNALLING, AND BROADCASTING RESPECTIVELY.

[24TH DECEMBER, 1926.]

BE IT ENACTED BY THE OIREACHTAS OF SAORSTÁT EIREANN AS FOLLOWS:—

PRELIMINARY

Short title

1.—This Act may be cited as the Wireless Telegraphy Act, 1926.

Definitions

2.—In this Act—

the expression "the Minister" means the Minister for Posts and Telegraphs;

the expression ['wireless telegraphy" means the emitting and receiving, or emitting only or receiving only, over paths which are not provided by any material substance constructed or arranged for that purpose, of electric, magnetic or electro-magnetic energy] of a frequency not exceeding 3 million megahertz, whether or not such energy serves the conveying (whether they are actually received or not) of communications, sounds, signs, visual images or signals, or the actuation or control of machinery or apparatus.]

the expression ['apparatus for wireless telegraphy' means apparatus capable of emitting and receiving, or emitting only or receiving only, over paths which are not provided by any material substance constructed or arranged for that purpose, electric, magnetic or electro-magnetic energy, of a frequency not exceeding 3 million megahertz, whether or not such energy serves the conveying (whether they are actually received or not) of communications, sounds, signs, visual images or signals, or the actuation or control of machinery or apparatus, and includes any part of such apparatus, or any article capable of being used as part of such apparatus, and also includes any other apparatus which is associated with, or electrically coupled to, apparatus capable of so emitting such energy]

the word ['broadcast' means the transmission, relaying or distributing by wireless telegraphy of communications, sounds, signs, visual images or signals, intended for direct reception by the general public whether such communications, sounds, signs, visual images or signals are actually received or not;]

the expression "broadcasting station" means a building or other place fitted and equipped for broadcasting [or for repeating broadcasting];

the expression "broadcast matter" means and includes any lectures, speeches, news, reports, advertisements, recitations, dramatic entertainments, and other spoken words and any music (whether vocal or instrumental) and other sounds approved by the Minister as suitable for being broadcasted from a broadcasting station maintained under this Act [or the Broadcasting Authority Act, 1960, and also includes images];

the expression "signalling station" means any fixed or not easily movable apparatus for signalling by means of visible signals or for signalling by means of audible signals.

[For the purposes of this Act, any apparatus which—

(a) is electrically coupled to wireless telegraphy apparatus, and

(b) is used in receiving and conveying messages, sounds or visual images sent by wireless telegraphy, shall be regarded as being wireless telegraphy apparatus.]

Amendment history

The expression for broadcasting station was amended by s.34(b) and the expression for broadcasting matter amended by s.34(c) of the Broadcasting Authority Act 1960. The definition of "apparatus for wireless telegraphy" and "wireless telegraphy" was amended by s.2 of the Broadcasting and Wireless Telegraphy Act 1988, which came into operation on December 31, 1988. The definition of "broadcast" was amended by s.19 of the Radio and Television Act 1988. The definitions of "broadcasting station" and "broadcasting matter" were amended by s.34 of the Broadcasting Authority Act 1960.

PART I

WIRELESS TELEGRAPHY AND SIGNALLING

Restrictions on possession of wireless telegraphy apparatus

3.—(1) Subject to the exceptions hereinafter mentioned, no person shall keep or have in his possession anywhere in Saorstát Eireann or in any ship or aircraft to which this section applies any apparatus for wireless telegraphy save in so far as such keeping or possession is authorised by a licence granted under this Act and for the time being in force.

(2) No person having possession of apparatus for wireless telegraphy under a licence granted under this Act shall [work or use] such apparatus otherwise than in accordance with the terms and conditions subject to which such licence is [by virtue of this Act deemed to have been] granted.

[(3)(a) Every person who keeps, has in his possession, installs, maintains, works or uses any apparatus in contravention of this section shall be guilty of an offence and shall be liable—

(i) in case the apparatus in respect of which the offence was committed is a television set, on summary conviction thereof—

(I) in the case of a first such offence, to a fine not exceeding £500,

(II) in the case of a second or subsequent such offence, to a fine not exceeding £1,000,

(ii) in case the apparatus in respect of which the offence was committed is not a television set—

(I) on summary conviction to a fine not exceeding £1,000,

(II) on conviction on indictment to a fine not exceeding £20,000.

(b) In this subsection 'television set' has the meaning assigned to it by section 1 (1) of the Wireless Telegraphy Act, 1972, as amended by section 2 (2) of the Broadcasting and Wireless Telegraphy Act, 1988.]

(3A)(a) Where a person is convicted on indictment of an offence under this section, the interest of the person, whether as owner or otherwise, in the following apparatus shall stand forfeited as a statutory consequence of conviction:

(i) in case the apparatus in respect of which the offence was committed is a wired broadcast relay station, the part or parts thereof comprised in the station between the station's initial point of reception of television programmes, sound programmes or television programmes and sound programmes, as the case may be, and the point at which such programmes are fed into the station's trunk cable for conveyance by wire,

(ii) in case the apparatus in respect of which the offence was committed is not a wired broadcast relay station, the apparatus in respect of which the offence was committed.

(b) In this subsection—

'service point' means a point in a premises or part of a premises which is connected by wire to a wired broadcast relay station and to which television programmes, sound programmes or both television programmes and sound programmes are conveyed by the wire for reception on wireless telegraphy apparatus in the possession of the occupier of the premises or part;

'wired broadcast relay station' means wireless telegraphy apparatus capable of receiving television programmes, sound programmes or both television programmes and sound programmes by means of wireless telegraphy and then conveying the programmes by wire for reception on wireless telegraphy apparatus, and includes any aerials and the wires connected to any service point served by such station.

(3B) Where anything is, as a statutory consequence of conviction, forfeited under this section, the Minister may direct that such thing shall be destroyed or be sold or otherwise disposed of in such manner as he thinks fit.

(3C) Where the Minister, in pursuance of subsection (3B) of this section, directs a thing to be sold, the net proceeds of the sale shall be paid into or disposed of for the benefit of the Exchequer in such manner as the Minister for Finance shall direct.";

(4) Apparatus for wireless telegraphy affixed to a ship to which this section applies or kept in any such ship for the use or general purposes of the ship in contravention of this section shall, for the purposes of a prosecution under this section, be deemed to be kept by and in the possession of the master of such ship and also to be kept by and

in the possession of the owner of such ship.

(5) Subject to the exceptions hereinafter mentioned this section applies to—

(a) every ship registered in Saorstát Eireann, and

(b) every unregistered ship or other vessel which is usually kept in or which frequents the waters (whether inland or territorial) of Saorstát Eireann, and

(c) every ship or vessel not coming within either of the foregoing paragraphs which is for the time being in the waters (whether inland or territorial) of Saorstát Eireann and in respect of which no licence then in force for the possession or working of apparatus for wireless telegraphy has been granted in any other country or state, and

(d) every aircraft owned by a person who, in the case of an individual, has his usual place of residence in Saorstát Eireann or, in the case of an association, company, or other body (whether corporate or incorporate), has its principal office in Saorstát Eireann, and

(e) every aircraft not coming within the foregoing paragraph which is for the time being in or over Saorstát Eireann or the waters thereof and in respect of which no licence then in force for the possession or working of apparatus for wireless telegraphy has been granted in any other country or state.

[(6) This section shall not apply to apparatus for wireless telegraphy which is—

(a) of a class or description for the time being declared by an order of the Minister (which may be revoked or amended by a further order) to be a class or description of apparatus for wireless telegraphy to which this section is not to apply,

(b) kept by or in the possession of the Minister for Defence for the purposes of the Defence Forces, or

(c) in any ship of war belonging to the State or any other country or state.]

(7) For the purposes of this section the expression "unregistered ship or other vessel" means a ship or other vessel which is not registered under the laws for the time being in force in relation to the registration of ships in Saorstát Eireann or any other country or state.

[3A.—(1) The Minister may by order fix a day to be the appointed day for the purposes of this section, and the day so fixed is in this section subsequently referred to as the appointed day.

(2) On and after the appointed day a person shall not provide or distribute, otherwise than pursuant to and in accordance with a licence granted by the Minister under this section, for ultimate reception, through the agency of electric, magnetic, electro-magnetic, electrochemical or electro-mechanical energy, on,

(a) apparatus for wireless telegraphy for receiving only sound and visual images, or

(b) apparatus for wireless telegraphy for receiving only sound, any local programme matter.

(3) A person who provides or distributes local programme matter contrary to

subsection (2) of this section shall be guilty of an offence.

(4) Where local programme matter is distributed or provided contrary to subsection (2) of this section, the person who directed or produced, or who was in overall control or otherwise in charge of, the local programme matter shall be guilty of an offence.

(5) A person who is guilty of an offence under this section shall be liable on summary conviction to a fine not exceeding one hundred pounds.

(6) In this section—

'local programme matter' means any programme matter which—

(a) serves either by means of visual images with or without sounds, or only by means of sounds to inform persons of anything or to educate or entertain them, and

(b) is conveyed by wire from or through a station to service points, and

(c) is not transmitted, relayed or distributed solely by wireless telegraphy;

'service points' means points in a premises or part of a premises which are connected by wire to a station and to which programme matter is conveyed by the wire for reception on wireless telegraphy apparatus in the possession of the occupier of the premises or part;

'station' means any apparatus (including wireless telegraphy apparatus) used to relay programme matter to service points.]

Amendment History:

Subsection 3(2) were amended and subss.3(3) and 3(6) replaced by s.11 of the Wireless Telegraphy Act 1972. Section 3A is inserted by s.17 of the Broadcasting Authority (Amendment) Act 1976. Subsection 3 substituted by s.12 of the Broadcasting and Wireless Telegraphy Act 1988, which came into operation on December 31, 1988. Transfer of function from the Minister to the Director by s.4 of the Telecommunications (Miscellaneous Provisions) Act 1996 (No. 34 of 1996).

Note

No. 34 of 1996 transfers the function described in Pt I of the Second Sched. from the Minister to the Director of ODTR, now ComReg.

Restrictions on maintenance of signalling stations

4.—(1) No person shall maintain a signalling station which is intended to be used or is capable of being used for the purpose of communication with ships at sea save in so far as such maintenance is authorised by a licence granted under this Act and for the time being in force.

(2) No person shall work or use any such signalling station as aforesaid the maintenance of which is not authorised by a licence granted under this Act and for the time being in force nor shall any person work or use any such signalling station in any manner contrary to the licence granted under this Act in respect thereof.

(3) Every person who maintains, works, or uses any such signalling station as aforesaid in contravention of this section shall be guilty of an offence under this section and shall be liable on summary conviction thereof to a fine not exceeding ten pounds together with, in the case of a continuing offence, a further fine not exceeding one pound for every day during which the offence continues.

(4) Nothing in this section shall apply to any signalling station maintained under Lloyd's Signal Station Act, 1888 or maintained by or under the control of the Minister for Industry and Commerce or the Commissioners of Irish Lights or any person having by law authority over local lighthouses, buoys, and beacons.

Grant of licences

5.—(1) The Minister may, subject to the provisions of this Act and on payment of the prescribed fee (if any) grant to any person a licence to keep and have possession of apparatus for wireless telegraphy in any specified place in Saorstát Eireann or to keep and have possession of apparatus for wireless telegraphy in any specified ship or other vessel or aircraft or to maintain a signalling station at any place in Saorstát Eireann.

[(1A) For the purposes of this Act and any regulations under section 6 of this Act, a vehicle shall itself be deemed to be a place separate and distinct from the premises in which such vehicle is ordinarily kept, and the word 'place' and the expression 'specified place' shall in this Act and in any such regulations be construed accordingly.]

[(1B) The Minister may by order (which he may at any time revoke by a further order) declare that the grant of licences under this Act in respect of apparatus for receiving only, and the collection on behalf of the Minister of fees on such grants, shall be carried out by Radio Éireann and, so long as any such order remains in force,—

(i) such grant and collection shall, notwithstanding subsection (1) of this section, be carried out by Radio Éireann and not otherwise,

(ii) Radio Éireann shall have all powers appropriate for enforcing subsection (1) of section 3 of this Act in relation to apparatus for receiving only,

(iii) sections 7 and 8 of this Act shall have effect in relation to apparatus for receiving only as if each reference therein to the Minister included a reference to Radio Éireann, and

(iv) prosecutions under subsection (3) of section 3 of this Act in relation to apparatus for receiving only, and prosecutions under subsection (3) of section 7 of this Act in relation to a notice served by Radio Éireann, shall, notwithstanding section 13 of this Act, be prosecuted by the Minister or Radio Éireann and not otherwise.]

Amendment history

Section 1A was inserted by s.2 of the Wireless Telegraphy Act 1956, which came into force on February 21, 1956. Section 3 of the Act of 1956 is inserted after the new s.1A. The insertion of s.1A is deemed to have come into operation immediately after the commencement of the Wireless Telegraphy Act 1926. Subsection (1B) inserted by s.34 and Sched.3, Pt 1 of the Broadcasting Authority Act 1960. Section 7 of the Broadcasting Authority (Amendment) Act 1966 renamed subs.(1A) as (1B). Section 3 of the Wireless Telegraphy Act 1956 specifies that the new section 1A came into operation immediately after the commencement of the Principal Act and accordingly—

(a) any regulations made before the passing of this Act and framed as regulations under section 6 of the Principal Act or subsection (1) of that section,

(b) any licences issued before the passing of this Act and framed as licences issued subject to any such regulations, and

(c) the collection and payment of any fees paid in respect of any such licences,

shall be, and shall be deemed always to have been, as valid for all purposes as if section 2 (note: i.e. the inserted text) of this Act had come into operation immediately after the commencement of The Principal Act.]

Every licence granted under this Act shall be in such form, continue in force for such period, and be subject to such conditions and restrictions (including conditions as to suspension and revocation) as shall be prescribed in regard thereto by regulations made by the Minister under this Act.

Regulations in regard to licences

6.—(1) The Minister may by order make regulations prescribing in relation to all licences granted under this Act or any particular class or classes of such licences all or any of the matters following that is to say:—

(a) the form of such licences,

(b) the period during which such licences continue in force,

(c) the manner in which, the terms on which, and the period or periods for which such licences may be renewed,

(d) the circumstances and manner in which such licences may be suspended or revoked by the Minister,

(e) the terms and conditions to be observed by the holders of such licences and subject to which such licences are deemed to be granted,

(f) the fees to be paid on the grant or renewal of such licences and the time and manner at and in which such fees are to be paid,

(g) any other matter relating to such licences in respect of which it shall appear to the Minister to be necessary or desirable to make provision by regulations made under this section.

(2) Regulations made under this section may authorise and provide for the granting of a licence under this Act subject to special terms, conditions, and restrictions to any person who satisfies the Minister that he requires the licence solely for the purpose of conducting experiments in wireless telegraphy.

"(2A) Where it appears to be expedient to the Minister he may by instrument in writing recognise as valid a licence issued by another country in respect of a class or classes of apparatus for wireless telegraphy subject to such conditions or restrictions as to the use of such apparatus as the Minister sees fit."

(3) (*Note: repealed with savings*) No regulation shall be made under this section in relation to fees without the previous consent of the Minister for Finance.

(Note: repealed except as regards licences in respect of television sets).

(4) Every regulation made under this section shall be laid before each House of the Oireachtas as soon as may be after it is made and if either such House shall, within twenty-one days on which either such House has sat next after the regulation was laid before such Houses, pass a resolution annulling such regulation, such regulation shall be annulled accordingly but without prejudice to the validity of anything previously done under such regulation.

Amendment History

Subsection 2A inserted by s.17 of the Broadcasting Act 1990. Subsection 6(3) repealed with savings by s.14 of the Telecommunications (Miscellaneous Provisions) Act 1996. This section is amended by s.13 of the Broadcasting and Wireless Telegraphy Act 1988, which came into operation on December 31, 1988, and which states that any sum due in respect of a fee prescribed under s.6 of the Act of 1926 shall be recoverable by the Minister as a simple contract debt in any court of competent jurisdiction. This section is also amended by s.20 of the Broadcasting and Wireless Telegraphy Act 1988, which came into operation on December 31, 1988, and which states that the Minister may by regulations prescribe the fee to be paid in respect of applications for licences or any class of licence under s.5 of the Act of 1926, subject to such exceptions as he may prescribe, and subss.(3) and (4) of s.6 of that Act shall apply to any such regulation. Section 4(8) of Telecommunications (Miscellaneous Provisions) Act 1996 states that Regulations shall not be made by the Director under s.6 of the Wireless Telegraphy Act 1926, other than with the consent of the Minister.

Obligation to furnish certain information

7.—(1) The Minister may, if and whenever he thinks proper so to do, cause a special notice in writing (accompanied by or having annexed thereto a form of declaration) to be served by registered post on any person requiring such person within fourteen days after the service of the notice on him to state on the said form of declaration such one or more of the matters hereinafter mentioned as shall be specified in the notice and to sign and otherwise complete such declaration and to give the same or send the same by post to a specified officer of the Minister.

(2) The matters which a person may be required under this section to state in a declaration are—

(a) whether he does or does not keep or has or has not in his possession any apparatus for wireless telegraphy,

(b) If he keeps or has in his possession any such apparatus, the nature of such apparatus, the name and address of the person by whom such apparatus was sold, let, hired or otherwise supplied to him and the place at which he keeps or has the same.

(c) whether he has or has not a licence granted under this Act and then in force,

(d) if he has such a licence, the number, date, and office of issue of such licence,

(e) any other matter relating to wireless telegraphy,

[(f) any matter which the Minister may require for the purpose of clarifying particulars recorded or notified by the person in purported compliance with section 2 of the Wireless Telegraphy Act, 1972, or an order under section 5 of that Act.]

(3) Every person on whom a special notice is duly served under this section shall within the time aforesaid duly and correctly complete in accordance with such notice and this section the form of declaration accompanying or annexed to such notice and give or send such declaration to the officer named in that behalf in such notice, and if any such person shall fail or neglect so to complete and give or send such declaration or shall make in such declaration any statement which is to his knowledge false or misleading he shall be guilty of an offence under this section and shall be liable on summary conviction thereof to a penalty not exceeding [two hundred and fifty pounds].

Amendment history

Section 7(2f) inserted by s.12 of the Wireless Telegraphy Act 1972. Amended by ss.12 and 17 of the Broadcasting and Wireless Telegraphy Act 1988, which came into operation on December 31, 1988. Section 20 of the Broadcasting Authority (Amendment) Act 1976 states that a person may be required under section 7 of the Act of 1926 to state in a declaration, (a) whether he does or does not keep or has or has not in his possession regulated apparatus, (b) if he keeps or has in his possession any such apparatus, the nature of such apparatus and the place at which he keeps or has the same.

Issue of search warrants

8.—(1) A Justice of the District Court may, upon the information on oath of an officer of the Minister or of a member of the Gárda Síochána that there is reasonable ground for believing that apparatus for wireless telegraphy is being kept or is being worked or used at any specified place "or in any specified vehicle" or in any specified ship in contravention of any provision of this Act or any regulation made or condition imposed under this Act, grant to such officer of the Minister or (with the consent of the Minister) to such member of the Gárda Síochána (as the case may be) a search warrant which shall be expressed and shall operate to authorise the officer of the Minister or member of the Gárda Síochána to whom the same is granted to enter, and if need be by force, the place "or in any specified vehicle" or ship named in the said information and there to search for apparatus for wireless telegraphy and to examine all such apparatus there found and to seize and take away all or any part of such apparatus "or any such vehicle" which appears to such officer or member to be kept, worked or used in contravention of any provision of this Act or any regulation made or condition imposed under this Act.

[(2) A search warrant granted under this section shall operate to authorise any one or more of the following, namely, any member of the Garda Siochána or officer of the Minister or other person authorised by the person to whom the warrant is granted to accompany and assist him in the exercise of the powers thereby conferred on him.

(3)(a) An officer of the Minister may retain anything seized under this section which he believes to be evidence of any offence or suspected offence under the Wireless Telegraphy Acts, 1926 to 1988, or the Broadcasting (Offences) Acts, 1968 and 1988, for use as evidence in proceedings in relation to any such offence, for such period from the date of seizure as is reasonable, or, if proceedings are commenced in which the thing so seized is required for use in evidence, until the conclusion of the proceedings, and, subject to section 3 (3A) of the Act of 1926, inserted by section 12 (1) (a) of the Broadcasting and Wireless Telegraphy Act, 1988, thereafter the Minister shall, as soon as may be, deliver any such thing to the person who in his opinion is the owner thereof, and in case the Minister decides that he is unable to ascertain such person, then, on and from the date of his decision, the Act of 1897 shall apply to the thing so seized.

(b) Where, by virtue of paragraph (a) of this subsection, the Act of 1897 is applied to any thing, then, without prejudice to the right of any claimant of the thing to make an application under that Act in regard thereto, the Minister shall, as soon as may be, make such an application.

(c) For the purpose of giving effect to the foregoing paragraphs of this subsection the Act of 1897 shall be construed and have effect subject to any modification which is necessary to give such effect.

(d) In this subsection, 'the Act of 1897' means the Police (Property) Act, 1897.

(4)(a) Any person who by act or omission impedes or obstructs an officer of the Minister or a member of the Garda Síochána or any other person in the exercise of a power conferred by a search warrant granted under this section shall be guilty of an offence.

(b) Any person who with intent to impede or obstruct an officer of the Minister or a member of the Garda Síochána or any other person in the exercise of a power conferred by a search warrant granted under this section places, erects, instals, keeps or maintains any thing shall be guilty of an offence and if, in the case of a continuing offence, the impediment or obstruction is continued after conviction, he shall be guilty of a further offence.

(c) Every person guilty of an offence under this subsection shall be liable on summary conviction to a fine not exceeding £500.]

Amendment history

Subsections 2, 3 and 4 inserted by s.17 of the Broadcasting and Wireless Telegraphy Act 1988, which came into operation on December 31, 1988. Section 20 of the Broadcasting Authority (Amendment) Act 1976 states that the powers conferred by s.8 of the Act of 1926 on a Justice of the District Court to grant a search warrant shall also be exercisable in accordance with that section by such Justice in relation to regulated apparatus and, accordingly, the first reference in subs.(1) of the said s.8 to apparatus for wireless telegraphy shall be construed as including a reference to regulated apparatus. Any search warrant granted in relation to regulated apparatus under the said s.8, as applied by para.(a) of this subsection, shall, in relation to such apparatus, be expressed and operate in the manner specified in subs.(1) of that section with, and subject to the modification that, for the purposes of this paragraph, the second reference in that subsection to apparatus for wireless telegraphy shall be construed as a reference to regulated apparatus.

Regulations as to wireless telegraphy in ships and aircraft

9.—(1) The Minister may by order made after consultation with the Minister for Industry and Commerce make regulations in respect of all or any of the following matters, that is to say:—

(a) requiring operators and other persons engaged in the working of apparatus for wireless telegraphy on all or any classes or class of ships registered in Saorstát Eireann to hold certificates of competency;

(b) requiring operators and other persons engaged in the working of apparatus for wireless telegraphy on all or any classes or class of aircraft owned in Saorstát Eireann to hold certificates of competency;

(c) the grant and renewal of such certificates of competency, the terms and conditions on which such certificates will be granted, and the qualifications to be possessed and the examinations and other tests to be undergone by persons to whom such certificates are granted;

(d) the duration, revocation and suspension of certificates of competency granted under the regulations;

(e) the validity, duration, renewal, revocation, and suspension of certificates of competency granted otherwise than under the regulations whether by the Minister or any other person and whether before or after the passing of this Act;

(f) subject to the sanction of the Minister for Finance, the fees to be charged for or in connection with the granting and renewal of any such certificates of competence as aforesaid and the collection and disposal of such fees;

(g) regulating and controlling the times and manner of working apparatus for wireless telegraphy in ships registered in Saorstát Eireann and, while they are in the territorial waters of Saorstát Eireann, ships registered outside Saorstát Eireann and unregistered ships and other vessels;

(h) regulating and controlling the times and manner of working apparatus for wireless telegraphy in aircraft owned in Saorstát Eireann and, while they are in or over Saorstát Eireann or the territorial waters thereof, aircraft not so owned;

(i) giving effect to and securing compliance with the provisions (save in so far as the same relate to ships to which this section and regulations made thereunder do not apply) of any international convention in relation to wireless telegraphy entered into by the Government of Saorstát Eireann.

[(2) Regulations made under this section may—

(a) provide that a breach or contravention of any specified such regulation shall be an offence,

(b) in relation to convictions on indictment for such an offence, provide that the court by whom the defendant is convicted may order the interest of the defendant, whether as owner or otherwise, in all or any apparatus in respect of or by means of which the court is satisfied a breach or contravention of a specified such regulation was committed to be forfeited.]

(3) Every regulation made under this section shall be laid before each House of the Oireachtas as soon as may be after it is made and if either such House shall, within twenty-one days on which either such House has sat next after the regulation was laid before such Houses, pass a resolution annulling such regulation such regulation shall be annulled accordingly but without prejudice to the validity of anything previously done under such regulation.

(4) For the purposes of this section an aircraft shall be deemed to be owned in Saorstát Eireann if but only if it is owned by a person who, in the case of an individual, has his usual place of residence in Saorstát Eireann or, in the case of an association, company, or other body (whether corporate or unincorporate), has its principal office in Saorstát Eireann.

(5) Neither this section nor any regulation made thereunder shall apply to any ship to which the Merchant Shipping (Wireless Telegraphy) Act, 1919 applies.

[(6) A person guilty of an offence by reason of a breach or contravention of a regulation specified, by virtue of paragraph (a) of subsection (2) of this section, in regulations made under this section shall be liable—

(a) on summary conviction, to a fine of one thousand pounds together with, in the case of a continuing such breach or contravention, a further fine (not exceeding one thousand pounds in all) not exceeding one hundred pounds for each day during which the offence is continued, and

(b) on conviction on indictment, to a fine of twenty thousand pounds together with, in the case of a continuing such breach or contravention, a further fine not exceeding two thousand pounds for each day during which the offence is continued.]

Amendment history

Subsection 2 substituted and subs.6 inserted by s.12 of the Broadcasting and Wireless Telegraphy Act 1988, which came into operation on December 31, 1988.

Government control of wireless telegraphy, etc., in emergencies

10.—(1) If at any time the Executive Council is of opinion that a national emergency has arisen of such character that it is expedient in the public interest that the Executive Council should have full control over the sending and receiving of messages, signals, and other communications by means of wireless telegraphy and of signalling stations capable of being used for communicating with ships at sea, the Executive Council may, if they so think fit, publish in the Iris Oifigiúil a notice declaring that such emergency has arisen.

(2) At any time during the continuance of any such emergency as aforesaid the Minister shall by order make such regulations as appear to the Executive Council to be necessary in the circumstances of such emergency with respect to the possession, sale, purchase, construction or use of apparatus for wireless telegraphy or for the generation and distribution of electro-magnetic radiation and of such signalling stations as aforesaid and apparatus for use therein.

[(3) Regulations made under this section may—

(a) provide that a breach or contravention of any specified such regulation shall be an offence,

(b) in relation to convictions on indictment for such an offence, provide that the court by whom the defendant is convicted may order the interest of the defendant, whether as owner or otherwise, in all or any apparatus in respect of or by means of which the court is satisfied a breach or contravention of a specified such regulation was committed to be forfeited.]

(4) Regulations made under this section shall continue in force for so long only as the emergency during which they are made continues, save that such regulations shall be deemed to continue in force after the termination of such emergency so far as may be necessary for the trial under such regulations of persons accused of having committed during such emergency a breach or contravention of any such regulation and the punishment of such persons (if convicted) under and in accordance with such regulations.

(5) For the purposes of this section—

(a) every such emergency shall, unless continued or sooner terminated under this sub-section, terminate at the expiration of three months from the publication in the Iris Oifigiúil of the notice mentioned in sub-section (1) of this section or, when the emergency has been continued under this sub-section, at the expiration of three months from the publication in the Iris Oifigiúil of the last notice of such continuance, and

(b) any such emergency may be terminated at any time by the publication by the Executive Council in the Iris Oifigiúil of a notice declaring that the emergency has terminated, and

(c) any such emergency may be continued by the publication by the Executive Council in the Iris Oifigiúil before the termination of the emergency of a notice declaring that the emergency still continues.

(6) Every regulation made under this section shall be laid before each House of the Oireachtas as soon as may be after it is made and if either such House shall, within twenty-one days on which that House has sat next after the regulation was laid before it, pass a resolution annulling such regulation such regulation shall be annulled accordingly but without prejudice to the validity of anything previously done under such regulation.

(7) No regulation which applies or relates to any ships to which the Merchant Shipping (Wireless Telegraphy) Act, 1919 applies shall be made by the Minister under this section without previous consultation with the Minister for Industry and Commerce.

[(8) A person guilty of an offence, by reason of a breach or contravention of a regulation specified, by virtue of paragraph (a) of subsection (3) of this section, in regulations made under this section, shall be liable—

(a) on summary conviction, to a fine of one thousand pounds, or, at the discretion of the court, to imprisonment for a term not exceeding six months, or, at such discretion, to both such fine and such imprisonment, together with, in the case of a continuing such breach or contravention, a further fine (not exceeding one thousand pounds in all) not exceeding one hundred pounds for each day during which the offence is continued, and

(b) on conviction on indictment, to a fine of twenty thousand pounds, or, at the discretion of the court, to imprisonment for a term not exceeding twelve months, or, at such discretion, to both such fine and such imprisonment, together with, in the case of a continuing such breach or contravention, a further fine not exceeding two thousand pounds for each day during which the offence is continued.]

[Forfeiture of apparatus; supplementary provisions

10A.—(1) A court shall not order anything to be forfeited pursuant to regulations under section 9 (2) or 10 (3) of this Act if a person claiming to be the owner of or otherwise interested in it applies to be heard by the court, unless an opportunity has been given to him to show cause why the order should not be made.

(2) Where—

(a) a person is convicted on indictment of an offence under section 3 of this Act, or

(b) an order is made pursuant to regulations under section 9 (2) or 10 (3) of this Act, the apparatus to which the forfeiture under the said section 3 or, as may be appropriate, the order relates shall be sold or disposed of in such other manner as the Minister thinks fit.

(3) Where the apparatus is sold pursuant to this section, the net proceeds of the sale shall be paid into or disposed of for the benefit of the Exchequer in such manner as the Minister for Finance shall direct.]

Amendment history

Subsection 3 substituted by s.12 of the Broadcasting and Wireless Telegraphy Act 1988, which came into operation on December 31, 1988. Subsection 8 inserted by s.12 of the Broadcasting and Wireless Telegraphy Act 1988. Section 10A inserted by s.12 of the Broadcasting and Wireless Telegraphy Act 1988. Section 20 of the Broadcasting Authority (Amendment) Act 1976 states that subs.(2) of s.10 of the Act of 1926 shall apply to regulated apparatus in the manner it applies to apparatus for wireless telegraphy, and, accordingly, that subsection shall have effect as if ", of regulated apparatus within the meaning of section 20 of the Broadcasting Authority (Amendment) Act, 1976" were inserted after "electro-magnetic radiation".

Prohibition of certain classes of messages, etc.

11.—(1) No person shall send or attempt to send by wireless telegraphy from any place in Saorstát Eireann or any ship or other vessel in the inland or the territorial waters of Saorstát Eireann or any ship registered in Saorstát Eireann wherever such ship may be or any aircraft in or over Saorstát Eireann or the territorial waters thereof—

(a) any message or communication of an indecent, obscene, or offensive character, nor

(b) any message or communication subversive of public order, nor

(c) any false or misleading signal of distress, nor

(d) any false or misleading message, signal, or communication to a ship or other vessel or an aircraft in distress.

(2) No person shall improperly divulge the purport of any message, communication, or signal sent or proposed to be sent by wireless telegraphy.

[(3) Every person who sends or attempts to send, or divulges the purport of, any message, communication or signal in contravention of this section shall be guilty of an offence and shall be liable—

(a) on summary conviction, to a fine not exceeding one thousand pounds, or, at the discretion of the court, to a term of imprisonment not exceeding six months, or, at such discretion, both to such fine and such imprisonment,

(b) on conviction on indictment, to a fine not exceeding twenty thousand pounds, or, at the discretion of the court, to a term of imprisonment not exceeding twelve months, or, at such discretion, to both such fine and such imprisonment.]

(4) (Note: repealed by s.26 of No. 2 of 1951).

Amendment history

Subsections (3) and (4) substituted by s.12 of the Broadcasting and Wireless Telegraphy Act 1988, which came into operation on December 31, 1988. Subsection (4) repealed by s.26 of the Criminal Justice Act 1951. Offences committed under s.11 of the Wireless Telegraphy Act 1926 are defined as scheduled offences under s.2(2)(a) of the Criminal justice Act 1951, which states that the District Court may try summarily a person charged with a scheduled offence if, (i) the Court is of opinion that the facts proved or alleged constitute a minor offence fit to be so tried, and (ii) the accused, on being informed by the Court of his right to be tried with a jury, does not object to being tried summarily. Section 2(2)(b) the Criminal Justice Act 1951 states that a person shall not be tried summarily for an offence specified in the First Sched. at reference numbers 1, 2 or 3 (note: which includes a reference to the Wireless Telegraphy Act 1926) or for an attempt to commit such an offence unless the Attorney General has consented to his being so tried. Section 4(2) of the Criminal Justice Act 1951 states that in the case, however, of an offence under s.11 of the Wireless Telegraphy Act 1926, (No. 45 of 1926), the District Court shall not impose a fine exceeding ten pounds or a term of imprisonment exceeding one month.

Restrictions on user of apparatus for wireless telegraphy

12.—(1) It shall not be lawful for any person so to work or use any apparatus for wireless telegraphy that electro-magnetic radiation therefrom interferes with the working of or otherwise injuriously affects any apparatus for wireless telegraphy in respect of which a licence has been granted under this Act and is in force or any apparatus for wireless telegraphy lawfully maintained or worked without any such licence or any broadcasting station maintained under Part II. of this Act [or under the Broadcasting Authority Act, 1960].

(2) Whenever the Minister is of opinion that a person is working or using any apparatus for wireless telegraphy in contravention of this section he may serve on or send by registered post to such person a notice requiring such person within a time (not being less than seven days) specified in the notice to take such steps (including where necessary the complete stoppage of the working or user of the apparatus) as shall be specified in the notice to terminate the interference or injurious affection which contravenes this section.

(3) Every person who works or uses any apparatus for wireless telegraphy in contravention of this section and, having been served with a notice under this section requiring him to terminate the interference or injurious affection which contravenes this section, does not within the time specified in that behalf in such notice terminate by the means specified in such notice or by some other means such interference or injurious affection shall be guilty of an offence under this section and shall be [liable—

(a)on summary conviction, to a fine not exceeding one thousand pounds together with, in the case of a continuing offence, a further fine (not exceeding one thousand pounds in all) not exceeding one hundred pounds for every day during which the offence is continued,

(b) on conviction on indictment, to a fine not exceeding twenty thousand pounds together with, in the case of a continuing offence, a further fine not exceeding two thousand pounds for every day during which the offence is continued.]

(4) No notice shall be served under this section in respect of the working or using of apparatus for wireless telegraphy in contravention of this section in a ship to which the Merchant Shipping (Wireless Telegraphy) Act, 1919 applies without the previous consent of the Minister for Industry and Commerce.

(5) Nothing in this section shall operate to prejudice or affect any power or right vested in the Minister under or by virtue of the Telegraphy Acts, 1863 to 1921.

Amendment history

Subsection 3 amended by s.12 of the Broadcasting and Wireless Telegraphy Act 1988, which came into operation on December 31, 1988.

Regulations as to radiation of electro-magnetic energy, etc.

[12A.(1) The Minister may make regulations for any or all of the following purposes:

(a) for prescribing the requirements to be complied with in the case of any apparatus to which this section applies if the apparatus is to be used;

(b) for prescribing the requirements to be complied with in the case of any apparatus to which this section applies if the apparatus is to be sold otherwise than for export, or offered or advertised for sale otherwise than for export, or let on hire or offered or advertised for letting on hire by any person who in the course of business manufactures, assembles or imports such apparatus;

(c) for prescribing the requirements to be complied with in the case of any apparatus to which this section applies if the apparatus is to be sold for export to a country or territory which is for the time being declared under this section by the Minister to be a country or territory to which this paragraph applies or offered or advertised for such sale, by any person mentioned in paragraph (b) of this subsection.]

(2) The said requirements shall be such requirements as the Minister thinks fit for the purpose of ensuring that the use of the apparatus does not cause undue interference with wireless telegraphy, and may in particular include—

(a) requirements as to the maximum intensity of electro-magnetic energy of any specified frequencies which may be radiated in any direction from the apparatus while it is being used; and

(b) in the case of an apparatus the power for which is supplied from electric lines, requirements as to the maximum electro-magnetic energy of any specified frequencies which may be injected into those lines by the apparatus, and, in so far as appears to the Minister necessary or expedient in the case of the regulations in question, different requirements may be prescribed for different circumstances and in relation to different classes or descriptions of apparatus, different districts or places and different times of use.

(3) The apparatus to which this section applies shall be such apparatus as may be specified in the regulations made thereunder, being apparatus generating, or designed to generate, or liable to generate fortuitously, electro-magnetic energy at frequencies of not more than three million megacycles per [second. The references in this subsection to apparatus include references to apparatus for wireless telegraphy and references to any form of electric line.]

The references in this subsection to apparatus include references to any form of electric line.

(4) Where the Minister proposes to make regulations under this section—

(a) he shall cause a draft of the proposed regulations to be prepared and shall cause the draft to be published and placed on sale by the Stationery Office,

(b) he shall give notice to the public, in such manner as he considers suitable, of his intention to make the regulations,

(c) the notice shall contain an intimation that copies of the draft of the regulations are available for purchase and that, during a specified period of not less than two months, representations suggesting variations of the draft may be made to the Minister.

(5) Regulations under this section shall not be made until after the expiration of the period for making representations specified in the relevant notice under paragraph

(b) of subsection (4) of this section and the Minister shall consider any representations made to him pursuant to the notice.

(6)(a) The Minister may appoint an advisory committee or advisory committees to advise him in relation to the making of regulations under this section and in relation to the consideration of representations referred to in the foregoing subsection.

(b) A committee under this subsection shall consist of so many members (not being less than three) as the Minister considers proper.

(c) A member of a committee under this subsection shall, unless he previously dies or resigns, retain his membership of the committee for the period determined by the Minister when appointing him and no longer, but shall be eligible for re-appointment.

(d) A committee under this subsection shall meet whenever summoned the Minister.

(7) Whenever the Minister is of opinion that a person is working or using apparatus not complying with the requirements applicable to it under regulations made for the purposes specified in paragraph (a) of subsection (1) of this section, he may serve on or send by registered post to such person a notice—

(a) requiring such person to take such steps (including where necessary the complete stoppage of the working or user of the apparatus) as shall be specified in the notice to terminate the relevant undue interference with wireless telegraphy, and

(b) requiring such person to take the said steps either—

(i) forthwith in a case in which the Minister is of opinion that the relevant undue interference with wireless telegraphy consists of or includes undue interference with wireless telegraphy used for the purposes of any safety of life service or any purpose on which the safety of any person or of any vessel, aircraft or vehicle may depend, and

(ii) in any other case, within a period (not being less than seven days) specified in the notice.

(8)(a) Where—

(i) a notice under subsection (7) of this section has been served on or sent to a person and the notice requires the complete stoppage forthwith of the working or user of apparatus, and

(ii) such person works or uses the apparatus,

such person shall be guilty of an offence.

(b) Where—

(i) a notice under subsection (7) of this section has been served on or sent to a person and the notice requires the complete stoppage, within a specified period, of the working or user of apparatus, and

(ii) such person works or uses the apparatus after the expiration of that period,

such person shall be guilty of an offence.

(c) Where—

(i) a notice under subsection (7) of this section has been served on or sent to a person and the notice requires the taking forthwith of steps to terminate undue interference with wireless telegraphy by any apparatus (not being steps consisting of the complete stoppage of the working or user of the apparatus), and

(ii) such person works or uses the apparatus without having taken the said steps,

such person shall be guilty of an offence.

(d) Where—

(i) a notice under subsection (7) of this section has been served on or sent to a person and the notice requires the taking, within a specified period, of steps to terminate undue interference with wireless telegraphy by any apparatus (not being steps consisting of the complete stoppage of the working or user of the apparatus), and

(ii) such person works or uses the apparatus without having taken the said steps, such person shall be guilty of an offence.

[(9) Whenever the Minister is of the opinion that any apparatus does not comply with the requirements applicable to it under regulations under this section for the purposes specified in paragraphs (b) or (c) of subsection (1) of this section—

(a) in case the Minister is of the opinion that the apparatus does not comply with the requirements applicable to it under regulations so made for the purposes specified in the said paragraph (b), he may serve on or send by registered post to any person who has manufactured or imported the apparatus in the course of business a notice prohibiting the person, as from the expiration of a period (not being less than seven days) specified in the notice, from selling the apparatus, otherwise than for export, or offering or advertising it for such sale, or letting it on hire or advertising it for letting on hire,

(b) in case the Minister is of the opinion that the apparatus does not comply with the requirements applicable to it under regulations so made for the purposes specified in the said paragraph (c), he may serve on or so send to any person who has manufactured or exported the apparatus in the course of business a notice prohibiting the person, as from the expiration of a period (not being less than seven days) specified in the notice, from selling the apparatus for export to the countries or territories specified in the relevant regulations under this section, or offering or advertising it for such sale, and in any such case requiring the person within such a period so specified,—

(i) to make the apparatus available for inspection by an officer of the Minister and authorised by him, or in case an order made under subsection (14) of this section is for the time being in force, an officer or servant of the Authority or any other body specified in the order and authorised by the Authority or the other body, as may be appropriate, to make the inspection,

(ii) if requested by such officer or servant to transport, at the expense of the person, to a place specified by the officer or servant a sample or samples (which such officer or servant is hereby empowered to select) of the apparatus, or of any part of the apparatus specified by such officer or servant, for testing pursuant to subsection (9A) of this section.

(9A) Where apparatus or any other thing is transported pursuant to a request made under subsection (9) of this section, the apparatus or other thing may be subjected by the person by whom the request was made or by any other officer or servant of the Minister, the Authority or the other body, as may be appropriate, to tests for the purpose of ascertaining whether or not the apparatus or other thing complies with the requirements applicable to it under the relevant regulations under this section.]

(10) Where—

(a) a notice under subsection (9) of this section has been served on or sent to a person, and

"(b) after the expiration of the period specified in the notice, such person contravenes the provisions, or fails to comply with the requirements, of the notice,"

such person shall be guilty of an offence.

(11)(a) A Justice of the District Court may, upon information on oath of an officer of the Minister or of a member of the Gárda Síochána that there is reasonable ground for believing that, at any specified place, apparatus to which this section applies is to be found which does not comply with the requirements applicable to it under regulations made under this section, grant to such officer of the Minister or (with the consent of the Minister) to such member of the Gárda Síochána a search warrant which shall be expressed and shall operate to authorise the officer of the Minister or member of the Gárda Síochána to whom it is granted to enter, and if need be by force, the place named in the said information and there to search for apparatus to which this section applies and to examine and test all such apparatus there found.

(b) A search warrant granted under this subsection to an officer of the Minister may authorise or, if the Justice granting it so thinks proper, require such officer to be accompanied by one or more members of the Gárda Síochána when making the search under the warrant.

(c) Where, under a warrant under this section, a person has a right to examine and test any apparatus at any place, it shall be the duty of any person who is at that place to give him any such assistance as he may reasonably require in the examination or testing of the apparatus.

(d) Any person who—

(i) obstructs any person in the exercise of the powers conferred on him by a warrant under this subsection, or

(ii) fails or refuses to give to any such Person any assistance which he is under this subsection under a duty to give to him, shall be guilty of an offence.

[(12) A person guilty of an offence under this section shall be liable—

(a) on summary conviction, to a fine not exceeding one thousand pounds together with, in the case of a continuing offence, a further fine (not exceeding one thousand pounds in all) not exceeding one hundred pounds for every day during which the offence is continued,

(b) on conviction on indictment, to a fine not exceeding twenty thousand pounds together with, in the case of a continuing offence, a further fine not exceeding two thousand pounds for every day during which the offence is continued.]

(13)The Minister may by order (which he may at any time revoke by a further order) declare that Radio Éireann shall have all powers appropriate for the investigation and detection of interference with wireless telegraphy apparatus for receiving only and, whenever such an order is for the time being in force,—

(a) Radio Éireann shall have those powers,

(b) subsection (2) of section 12 of this Act and subsection (7) of this section shall have effect as if each of the references therein to the Minister included a reference to Radio Éireann, and

(c) subsection (11) of this section shall have effect as if each of the references therein to the Minister included, in relation to regulations made for the purposes specified in paragraph (a) of subsection (1) of this section, a reference to Radio Éireann.

[(14) The Minister may by order (which he may at any time revoke or amend by a further order) declare that the Authority or any other body specified in the order shall have all the powers which the Minister may exercise under subsection (9) of this section and, whenever such an order is for the time being in force, the Authority or the other body so specified shall have those powers and subsection (9) of this section shall have effect as if each of the references therein to the Minister included a reference to the Authority or to the other body so specified, as may be appropriate.

(15)The Minister may by regulations declare any country or territory specified in the regulations to be a country or territory to which paragraph (c) of subsection (1) of this section applies.

(16)In this section 'the Authority' means Radio Telefís Éireann.]

Amendment History

Section 12A inserted by s.34 of the Broadcasting Authority Act 1960. Subsections (1) and (9) substituted and subs.(14) inserted by s.19 of the Broadcasting Authority (Amendment) Act 1976. Section 12A subss.(2) and (3) amended by s.13 of the Wireless Telegraphy Act 1972. Subsection (12) substituted by s.12 of the Broadcasting and Wireless Telegraphy Act 1988, which came into operation on December 31, 1988.

Deliberate interference

[12B.(1) Any person who uses any apparatus for the purpose of interfering with any wireless telegraphy shall be guilty of an offence.

(2) Subsection (1) of this section shall apply whether or not the apparatus in question is wireless telegraphy apparatus or apparatus to which section 12A of this Act applies and whether or not any notice under subsection (7) or subsection (9) of that section has been given with respect to the apparatus.

[(3) A person guilty of an offence under this section shall be liable—

(a) on summary conviction, to a fine not exceeding one thousand pounds together with, in the case of a continuing offence, a further fine (not exceeding one thousand pounds in all) not exceeding one hundred pounds for every day during which the offence is continued,

(b) on conviction on indictment, to a fine not exceeding twenty thousand pounds together with, in the case of a continuing offence, a further fine not exceeding two thousand pounds for every day during which the offence is continued.]]

Amendment history

Section 12B inserted by s.34 of the Broadcasting Authority Act 1960. Subsection (3) substituted by s.12 of the Broadcasting and Wireless Telegraphy Act 1988, which came into operation on December 31, 1988. Section 20 of the Broadcasting Authority (Amendment) Act 1976 states that s.12 of the Act of 1926 shall apply to regulated apparatus in the manner in which it applies to apparatus for wireless telegraphy, and, accordingly, the first reference in subs.(1) of the said s.12 and every reference in subss.(2), (3) and (4) of that section to apparatus for wireless telegraphy shall be construed as including a reference to regulated apparatus.

Prosecution of offences

13.—All prosecutions under this Act in a court of summary jurisdiction shall be prosecuted at the suit of the Minister and not otherwise.

Offences committed in ships or aircraft

14.—(1) For the purposes of sections 53 of the Courts of Justice Act, 1924 (No. 10 of 1924) and section 6 of the Courts of Justice Act, 1926 (No. 1 of 1926) any act which is by virtue of this Act or any regulation made thereunder a misdemeanour or an offence triable summarily shall, if committed in a ship, vessel, or aircraft, be deemed to have been committed in any place in which the accused person may be, and, if committed in a ship or vessel which was within the territorial waters of Saorstát Eireann when the act was committed or when the accused person was arrested, may be deemed to have been committed in the court district abutting on that portion of the said waters in which such ship was when the act was committed or the accused person was arrested, as the case may require.

(2) Whenever a fine is imposed under this Act by any court on a person who is the owner or the master of a ship or other vessel and such fine is imposed for an offence committed in respect of such ship or vessel, such fine may (without prejudice to any other method for the time being authorised by law) be levied by distress and sale of such ship or vessel, her tackle, furniture, and apparel.

Note

In s.6 of the Courts of Justice Act 1926, as applied by s.48 of this Act, and in subs.(1) of s.14 of the Wireless Telegraphy Act 1926, the references to s.53 of the Act of 1924 shall be construed as references to subs.(3) of this section.

Repeals and preservation of existing licences and payments

15.—(1) The Wireless Telegraphy Act, 1904 and the Wireless Telegraphy Act, 1906 are hereby repealed.

(2) All licences for the possession of apparatus for wireless telegraphy which were granted under the said Acts hereby repealed and were in force at the passing of this Act shall, notwithstanding such repeal, continue in force for such time as they would have continued in force under the said Acts if this Act had not been passed, but all such licences shall for the purposes of this Act be deemed to have been granted under this Act and this Act shall apply to all such licences accordingly.

(3) No fee heretofore paid to the Minister in respect of a licence for the possession of apparatus for wireless telegraphy shall be recoverable on the ground that such fee was not legally chargeable.

Expenses

16.—All expenses of carrying this Part of this Act into effect shall, to such extent as shall be sanctioned by the Minister for Finance, be paid out of moneys to be provided by the Oireachtas.

PART II

BROADCASTING

Maintenance of broadcasting stations by the Minister

17.—(1) The Minister may, with the sanction of the Minister for Finance, acquire or establish such and so many broadcasting stations in such places in Saorstát Eireann as the Minister shall, with the sanction aforesaid, from time to time think proper.

(2) The Minister may, with the sanction of the Minister for Finance, maintain and work all broadcasting stations acquired or established by him under this section and there receive, transmit, relay, or distribute such broadcast matter as he shall think proper.

Charging of fees for broadcasting

18.—(1) The Minister may, if he so thinks fit, charge fees for the distribution from a broadcasting station maintained under this Act of any class or classes of broadcast matter.

(2) The amount of the fees to be charged under this section shall be fixed by the Minister with the sanction of the Minister for Finance and all such fees shall be paid into or disposed for the benefit of the Exchequer in such manner as the Minister for Finance shall direct.

Advisory committee

19.—(1) As soon as may be after the passing of this Act the Minister shall establish by order an advisory committee to advise and assist him in the conduct of the broadcasting stations maintained by him under this Act and the selection and control of the broadcast matter distributed from such broadcasting stations.

(2) The said advisory committee shall consist of so many (not being less than five) members as the Minister for Posts and Telegraphs shall think proper and of such members one shall be nominated by the Minister for Education, and one shall be nominated by the Minister for Lands and Agriculture, and the remainder shall be nominated by the Minister for Posts and Telegraphs.

(3) Each member of the said advisory committee shall, unless he previously dies or resigns, retain his membership of the committee for two years from the date of his nomination and no longer but shall be eligible for re-nomination.

(4) The said advisory committee shall meet whenever summoned by the Minister and also on such other occasions as the committee may from time to time determine.

Expenses

20.—All expenses of carrying this Part of this Act into effect shall, to such extent as shall be sanctioned by the Minister for Finance, be paid out of moneys to be provided by the Oireachtas.

WIRELESS TELEGRAPHY ACT 1956

(No. 4 of 1956)

AN ACT TO AMEND THE WIRELESS TELEGRAPHY ACT, 1926, WITH RETROSPECTIVE EFFECT AND TO PROVIDE FOR CERTAIN VALIDATIONS.

[21st February, 1956.]

(Note: All amendments completely applied)

BROADCASTING (OFFENCES) ACT 1968

(No. 35 of 1968)

ARRANGEMENT OF SECTIONS

AN ACT TO SUPPRESS BROADCASTING, FROM SHIPS, AIRCRAFT AND CERTAIN MARINE STRUCTURES

[16TH AUGUST, 1968.]

BE IT ENACTED BY THE OIREACHTAS AS FOLLOWS:

Interpretation

1.—(1) In this Act—

"broadcast" means a broadcast by wireless telegraphy of sounds or visual images intended for general reception (whether the sounds or images are actually received by any person or not), but does not include a broadcast consisting in a message or signal sent in connection with navigation or for the purpose of securing safety;

"sea waters adjacent to the State" comprises all sea areas which lie within the line specified by section 3 of the Maritime Jurisdiction Act, 1959, as being, for the purposes of that Act, the outer limit of the territorial seas and "the high seas" means the seas outside the line so specified or any line which, under the law of any country or territory outside the State, is the outer limit of the territorial waters of that country or territory;

"ship" includes every description of vessel used in navigation;

"wireless telegraphy", and "apparatus for wireless telegraphy" have the same meanings respectively as in the Wireless Telegraphy Act, 1926, and "wireless telegraphy licence" means a licence granted under that Act.

(2) Any reference in this Act to any other enactment shall be construed as a reference to that enactment as amended by or under any other enactment.

Prohibition of broadcasting from ships and aircraft

2.—(1) It shall not be lawful for a broadcast to be made from a ship or aircraft while it is in or over the State or sea waters adjacent to the State, nor shall it be lawful for a broadcast to be made from a ship registered in the State or an aircraft so registered while the ship or aircraft is elsewhere than in or over the State or sea waters adjacent to the State.

(2) If a broadcast is made from a ship in contravention of the foregoing subsection, the owner of the ship, the master of the ship and every person who operates, or participates in the operation of, the apparatus by means of which the broadcast is made shall be guilty of an offence; and if a broadcast is made from an aircraft in contravention of that subsection, the operator of the aircraft, the commander of the aircraft and every person who operates, or participates in the operation of, the apparatus by means of which the broadcast is made shall be guilty of an offence.

(3) A person who procures the making of a broadcast in contravention of subsection (1) of this section shall be guilty of an offence.

(4) In subsection (2) of this section—

(a) "master", in relation to a ship, includes any other person (except a pilot) having command or charge of the ship;

(b) "operator", in relation to an aircraft, means the person for the time being having the management of the aircraft.

Prohibition of broadcasting from marine structures

3.—(1) It shall not be lawful for a broadcast to be made from—

(a) a structure in sea waters adjacent to the State or in tidal waters in the State, being a structure affixed to, or supported by, the bed of those waters and not being a ship, or

(b) any other object in such waters, being neither a structure affixed or supported as aforesaid nor a ship or aircraft,

and if a broadcast is made in contravention of the foregoing provision, every person who operates, or participates in the operation of, the apparatus by means of which the broadcast is made shall be guilty of an offence.

(2) A person who procures the making of a broadcast in contravention of the foregoing subsection shall be guilty of an offence.

Prohibition of acts connected with broadcasting from certain ships and aircraft, and from marine structures outside the State

4.—(1) If a broadcast is made—

(a) from a ship other than one registered in the State while the ship is on the high seas,

(b) from an aircraft other than one so registered while the aircraft is on or over the high seas,

(c) from a structure on the high seas, being a structure affixed to, or supported by, the bed of those seas and not being a ship, or

(d) from any other object on those seas, being neither a structure affixed or supported as aforesaid nor a ship or aircraft,

any person being a citizen of Ireland who operates, or participates in the operation of, the apparatus by means of which the broadcast is made shall be guilty of an offence.

(2) A person who procures a broadcast to be made as mentioned in the foregoing subsection shall be guilty of an offence.

Prohibition of acts facilitating broadcasting from ships, aircraft, etc.

5.—(1) A person who does any of the acts mentioned in subsection (3) of this section, while satisfying the condition as to knowledge or belief mentioned in the case of that act, shall be guilty of an offence if—

(a) he does the act in the State or sea waters adjacent to the State or in a ship registered in the State or an aircraft so registered while the ship or aircraft is elsewhere than in or over the State or sea waters adjacent to the State, or

(b) being a citizen of Ireland, he does the act on or over the high seas.

(2) A person who, in the State, procures another person to do, outside the State, anything which, if it had been done in the State by the last-mentioned person, would have constituted an offence under the foregoing subsection shall be guilty of an offence.

(3) The acts, and conditions as to knowledge or belief, referred to in subsection (1), of this section are the following:

(a) furnishing or agreeing to furnish to another a ship or aircraft knowing, or having reasonable cause to believe, that broadcasts are to be made from it in contravention of section 2 (1) of this Act or while it is on or over the high seas;

(b) carrying or agreeing to carry in a ship or aircraft apparatus for wireless telegraphy knowing, or having reasonable cause to believe, that by means thereof broadcasts are to be made from the ship or aircraft as aforesaid;

(c) supplying to, or installing in, a ship or aircraft apparatus for wireless telegraphy knowing, or having reasonable cause to believe, that by means thereof broadcasts are to be made from the ship or aircraft as aforesaid;

(d) supplying any apparatus for wireless telegraphy for installation on or in, or installing any such apparatus on or in, any structure or other object (not being, in either case, a ship or aircraft) knowing, or having reasonable cause to believe, that by means of that apparatus broadcasts are to be made from the object in contravention of section 3 (1) of this Act or while the object is on the high seas;

(e) repairing or maintaining any apparatus for wireless telegraphy knowing, or having reasonable cause to believe, that, by means thereof, broadcasts are made, or are to be made, in contravention of section 2 (1) or 3 (1) of this Act or as mentioned in section 4 (1) of this Act;

(f) knowing, or having reasonable cause to believe, in the case of a ship or aircraft, that broadcasts are made, or are to be made, from it in contravention of section 2 (1) of this Act or while it is on or over the high seas—

(i) supplying any goods or materials for its operation or maintenance, for the operation or maintenance of apparatus for wireless telegraphy installed therein or for the sustentation or comfort of the persons on board of it;

(ii) carrying by water or air goods or persons to or from it;

(iii) engaging a person as an officer or one of the crew of it:

(g) knowing or having reasonable cause to believe, in the case of a structure or other object (not being, in either case, a ship or aircraft), that broadcasts are made, or are to be made, from it in contravention of section 3 (1) of this Act or while it is on the high seas—

(i) supplying any goods or materials for its maintenance, for the operation or maintenance of apparatus for wireless telegraphy installed therein or thereon or for the sustentation or comfort of the persons therein or thereon;

(ii) carrying by water or air goods or persons thereto or therefrom;

(iii) engaging a person to render services therein or thereon.

Prohibition of acts relating to matter broadcast from ships, aircraft, etc.

6.—(1) A person who does any of the acts mentioned in subsection (3) of this section, and, if any intent or circumstances is or are specified in relation to the act, does it with that intent or in those circumstances, shall be guilty of an offence if—

(a) he does the act in the State or sea waters adjacent to the State or in a ship registered in the State or an aircraft so registered while the ship or aircraft is elsewhere than in or over the State or sea waters adjacent to the State, or

(b) being a citizen of Ireland, he does the act on or over the high seas.

(2) A person who, in the State, procures another person to do, outside the State, anything which, if it had been done in the State by the last-mentioned person, would have constituted an offence under the foregoing subsection, shall be guilty of an offence.

(3) The acts, and, where relevant, the intent and circumstances, referred to in subsection (1) of this section are the following:

(a) supplying a cinematograph film or a record with intent that a broadcast of the film or, as the case may be, the recording embodied in the record may be made in contravention of section 2 (1) or 3 (1) of this Act or as mentioned in section 4 (1) thereof;

(b) making a literary, dramatic or musical work with intent that a broadcast of the work may be made as aforesaid;

(c) making an artistic work with intent that the work may be included in a television broadcast made as aforesaid;

(d) participating in a broadcast made as aforesaid, being actually present as an announcer, as a performer or one of the performers concerned in an entertainment given, or as the deliverer of a speech;

(e) advertising by means of a broadcast made as aforesaid or inviting another to advertise by means of a broadcast to be so made;

(f) publishing the times or other details of any broadcasts which are to be so made, or (otherwise than by publishing such details) publishing an advertisement of matter calculated to promote, directly or indirectly, the interests of a business whose activities consist in or include the operation of a station from which broadcasts are or are to be so made.

(4) For the purposes of this section if, by means of a broadcast made in contravention of section 2 (1) or 3 (1) of this Act or as mentioned in section 4 (1) thereof, it is stated, suggested or implied that any entertainment of which a broadcast is so made has been supplied by, or given at the expense of, a person, he shall, unless he proves that it was not so supplied or given, be deemed thereby to have advertised.

(5) For the purposes of this section advertising by means of a broadcast shall be deemed to take place as well wherever the broadcast is received as where it is made.

(6) In this section "speech" includes lecture, address and sermon, and references in this section to a cinematograph film, a record and a literary, dramatic, musical or artistic work shall be construed in like manner as references thereto in the Copyright Act, 1963.

Penalties and legal proceedings

7.—(1) A person guilty of an offence under this Act shall be liable—

(a) on summary conviction, to imprisonment for a term not exceeding three months or, at the discretion of the court, to a fine not exceeding [£1000] or to both such imprisonment and such fine, or

(b) on conviction on indictment, to imprisonment for a term not exceeding two years or, at the discretion of the court, to a fine not exceeding [£20,000] or to both such fine and such imprisonment.

(2) Where an offence under this Act which has been committed by a body corporate is proved to have been committed with the consent or connivance of, or to be attributable to any neglect on the part of, a director, manager, secretary or other similar officer of the body corporate, or any person who was purporting to act in any such capacity, he, as well as the body corporate, shall be guilty of that offence and shall be liable to be proceeded against accordingly.

(3) Proceedings for an offence under this Act may be taken, and the offence may for all incidental purposes be treated as having been committed, in any place in the State.

(4) Notwithstanding section 10 (4) of the Petty Sessions (Ireland) Act, 1851, summary proceedings for an offence under this Act may be instituted at any time within two years from the time when the offence was committed.

(5) Proceedings for an offence under this Act shall not be instituted otherwise than by or on behalf of the Attorney General; but this shall not prevent the issue or execution of a warrant for the arrest of any person in respect of such an offence or the remanding in custody or on bail of any person charged with such an offence.

(6) A member of the Garda Síochána shall, for the purpose of the enforcement of this Act, have in sea waters adjacent to the State all the powers, protection and privileges which he has in the State.

Amendment History

Subsection (1) amended by s.18 of the Broadcasting and Wireless Telegraphy Act 1988, which came into operation on December 31, 1988.

Special defence available in proceedings for carrying goods or persons in contravention of section 5

8.—(1) In any proceedings against a person for an offence under section 5 of this Act consisting in the carriage of goods or persons to or from a ship or aircraft, it shall be a defence for him to prove—

(a) that the ship or aircraft was, or was believed to be, wrecked, stranded or in distress, and that the goods or persons carried were carried for the purpose of preserving the ship or aircraft, or its cargo or apparel, or saving the lives of persons on board of it, or

(b) that a person on board of the ship or aircraft was, or was believed to be, suffering from hurt, injury or illness, and that the goods or persons were carried for the purpose of securing that the necessary surgical or medical advice and attendance were rendered to him.

(2) In any proceedings against a person for an offence under section 5 of this Act consisting in the carriage of goods or persons to or from an object other than a ship or aircraft, it shall be a defence for him to prove—

(a) that the object was, or was believed to be, unsafe, and that the goods or persons carried were carried for the purpose of saving the lives of persons therein or thereon, or

(b) that a person therein or thereon was, or was believed to be, suffering from hurt, injury or illness, and that the goods or persons were carried for the purpose of securing that the necessary surgical or medical advice and attendance were rendered to him.

(3) In any proceedings against a person for an offence under section 5 of this Act

consisting in the carriage of a person to or from a ship or aircraft or to or from an object other than a ship or aircraft, it shall be a defence for him to prove that the person carried was visiting the ship, aircraft or object, as the case may be, for the purpose of exercising or performing any power or duty conferred or imposed on him by law.

(4) The references in subsections (1) (a) and (2) (a) of this section to persons' having been carried for the purpose of saving lives shall not be construed so as to exclude the persons whose lives it was the purpose to save and the references in subsections (1) (b) and (2) (b) thereof to persons' having been carried as therein mentioned shall not be construed so as to exclude the person who was, or was believed to be, suffering as so mentioned.

Savings for things done under wireless telegraphy licence

9.—Nothing in this Act shall render it unlawful to do anything under and in accordance with a wireless telegraphy licence, or to procure anything to be so done.

Short title and commencement

10.—(1) This Act may be cited as the Broadcasting (Offences) Act, 1968.

(2) This Act shall not come into operation before the expiry of one month beginning with the day on which it is passed, but subject thereto it shall come into operation on such day as may be appointed by the Minister for Posts and Telegraphs by order.

WIRELESS TELEGRAPHY ACT 1972

(No. 5 of 1972)

ARRANGEMENT OF SECTIONS

AN ACT TO ENABLE THE MINISTER FOR POSTS AND TELEGRAPHS TO OBTAIN CERTAIN INFORMATION AS TO THE SALE AND HIRE OF TELEVISION RECEIVING SETS, TO ENABLE HIM TO PROHIBIT THE MANUFACTURE OR IMPORTATION OF CERTAIN APPARATUS FOR WIRELESS TELEGRAPHY AND TO MAKE CERTAIN DECLARATIONS IN RELATION TO THE ISSUE OF LICENCES FOR APPARATUS FOR WIRELESS TELEGRAPHY, TO AMEND AND EXTEND THE WIRELESS TELEGRAPHY ACTS, 1926 AND 1956, AND TO PROVIDE FOR OTHER MATTERS CONNECTED WITH THE MATTERS AFORESAID.

[3rd April, 1972]

BE IT ENACTED BY THE OIREACHTAS AS FOLLOWS:

Interpretation

1.—(1) In this Act—

"appointed day" means such day as the Minister may by order appoint under section 2 (4) of this Act;

"hire contract" means a contract for the letting of a television set on hire;

"hire-purchase agreement", "credit-sale agreement", "owner", "seller", and "buyer" have the meanings respectively assigned to them by section 1 of the Hire-Purchase Act, 1946;

"hirer" means—

(a) a person described in the definition of hirer in section 1 of the Hire-Purchase Act, 1946, and

(b) a person with whom a hire contract is made by a television dealer;

"manufacture" includes construction by any method and the assembly of component parts;

"prescribed" means prescribed by regulations made by the Minister under section 15 of this Act;

"the Principal Act" means the Wireless Telegraphy Act, 1926;

"registered dealer" has the meaning assigned to it by section 2 (3) of this Act;

"television dealer" means a person who by way of trade or business—

(a) sells television sets by wholesale or by retail,

(b) lets such sets on hire or hire-purchase,

(c) arranges for such sets to be sold or let as aforesaid by another television dealer,

(d) engages in the collection of instalments or other payments of or towards the price or by way of rent in respect of the sale or letting of any television set, or

(e) holds himself out as willing to engage in any of the foregoing activities;

"Television set" means any apparatus for wireless telegraphy [capable] of receiving and exhibiting television programmes broadcast for general reception (whether or not its use for that purpose is dependent on the use of anything else in conjunction therewith) and any assembly comprising such apparatus and other apparatus.

(2) In this Act references to sale by retail include references to sale by credit-sale agreement but do not include references to sale by auction unless the auctioneer is selling as principal.

(3) For the purposes of this Act a television set is sold or let on hire or hire-purchase when the contract of sale or, as the case may be, the contract of hire or hire-purchase is made.

Amendment History

Definition of "Television Set" amended by s.2 of the Broadcasting and Wireless Telegraphy Act 1988, which came into operation on December 31, 1988.

Registration of television dealers

2.—(1) The Minister shall establish and maintain a register of television dealers.

[(2) A person shall not act as a television dealer unless, prior to his so acting, he has given to the Minister a notice in the prescribed form, or in a form to the like effect, containing the following information—

(a) the person's name, and

(b) the place or places where the records which a television dealer is required by this Act to keep will be kept by him and be available for inspection,

and the information when received shall be entered in the register established and maintained under subsection (1) of this section.

(2A) In any proceedings in which a contravention of subsection (2) of this section is alleged, it shall be a defence for the defendant to prove—

(a) that, immediately before the commencement of the Broadcasting and Wireless Telegraphy Act, 1988, apart from sections 16 and 21 thereof, he was a television dealer,

(b) that he gave to the Minister, either before or after the commencement of that Act, the notice required to be so given by this section, and

(c) that such notice contained the information so referred to and was given by him to the Minister not later than thirty days after the defendant started to act as a television dealer.]

(3) If a person who has given a notice under subsection (2) of this section (in this Act referred to as a registered dealer) ceases to be a television dealer, or any change occurs in the matters with respect to which he has given information under this section, he shall give notice thereof to the Minister not later than thirty days after the date on which he so ceases or, as the case may be, the change in question, and the Minister shall cancel or alter, as may be appropriate, the entry in the register relating to that dealer.

(4) The Minister may by order appoint a day to be the appointed day for the purposes of this Act.

Amendment History

Subsections (2) and (2A) amended by s.19 of the Broadcasting and Wireless Telegraphy Act 1988, which came into operation on December 31, 1988.

Notification and recording of certain transactions

3.—(1) Subject to subsections (2) and (3) of this section, every registered dealer required to give a notice under section 2 of this Act who after the expiration of the period within which he is required to give that notice—

(a) sells a television set by wholesale or by retail;

(b) lets a television set on a hire contract or on a hire-purchase agreement; or

(c) arranges for a television set to be sold or let as aforesaid to any person by another television dealer, shall, in relation to that sale or letting, give to the

Minister a notice containing the particulars specified in Part I of the Schedule to this Act and make a record of the particulars specified in that Part, and the particulars shall be given to the Minister not later than—

(i) in case a time is specified in the said Schedule in relation to the particulars, that time, and

(ii) in any other case, the last day of the month which follows the month during which the sale or letting was made.

(2) Where a registered dealer sells or lets a television set to another registered dealer for sale or letting by that other dealer, the registered dealer who made the sale or letting shall not be required to comply with subsection (1) of this section but shall instead, in relation to the sale or letting, give to the Minister, not later than the last day of the month which follows the month during which the sale or letting was made, a notification of the name and address of the other registered dealer concerned and make a record of that name and address.

(3) Where pursuant to an arrangement of the kind specified in subsection (1) (c) of this section, a television set is sold or let by a registered dealer and subsection (1) of this section is required to be complied with as regards the sale or letting by the other dealer concerned—

(a) in relation to the sale or letting the registered dealer with whom the arrangement was made shall not be required to comply with subsection (1) of this section, and

(b) that registered dealer shall, unless all payments of or towards the price or by way of rent in respect of the sale or letting are to be received or collected on his behalf by the dealer who made the arrangement, in relation to the sale or letting, give to the Minister, within the time specified in subsection (2) of this section, a notification containing the particulars specified in Part II of the Schedule to this Act.

Notification of certain instalments and payments

4.—(1) Every registered dealer shall, within such period (not being less than 90 days) immediately following his registration as the Minister shall fix by order, notify the Minister whether, by virtue of a credit-sale agreement, hire contract or hire-purchase agreement relating to the sale or letting of a television set and made on or before the day on which the period within which he is required under section 2 of this Act to give notice expires, any instalment of the price or payment of rent fell or will fall, as may be appropriate, to be paid on or after the aforementioned day.

(2) In case an instalment or payment mentioned in subsection (1) of this section fell or will fall to be paid in the manner mentioned in that subsection, the registered dealer shall, with respect to the contract or agreement to which the instalment or payment relates, in addition give to the Minister a notice containing the particulars specified in Part III of the Schedule to this Act, and the particulars shall be given to the Minister within—

(a) in case a time is specified in the said Schedule in relation to the particulars, that time, and

(b) in any other case, the period mentioned in the said subsection (1).

Notification concerning apparatus or equipment capable of radiating certain radio frequency power

5.—For the purpose of facilitating the prompt detection of significant sources of interference with wireless telegraphy, the Minister may by order require any person who is in possession of any apparatus or equipment capable of radiating, in conditions specified in the order, radio frequency power equal to or greater than an amount so specified, to give to the Minister, within such period as shall be specified in the order, a notice containing the following information—

(a) that person's name and address;

(b) descriptive particulars of the apparatus or equipment; and

(c) the address of the premises at which it has been or is to be installed.

Notifications and records generally

6.—(1) Any notice to be given to the Minister under the foregoing provisions of this Act shall be in writing and be in the prescribed form (if any).

(2) Any record required by this Act to be made may be made either in the prescribed form (if any) or in any other form which enables the matters recorded to be readily ascertained by any person to whom the record is produced for inspection; and any matter required to be recorded by virtue of this Act shall be recorded by the person concerned—

(a) in case a time is specified in relation thereto in the Schedule to this Act, within that time, and

(b) in any other case, not later than the last day of the month which follows the month during which the relevant sale or letting was made.

(3) Any record required by this Act to be made by any person shall be kept at a place at which he carries on business and, unless he previously ceases to be a television dealer, shall be preserved by him—

(a) in case it relates to a sale and the sale price is not payable by instalments, for not less than twelve months from the date of the sale:

(b) in case it relates to a sale and the price is payable by instalments or to a letting, for twelve months from the date when the last instalment or payment of rent is due.

(4) The person having charge of any place where a record is kept under this section shall at any reasonable hour, if so required by an officer of the Minister duly authorised in that behalf by the Minister, produce the record for inspection.

Notice of no sales etc.

(b) Where a notice required by this section is given to the Minister, the person giving the notice shall make a record of the fact that such notice was given and of the date on which it was sent to the Minister and such record shall be kept by such person for a period of not less than twelve months, and for the purposes of subsection (4) of section 6 of the Act of 1972 the record shall be regarded as being kept under that section.

Failure to comply with certain requirements under section 6 (4) of Act of 1972 an offence

11.—Any person who without reasonable cause or excuse fails to comply with a requirement duly made under section 6 (4) of the Act of 1972, as extended by section 10 (2) (b) of this Act, shall be guilty of an offence and shall be liable on summary conviction to a fine not exceeding £1,000.

(5) Any notification required to be given to the Minister by or under this Act may be given by sending it to him by registered post.

Restriction of manufacture or importation of certain apparatus

7.—(1) Where it appears to the Minister to be expedient that the provisions of this section should, for the purpose of preventing or reducing the risk of interference with wireless telegraphy, or for such other purpose as the Minister shall specify, apply to any class or description of apparatus for wireless telegraphy, he may, with the consent of the Minister for Industry and Commerce, by order specify apparatus of that class or description for the purposes of this section.

(2) Subject to subsection (3) of this section, where any class or description of apparatus for wireless telegraphy is for the time being specified by an order under subsection (1) of this section—

(a) a person shall not sell, let on hire or manufacture, whether or not for sale, apparatus of that class or description, and

(b) a person shall not import apparatus of that class or description.

(3) An order under subsection (1) of this section may include provisions enabling the Minister—

(a) to grant licences exempting from the provisions of subsection (2) (a) of this section any apparatus for wireless telegraphy of a specified class or description which is manufactured in the State solely for export, and

(b) to issue any such licence subject to such terms and conditions (including terms and conditions as to sale) as may be specified in the licence.

(4) The Minister may by order revoke or amend an order under this section (including an order under this subsection).

Conservation of radio frequency spectrum and avoidance of undue interference with wireless telegraphy

8.—(1) For the purpose of conserving the radio frequency spectrum or avoiding undue interference with wireless telegraphy, the Minister may from time to time impose such special conditions mentioned in subsection (4) of this section as he shall think proper. When granting a licence under the Principal Act the Minister may declare that the licence is issued subject to compliance by the holder of the licence with any special conditions imposed under this section which apply to the apparatus for wireless telegraphy to which the licence relates and are in force at any time when the licence is in force. In case the Minister makes a declaration under this section in relation to a licence, he shall take such steps as are necessary to ensure that a copy of any special condition which is for the time being imposed under this subsection is available for inspection at all reasonable times by any person.

(2) Whenever the Minister imposes special conditions under this section, as soon as practicable he shall cause notice of that fact to be published in at least one daily newspaper published in the State and the notice shall contain a statement of the place where and the hours during which a copy of the special conditions may be inspected by any person.

(3) Whenever the Minister makes a declaration under this section. the licence to which the declaration relates, for so long as a special condition imposed under this subsection and relating to the relevant apparatus for wireless telegraphy remains in force, shall be deemed to be issued subject thereto.

(4) The conditions referred to in subsection (1) of this section are conditions (which may be restrictions) as to the installation, maintenance or use of apparatus for wireless telegraphy and such conditions may apply to a particular apparatus or to apparatus which is of a particular type or description.

(5) A prosecution for a contravention of or a failure to comply with the requirements of a special condition subject to which, by virtue of this section, a licence is deemed to have been granted shall not be brought against a person unless prior to the commission of the alleged offence—

(a) the Minister has given to the person notice in writing of the special condition to which the alleged offence relates, and

(b) the person has had a reasonable opportunity of complying with the requirement of the special condition.

Presumptions relating to offences under sections 3 and 7 of Principal Act

9.—(1) In a prosecution for an offence under section 3 of the Principal Act in which it is shown that an apparatus for wireless telegraphy was in a particular premises on a particular day, it shall be presumed, until the contrary is shown by the defendant, that on that day the apparatus was in the possession of the person who was then the occupier of the premises.

(2) In a prosecution for an offence under the said section 3 in which it appears (whether by virtue of subsection (1) of this section or otherwise) that a person kept or had in his possession an apparatus for wireless telegraphy at the time to which the prosecution relates, it shall be presumed, until the contrary is shown by the defendant, that he did not at such time hold a licence under the Principal Act then having effect and licensing him to keep or have in his possession the apparatus to which the prosecution relates.

(4) In this section—

"occupier" in relation to premises, means a person who as owner, tenant or otherwise is in occupation, whether solely, jointly or severally, of the premises;

"premises" means land and includes a part of a building occupied as a separate dwelling, whether or not the occupier shares with any other person any portion thereof or any accommodation, amenity or facility in connection therewith.

Offences and penalties

10.—(1) A person who—

(a) without reasonable cause or excuse, fails to comply with any of the requirements of section 2, 3 or 4 of this Act or a requirement of an order under section 5 of this Act, or

(b) in purported compliance therewith—

(i) furnishes any information which to his knowledge is false in a material respect, or

(ii) makes or causes to be made or knowingly allows to be made any record which to his knowledge is false in a material respect, shall be guilty of an offence under this subsection.

Notice of no sales etc.

(3) A person who—

(a) without reasonable cause or excuse fails to comply with any of the requirements of subsection (1) or (2) of this section, or

(b) in purported compliance therewith:

(i) furnishes any information which to his knowledge is false in a material respect, or

(ii) makes or causes to be made or knowingly allows to be made any record which to his knowledge is false in a material respect, shall be guilty of an offence under section 10 (1) of the Act of 1972.

(2) A person who—

(a) sells, lets on hire or manufactures any apparatus for wireless telegraphy in contravention of section 7 of this Act,

(b) imports any such apparatus in contravention of the said section 7,

(c) contravenes or fails to comply with any term or condition subject to which a licence is granted to him by the Minister under the said section 7, or

(d) contravenes or fails to comply with any special condition subject to which, by virtue of section 8 of this Act, a licence is deemed to have been granted to him by the Minister under the Principal Act,

shall be guilty of an offence under this subsection.

(3) A person guilty of an offence under subsection (1) of this section shall be liable on summary conviction to a fine not exceeding—

(a) in case the offence relates to a requirement of an order under the said section 5, five hundred pounds, and

(b) in any other case, one thousand pounds.

(3) Section 4 (2) of the Criminal Justice Act, 1951, and section 13 (3) (b) of the

Criminal Procedure Act, 1967 (which provide for maximum penalties under section 11 of the Act of 1926) are hereby repealed.

[(4)(a)(i) A person guilty of an offence under subsection (2) of this section shall be liable—

(I) on summary conviction to a fine not exceeding one thousand pounds,

(II) on conviction on indictment to a fine not exceeding twenty thousand pounds.

(ii) Where a person is convicted on indictment of an offence under subsection (2) of this section, the Court may, at its discretion, in addition to imposing any fine to which the person may be liable under this section, order that the interest of the person, whether as owner or otherwise, in any apparatus in relation to which the offence was committed be forfeited.

(b) A court shall not order any thing to be forfeited under paragraph (a) of this subsection if a person claiming to be the owner of or otherwise interested in it applies to be heard by the court, unless an opportunity has been given to him to show cause why the order should not be made.] and also, in every case, forfeiture of all the apparatus in respect of which the offence was committed.

(5) If a person is convicted of failing to comply with a requirement mentioned in subsection (1) of this section and the failure to comply with the requirement continues after the conviction, that person shall be guilty of a further offence of failing to comply with the requirement and shall be liable to be proceeded against and punished accordingly.

Amendment History

Subsection (4) replaced by s.12 of the Broadcasting and Wireless Telegraphy Act 1998. Section 10(3) of the Broadcasting and Wireless Telegraphy Act 1998 inserted here for clarity.

Amendment of section 3 of Principal Act

11.— (*note: amendments applied*)

Amendment of section 7 of Principal Act

12.— (*note: amendments applied*)

Amendment of section 12A of Principal Act

13.— (*note: amendments applied*)

Amendment of Schedule

14.—(1) The Minister may by order amend the Schedule to this Act.

(2) When an order under this section is proposed to be made, a draft of the order shall be laid before each House of the Oireachtas and the order shall not be made until

a resolution approving of the draft has been passed by each such House.

Regulations generally

15.—The Minister may make regulations for prescribing any matter referred to in this Act as prescribed.

Laying of orders and regulations

16.—The Minister shall cause every order, other than an order under section 14 of this Act, and regulation made under this Act to be laid before each House of the Oireachtas as soon as may be after being made and, if a resolution annulling the order or regulation is passed by either such House within the next twenty-one days on which that House has sat after the order or regulation is laid before it, the order or regulation shall be annulled accordingly but without prejudice to the validity of anything previously done thereunder.

Expenses of Minister

17.—The expenses incurred by the Minister in the administration of this Act shall, to such extent, as may be sanctioned by the Minister for Finance, be paid out of moneys provided by the Oireachtas.

Short title, collective citation and construction

18.—(1) This Act may be cited as the Wireless Telegraphy Act, 1972.

(2) The Wireless Telegraphy Acts, 1926 and 1956, the Broadcasting, Authority Acts, 1960 to 1971, in so far as they amend those Acts, and this Act may be cited together as the Wireless Telegraphy Acts, 1926 to 1972.

(3) The Principal Act (as amended by the Wireless Telegraphy Act, 1956, the Broadcasting Authority Act, 1960, and the Broadcasting Authority Act, 1966) and this Act shall be construed together as one Act.

SCHEDULE

Sections 3 and 4.

NOTIFICATIONS AND RECORDS

PART I

Particulars to be notified and recorded pursuant to section 3 (1).

1. The date of the sale or letting.
2. The name and address of the buyer or hirer.
3. The make and type of television set and in particular whether it is (a) designed for reception in colour, and (b) portable.
4. In the case of a sale, whether the price is payable by instalments and, in the case of a letting, whether it is a letting on hire or hire-purchase.
5. In the case of a credit sale or a letting, the name and address of the seller or owner and the name and address of any person who is to receive any

payment or instalment of or towards the price or by way of rent in respect of the credit sale or the letting.

6. If the set has been or is to be installed by the registered dealer or another person to his order, the address of the premises at which it has been or is to be installed and the name of the occupier (if known) of those premises.
7. Within 30 days of the knowledge coming to the information of the registered dealer concerned.
8. In case the dealer is himself the seller or owner or such payments or instalments are to be received by the dealer or collected by him on behalf of the seller or owner, any change in the address of the buyer or hirer.
9. If after the date of the sale or letting any payments of or towards the price or by way of rent in respect of the sale or letting which would otherwise be received or collected by the dealer are to be received or collected by another person, the name and address of that other person.

PART II

Particulars to be notified pursuant to section 3 (3).

1. The date of the hire contract, hire-purchase agreement or credit-sale agreement, as the case may be.
2. The name and address of the buyer or hirer.
3. The name and address of the registered dealer who arranged the sale or letting.
4. Within 30 days of the information coming to the knowledge of the other registered dealer concerned.
5. Any change in the address of the buyer or hirer.

PART III

Particulars to be notified pursuant to section 4 (2).

1. The name and address of the buyer or hirer.
2. The date of the hire contract, credit-sale agreement or hire-purchase agreement, as the case may be.
3. If after the date of the sale or letting any payments of or towards the price or by way of rent in respect of the sale or letting which would otherwise be received or collected by the dealer are to be received or collected by another person, the name and address that other person.
4. Within 30 days of the information coming to the knowledge of the registered dealer concerned.
5. Any change in the address of the buyer or hirer.
6. If after a notification pursuant to section 4 (2) of this Act has been given, any payments of or towards the price or by way of rent in respect of the sale or letting which would otherwise be received or collected by the dealer are to be received or collected by another person, the name and address of that other person.

BROADCASTING AND WIRELESS TELEGRAPHY ACT 1988

(No. 19 of 1988)

ARRANGEMENT OF SECTIONS

ACTS REFERRED TO

Broadcasting Authority Act, 1960	1960, No. 10
Broadcasting Authority (Amendment) Act, 1976	1976, No. 37

Broadcasting (Offences) Act, 1968	1968, No. 35
Companies Act, 1963	1963, No. 33
Copyright Act, 1963	1963, No. 10
Police (Property) Act, 1897	1897, c. 30
Postal and Telecommunications Services Act, 1983	1983, No. 24
Wireless Telegraphy Act, 1926	1926, No. 45
Wireless Telegraphy Act, 1972	1972, No. 5

AN ACT TO PROHIBIT BROADCASTING IN THE STATE SAVE UNDER AND IN ACCORDANCE WITH A LICENCE ISSUED BY THE MINISTER FOR COMMUNICATIONS AND TO AMEND AND EXTEND THE WIRELESS TELEGRAPHY ACTS, 1926 TO 1972, AND THE BROADCASTING (OFFENCES) ACT, 1968, AND TO PROVIDE FOR OTHER MATTERS CONNECTED WITH THE MATTERS AFORESAID.

[3RD JULY, 1988]

BE IT ENACTED BY THE OIREACHTAS AS FOLLOWS:

Definitions

1.—In this Act—

"the Act of 1926" means the Wireless Telegraphy Act, 1926;

"the Act of 1963" means the Copyright Act, 1963;

"the Act of 1968" means the Broadcasting (Offences) Act, 1968;

"the Act of 1972" means the Wireless Telegraphy Act, 1972;

"apparatus for wireless telegraphy" has the meaning assigned to it by virtue of section 2 (1) of this Act;

"artistic work" has the meaning assigned to it by section 9 of the Act of 1963;

"broadcast" means a broadcast by wireless telegraphy of communications, sounds, signs, visual images or signals, whether such communications, sounds, signs, visual images or signals are actually received or not;

"cinematograph film" means any sequence of visual images recorded (whether cinematographically or by means of any other process) on material of any description (whether translucent or not) so as to be capable, by the use of that material, of comprising, or being included in, a broadcast, and includes a video recording of any description;

"dramatic work" has the meaning assigned to it by section 2 (1) of the Act of 1963;

"literary work" includes any written table or compilation;

"the Minister" means the Minister for Communications;

"owner", in relation to premises, means—

(a) a person, other than a mortgagee not in possession, who, whether in his own right or as a trustee or agent for any other person, is entitled to receive the rack rent of the premises or, where the premises are not let at a rack rent, would be so entitled if they were so let, whether the interest of the person is held solely, jointly or severally, or

(b) a lessee or occupier, whether the lease is held or the occupier is in occupation solely, jointly or severally;

"premises" includes land not built on, land covered by water and a structure of any kind whether attached or affixed to the land or not;

"record", except where the context otherwise requires, has the meaning assigned to it by section 2 (1) of the Act of 1963;

"supply" includes giving without payment;

"telecommunications service" means a telecommunications service described in section 87 (1) of the Postal and Telecommunications Services Act, 1983;

"vehicle" includes vessel.

"Apparatus for wireless telegraphy", "wireless telegraphy" and "television set"

2.—(*note: amendments applied*)

Control of broadcasting

3.—(1) A broadcast shall not be made from any premises or vehicle in the State unless it is made pursuant to and in accordance with a licence issued by the Minister.

(2) Where a broadcast is made in contravention of subsection (1) of this section, each of the following shall be guilty of an offence:

(a) any person who is the owner of, or is in control or is concerned in the management of, any premises or vehicle from which the broadcast is made and who knowingly permits or suffers the broadcast to take place, and

(b) any person who operates, or assists in the operation of, the apparatus for wireless telegraphy by means of which the broadcast is made.

(3) Where in proceedings for an offence under this section it is proved that a broadcast took place from a particular premises or vehicle and that the defendant was, at the time of the alleged offence, the owner of, or in control or concerned in the management of, the premises or vehicle, then, unless there is sufficient other evidence to raise an issue as to whether the defendant knowingly permitted or suffered the broadcast to be made, he shall be treated as having so permitted or suffered the broadcast to be made.

(4) The provisions of subsection (1) of this section are in addition to those of sections 2 (1) and 3 (1) of the Act of 1968 and nothing in this section shall be construed as amending the said section 2 (1) or 3 (1).

Prohibition of acts facilitating broadcasting in contravention of section 3

4.—(1) A person who does any of the acts mentioned in subsection (2) of this section, while satisfying the condition as to knowledge or belief specified in relation to the act, shall be guilty of an offence.

(2) The acts, and the conditions as to knowledge or belief, referred to in subsection

(1) of this section are the following:

(a) making available to another any premises or vehicle or any other thing knowing, or having reasonable cause to believe, that broadcasts are to be made from it in contravention of section 3 (1) of this Act;

(b) having or keeping, or agreeing to have or to keep, apparatus for wireless telegraphy knowing, or having reasonable cause to believe, that by means thereof broadcasts have been, are being or are to be made in contravention of the said section 3 (1);

(c) supplying any apparatus for wireless telegraphy for installation on or in, or installing any such apparatus on or in, any premises or vehicle or any other thing knowing, or having reasonable cause to believe, that, by means of that apparatus, broadcasts are to be made in contravention of the said section 3 (1);

(d) repairing or maintaining any apparatus for wireless telegraphy knowing, or having reasonable cause to believe, that, by means of that apparatus, broadcasts have been, are being or are to be made in contravention of the said section 3 (1).

(3) Where in proceedings for an offence under this section it is proved that the defendant did an act mentioned in subsection (2) of this section and that in the particular circumstances of the case he ought to have had the knowledge specified in that subsection in relation to the act, then, unless there is sufficient other evidence to raise an issue as to whether the defendant had such knowledge at the relevant time, the act shall be treated as having been done by him with such knowledge.

(4) For the purposes of this section a broadcast shall be regarded as being made by means of an apparatus whether the broadcast is made by means of the apparatus alone or by means of the apparatus and other apparatus.

(5) In this section "apparatus for wireless telegraphy" has the same meaning as in section 2 of the Act of 1926, as amended by section 2 of this Act.

Prohibition of acts relating to matter broadcast in contravention of section 3

5.—(1) A person who does any of the acts mentioned in subsection (2) of this section, and, if any intent, knowledge or belief or circumstances is or are specified in relation to the act, does it with that intent, knowledge or belief or in those circumstances, shall be guilty of an offence.

(2) The acts, and, where relevant, the intent, knowledge, belief and circumstances, referred to in subsection (1) of this section are the following:

(a) supplying a cinematograph film or a record with intent that such film or the sound embodied in the record may comprise, or be included in, a broadcast made in contravention of section 3 (1) of this Act;

(b) making a literary, dramatic or musical work with intent that the work may comprise, or be included in, a broadcast made in contravention of the said section 3 (1);

(c) making an artistic work with intent that the work may comprise, or be included in, a broadcast made in contravention of the said section 3 (1);

(d) participating in a broadcast made in contravention of the said section 3 (1) whether as a director, producer or announcer or as the deliverer of a speech or otherwise;

(e) participating, whether as a director, producer or announcer or as the deliverer of a speech or otherwise, in the making of a cinematograph film or record made in the State knowing, or having reasonable cause to believe, that such film or record is to comprise, or to be included in, a broadcast made in contravention of the said section 3 (1);

(f) advertising by means of a broadcast made in contravention of the said section 3 (1), inviting another to advertise by means of a broadcast to be so made or making an advertisement with the intent that it may comprise, or be included in, a broadcast to be so made;

(g) publishing dates, times or programme schedules which relate to broadcasts which, if made, would be made in contravention of the said section 3 (1) or (otherwise than by publishing such particulars) publishing an advertisement of matter calculated to promote, directly or indirectly, the interests of a business whose activities consist of or include the operation of a station from which broadcasts are, or are to be, made in contravention of the said section 3 (1).

(3)(a) Where in proceedings for an offence under this section it is proved that, by means of a broadcast made in contravention of section 3 (1) of this Act, it was stated, suggested or implied that any matter which comprised, or was included in, the broadcast was supplied by, or given at the expense, whether wholly or partly, of the defendant, then, unless there is sufficient other evidence to raise an issue as to whether the defendant advertised by means of the broadcast, he shall be treated as having so advertised.

(b) Where in proceedings for an offence under this section it is proved that the defendant did an act mentioned in subsection (2) of this section and that in the particular circumstances of the case he ought to have had the knowledge specified in that subsection in relation to the act, then, unless there is sufficient other evidence to raise an issue as to whether the defendant had such knowledge at the relevant time, the act shall be treated as having been done by him with such knowledge.

(4) Where in proceedings for an offence under this section—

(a) it is proved that a broadcast was made in contravention of section 3 (1) of this Act and that the broadcast was wholly or partly comprised of an advertisement, and

(b)(i) there is produced in court anything which both—

(I) by reason of something printed thereon, or on a label attached thereto, purports to relate to the goods, service, accommodation, facility, entertainment or other event, or other thing, to which the advertisement relates, and

(II) has something printed thereon, or on a label attached thereto, which is such as to seem to the court to be likely to be taken as an indication that the defendant prepares, manufactures, assembles, imports, provides, supplies, promotes, organises or is otherwise connected with the provision of the goods, service, accommodation, facility, entertainment or other event, or other thing, to which the advertisement relates,

(ii) there is contained in the advertisement a reference which, in the opinion of the court, is a reference to the defendant,

then, unless there is sufficient other evidence to raise an issue as to whether the defendant advertised by means of the broadcast, he shall be treated as having so advertised.

(5) In this section, "speech" has the meaning assigned to it by section 6 (6) of the Act of 1968.

Penalties and legal proceedings

6.—(1) A person guilty of an offence under section 3, 4 or 5 of this Act shall be liable—

(a) on summary conviction, to imprisonment for a term not exceeding three months or, at the discretion of the court, to a fine not exceeding £1,000 or to both such imprisonment and such fine, or

(b) on conviction on indictment, to imprisonment for a term not exceeding two years or, at the discretion of the court, to a fine not exceeding £20,000 or to both such fine and such imprisonment.

(2)(a) On conviction on indictment of a person for an offence under section 3 or section 4 of this Act in relation to a vehicle the court may, at its discretion, in addition to any punishment to which that person may be liable under subsection (1) of this section, order the vehicle to be forfeited.

(b) Where a vehicle is forfeited under this subsection, the Minister way direct that it be sold or otherwise disposed of in such manner as he thinks fit.

(3) Where an offence under section 3, 4 or 5 of this Act which has been committed by a body corporate is proved to have been committed with the consent or connivance of, or to be attributable to any neglect on the part of, a director, manager, secretary or other similar officer of the body corporate, or any person who was purporting to act in any such capacity, he, as well as the body corporate, shall be guilty of that offence and shall be liable to be proceeded against accordingly.

(4) Notwithstanding section 10 (4) of the Petty Sessions (Ireland) Act, 1851, summary proceedings for an offence under section 3, 4 or 5 of this Act [or under section 3 of the Act of 1926 as amended by section 12 of this Act] may be instituted at any time within two years from the time when the offence was committed.

Amendment History

Subsection (4) amended by the Broadcasting Act 1990.

Prohibition notice

7.—(1)(a) Where the Minister is of opinion that a broadcast has been made from any premises or vehicle in contravention of section 3 (1) of this Act, he may by a notice in writing (in this section referred to as a "prohibition notice") addressed to and served on either or both of the following, namely, Bord Telecom Éireann and the Electricity Supply Board require the person to whom it is addressed to comply with the requirements of the notice.

(b) A person to whom a prohibition notice is addressed and on whom it is served shall, for so long as the notice is in operation, comply with the requirements of the notice.

(2) A prohibition notice shall—

(a) specify—

(i) the person or persons to whom it is addressed,

(ii) the premises from which the Minister is of opinion the broadcast to which it relates was made, and

(iii) the date or dates on which the Minister is of opinion such broadcast was made, and

(b) require a person to whom it is addressed, for so long as the notice is in operation, not to offer to provide, or provide or maintain, to a connection point in the premises specified in the notice,

(i) in case such a person is Bord Telecom Éireann, a telecommunications service,

(ii) in case such a person is the Electricity Supply Board, a supply of electricity.

(3) A person on whom a prohibition notice is served pursuant to subsection (1) of this section shall be immune from liability in respect of anything done or omitted to be done by that person in pursuance of the notice.

(4) Where a prohibition notice is served pursuant to subsection (1) of this section and a premises is specified in the notice, the Minister shall, as soon as may be, serve a copy of the notice on the occupier of the premises together with a statement that such occupier may, within the period of fourteen days beginning on the date of the notice, make representations to the Minister showing why the prohibition notice should not come into operation (which representations are hereby authorised to be made).

(5) Unless it is previously withdrawn, a prohibition notice shall come into operation on such day as the Minister shall determine (being a day not earlier than the day immediately following the expiration of the period of fourteen days referred to in subsection (4) of this section).

(6) When a prohibition notice comes into operation—

(a) it shall remain in operation until it is withdrawn, and

(b) for so long as it remains in operation, a person to whom the notice is addressed shall not offer to provide, or provide or maintain to a connection point in the premises specified in the notice a telecommunications service or a supply of electricity, as may be appropriate having regard to the terms of the notice.

(7) A notice or copy of a notice required to be served on a person by this section shall be served on him in some one of the following ways:

(a) where it is addressed to him by name, by leaving it at his registered or principal office or at his principal place of business,

(b) by sending it by post in a prepaid registered letter addressed to him at the address at which he ordinarily resides or at his registered or principal office, or at his principal place of business or, in a case in which an address for service has been furnished, at that address.

(8) Where a copy of a prohibition notice is required by this section to be served on an occupier of any premises and the name of the occupier cannot be ascertained by reasonable inquiry, it may be addressed to "the occupier" without naming him.

(9) For the purposes of this section, a company within the meaning of the Companies Act, 1963, shall be deemed to be ordinarily resident at its registered office, and every other body corporate and every unincorporated body shall be deemed to be ordinarily resident at its principal office or place of business.

Use of certain services to promote, further or facilitate certain interests an offence

8.—Any person who—

(a) by using either a telecommunications service as regards which he is the subscriber or a supply of electricity supplied to him; or

(b) by enabling or permitting such a supply of electricity or such a telecommunications service to be used by another, promotes, furthers or facilitates, directly or indirectly, the interests of a business whose activities consist of or include the operation of a station from which broadcasts are, or are to be, made in contravention of section 3 (1) of this Act shall be guilty of an offence and shall be liable on summary conviction to a fine not exceeding £1,000.

Production of licence granted under Act of 1926 required in certain circumstances

9.—(1) Subject to subsection (2) of this section, a person shall not, pursuant to a sale or to an agreement to sell, let on hire or hire purchase or otherwise to supply, deliver any apparatus for wireless telegraphy other than a television set which is of a particular class or description unless within the relevant period there has been produced by or on behalf of the purchaser, hirer, or the party to whom the apparatus is to be otherwise supplied, as may be appropriate, for inspection by the person making the delivery or by his agent, a licence granted under the Act of 1926 which—

(a) was issued to the purchaser or hirer, or the party so supplied, as may be appropriate, and

(b) relates to apparatus for wireless telegraphy which is of such class or description, and

(c) is for the time being in force.

(2) The Minister may by order exempt from the provisions of subsection (1) of this section apparatus for wireless telegraphy which is of a class or description specified in the order, and in case an order under this subsection is for the time being in force, subsection (1) of this section shall be construed and have effect subject to the terms of the order.

(3) In any proceedings in which a contravention of subsection (1) of this section is alleged it shall be a defence for the defendant to—

(a) prove that—

(i) the relevant purchaser, hirer or party supplied produced to the defendant or to his agent a document purporting to be the licence the production of which would have satisfied the requirements of the said subsection (1), and

(ii) such document was inspected by the defendant or by his agent, and

(iii) the defendant, or, in case the document was produced to his agent, his agent, reasonably believed the document to be such licence, and

(iv) the document was so produced within the period which would have been appropriate having regard to the said subsection (1), and

(b) satisfy the court that such belief was reasonable.

(4) Any person who contravenes subsection (1) of this section shall be guilty of an offence and shall be liable—

(a) on summary conviction, to a fine not exceeding £1,000,

(b) on conviction on indictment, to a fine not exceeding £20,000.

(5) In this section—

"the relevant period" means in relation to a delivery the period beginning on the day which is three days prior to the date on which the delivery is made and ending immediately before the making of the delivery;

"television set" has the meaning assigned to it by section 1 (1) of the Wireless Telegraphy Act, 1972, as amended by section 2 (2) of this Act.

Notice of no sales etc.

10.—(1) In case during a particular month a television dealer—

(a) sells or lets no television set in a manner mentioned in paragraph (a) or (b) of section 3 (1) of the Act of 1972, or

(b) makes no arrangement described in paragraph (c) of the said section 3 (1),

he shall give to the Minister a notice in writing stating that during that month no such sale, letting or arrangement was made by him.

(2)(a) Where a notice is by this subsection required to be given to the Minister, the notice shall be so given not later than the last day of the month which follows the month to which the notice relates.

(b) Where a notice required by this section is given to the Minister, the person giving the notice shall make a record of the fact that such notice was given and of the date on which it was sent to the Minister and such record shall be kept by such person for a period of not less than twelve months, and for the purposes of subsection (4) of section 6 of the Act of 1972 the record shall be regarded as being kept under that section.

(3) (*note: applied to s.10 of the Wireless Telegraphy Act 1972*)

Failure to comply with certain requirements under section 6 (4) of Act of 1972 an offence

11.—(*note: applied to s.6 of the Wireless Telegraphy Act 1972*)

Penalties for certain offences under Act of 1926 and Act of 1972 altered

12.—(1) The Act of 1926 is hereby amended by—

(a) (*note: amendments applied*)

(b) (*note: amendments applied*)

(c) in section 9—

(i) (*note: amendments applied*)

(ii) (*note: amendments applied*)

(d) in section 10—

(i) (*note: amendments applied*)

(ii) (*note: amendments applied*)

(e) (*note: amendments applied*)

(f) (*note: amendments applied*)

(g) (*note: amendments applied*)

(h) (*note: amendments applied*)

(i) (*note: amendments applied*)

(2) Section 10 of the Act of 1972 is hereby amended by—

(a) (*note: amendments applied*)

(b) (*note: amendments applied*)

Recovery of licence fees

13.—(*note: moved to s.6 of the Wireless Telegraphy Act 1926*)

Prosecution of offences

14.—Summary proceedings for an offence under this Act may be prosecuted by the Minister.

Onus of proof

15.—In proceedings for an offence under this Act it shall not be necessary to negative by evidence the existence either of any order under section 9 (2) of this Act or of any licence to broadcast and accordingly the onus of proving the existence of such an order, or the issue of such a licence to the defendant, shall be on the defendant.

Subsections (1), (2) and (3) of section 3 of Act of 1926 applied to Bord Telecom Éireann (Irish Telecommunications Board)

16.—For the avoidance of doubt it is hereby declared that subsections (1), (2) and (3) of section 3 of the Act of 1926 apply to Bord Telecom Éireann (The Irish Telecommunications Board).

Amendment of sections 7 and 8 of Act of 1926

17.—(1) (*note: amendments applied*)

(2) (*note: amendments applied*)

(3) (*note: amendments applied*)

Amendment of section 7 of Act of 1968

18.—(*note: amendment applied*)

Amendment of section 2 of Act of 1972

19.—(*note: amendment applied*)

Fees on application for licence

20.—(*note: moved to s.6 of the Wireless Telegraphy Act 1926*)

Short title, commencement and collective citations

21.—(1) This Act may be cited as the Broadcasting and Wireless Telegraphy Act, 1988.

(2) This Act, other than this section and section 16, shall not come into operation before the expiry of one month beginning on the day on which it is passed, but subject to the foregoing it (apart from this section and section 16) shall come into operation on the 31st day of December, 1988, or on such earlier day as may be appointed by the Minister by order.

(3)(a) The Act of 1968 and this Act, other than sections 2, 9, 10, 11, 12, 16, 17 and 19 of this Act, may be cited together as the Broadcasting (Offences) Acts, 1968 and 1988.

(b) The Wireless Telegraphy Acts, 1926 to 1972, and sections 2, 9, 10, 11, 12, 14, 15, 16, 17 and 19 of this Act may be cited together as the Wireless Telegraphy Acts, 1926 to 1988.

SECTION 2

BROADCASTING AUTHORITY ACT 1960

(No. 10 of 1960)

ARRANGEMENT OF SECTIONS

AN ACT TO ENABLE AN AUTHORITY TO BE ESTABLISHED FOR THE PURPOSE OF PROVIDING A NATIONAL TELEVISION AND SOUND BROADCASTING SERVICE, TO AMEND AND EXTEND THE WIRELESS TELEGRAPHY ACTS, 1926 AND 1956, AND TO PROVIDE FOR MATTERS CONNECTED WITH THE MATTERS AFORESAID.

[12TH APRIL, 1960.]

BE IT ENACTED BY THE OIREACHTAS AS FOLLOWS:—

Interpretation

1.—(1) In this Act—

"the Act of 1926" means the Wireless Telegraphy Act, 1926; 1926, No. 45.

"the Authority" has the meaning specified in subsection (1) of section 3 of this Act;

"broadcast" and "broadcasting station" have the same meanings as in the Act of 1926, as amended by this Act;

"broadcasting licence fee" means a fee paid on a licence granted under section 5 of the Act of 1926 in respect of apparatus for receiving only;

"the Commissioners" means the Commissioners of Public Works in Ireland;

"the Director-General" has the meaning specified in section 11 of this Act;

"the establishment day" means the day appointed to be the establishment day for the purposes of this, Act by order of the Minister under section 2 of this Act;

"functions" includes powers and duties;

"the Minister" means the Minister for Posts and Telegraphs.

(2) A reference in this Act to performance of functions includes, with respect to powers, a reference to exercise of powers.

Appointment of establishment day

2.—The Minister may by order appoint a day to be the establishment day for the purposes of this Act.

Establishment of Authority

3.—(1) There shall, by virtue of this section, be established on the establishment day an authority to be known as Radio Éireann (in this Act referred to as the Authority).

(2) The Authority shall be a body corporate with perpetual succession and power to sue and be sued in its corporate name and to acquire, hold and dispose of land.

Members of Authority

4.—(1) The members of the Authority shall be appointed by the Government and shall be not less than seven and not more than nine in number.

(2) The period of office of a member of the Authority shall be such period, not exceeding five years, as the Government may determine when appointing him.

(3) A member of the Authority whose term of office expires by effluxion of time shall be eligible for re-appointment.

(4) A member of the Authority may at any time resign his office as member by letter sent to the Government, and the resignation shall take effect on receipt of the letter.

(5) Where a member of the Authority is nominated either as a candidate for election to either House of the Oireachtas or as a member of Seanad Éireann, he shall thereupon cease to be a member of the Authority.

(6) A person who is for the time being entitled under the Standing Orders of either House of the Oireachtas to sit therein shall, while so entitled, be disqualified from becoming a member of the Authority.

Remuneration and terms of office of members of Authority

5.—(1) A member of the Authority shall be paid, out of funds at the disposal of the Authority—

(a) such remuneration as may be fixed from time to time by the Government, and

(b) such amounts in respect of expenses as the Authority considers reasonable.

(2) Subject to subsection (1) of this section, a member of the Authority shall hold office on such terms as the Government may determine from time to time.

(3) The Minister shall cause the terms of employment and remuneration of the members of the Authority to be laid before both Houses of the Oireachtas.

Removal of member of Authority

6.—Repealed by section 21 of the Broadcasting Authority (Amendment) Act, 1976 No. 37 of 1976

Chairman of Authority

7.—(1) The Government shall from time to time as occasion requires appoint a member of the Authority to be chairman thereof.

(2) The chairman of the Authority shall, unless he sooner dies, resigns the office of chairman or ceases to be chairman under subsection (4) of this section, hold office until the expiration of his period of office as a member of the Authority.

(3) The chairman of the Authority may at any time resign his office as chairman by letter sent to the Government, and the resignation shall, unless it is previously withdrawn in writing, take effect at the commencement of the meeting of the Authority held next after the Authority has been informed by the Government of the resignation.

(4) Where the chairman of the Authority ceases during his term of office as chairman to be a member of the Authority, he shall also then cease to be chairman of the Authority.

Disclosure by member of the Authority of interest in proposed in contract

8.—A member of the Authority who has—

(a) any interest in any company or concern with which the Authority proposes to make any contract, or

(b) any interest in any contract which the Authority proposes to make, shall disclose to the Authority the fact of the interest and the nature thereof, and shall take no part in any deliberation or decision of the Authority relating to the contract, and the disclosure shall be recorded in the minutes of the Authority.

Seal of Authority

9.—(1) The Authority shall as soon as may be after its establishment provide itself with a seal.

(2) The seal of the Authority shall be authenticated by the signature of the chairman of the Authority or some other member thereof authorised by the Authority to act in that behalf and the signature of an officer of the Authority authorised by the Authority to act in that behalf.

(3) Judicial notice shall be taken of the seal of the Authority, and every document purporting to be an instrument made by the Authority and to be sealed with the seal (purporting to be authenticated in accordance with this section) of the Authority shall be received in evidence and be deemed to be such instrument without further proof unless the contrary is shown.

Meetings and procedure of Authority

10.—(1) The Authority shall hold such and so many meetings as may be necessary for the due fulfilment of its functions.

(2) The Minister may fix the date, time and place of the first meeting of the Authority.

(3) At a meeting of the Authority—

(a) the chairman of the Authority shall, if present, be chairman of the meeting,

(b) if and so long as the chairman of the Authority is not present or if the office of chairman is vacant, the members of the Authority who are present shall choose one of their number to be chairman of the meeting.

(4) Every question at a meeting of the Authority shall be determined by a majority of the votes of the members present and voting on the question, and in the case of an equal division of votes, the chairman of the meeting shall have a second or casting vote.

(5) The Authority may act notwithstanding one or more vacancies among its members.

(6) Subject to the provisions of this Act, the Authority shall regulate its procedure by rules.

(7) The quorum of the Authority shall be fixed by the rules made under the foregoing subsection, but—

(a) it shall not be less than three, and

(b) until it is so fixed, it shall be three.

Director-General

11.—The Authority shall from time to time appoint a person to be the chief executive officer of the Authority, and such person shall be known, and is in this Act referred to, as the Director-General.

Officers and servants (other than the Director-General) of Authority

12.—(1) The Authority shall, as well as appointing the Director-General, appoint such and so many other persons to be officers and servants of the Authority as the Authority from time to time thinks proper, but, subject to subsection (2) of this section, a person shall not be appointed under this section to be an officer of the Authority unless he has been selected by means of a public competition.

(2) The requirement under subsection (1) of this section of being selected by means of a public competition shall not apply in relation to:

(i) a person who, immediately before the establishment day, was an officer of the Minister employed in the broadcasting service,

(ii) an appointment consisting of the promotion of a person who is already an officer of the Authority,

"(iiA) an appointment consisting of the promotion of a person who is already a servant of the Authority,".

(iii) an office for which, in the opinion of the Authority, specialised qualifications not commonly held are required, or

(iv) an office to which appointments are made for limited periods only, being periods not exceeding two years.

Amendment History

Section 12(2)(iiA) inserted by s.4 of the Broadcasting Authority (Amendment) Act 1966.

Tenure of office or employment, etc.

13.—(1) An officer or servant of the Authority shall hold his office or employment on such terms and conditions as the Authority from time to time determines.

(2) There shall be paid by the Authority to its officers and servants such remuneration and allowances as the Authority from time to time determines.

(3) The Authority may at any time remove any officer or servant of the Authority from being its officer or servant.

(4) Notwithstanding the foregoing subsections of this section, the consent of the Minister shall be necessary before the Authority appoints or removes the Director-General, or alters his remuneration or his terms and conditions of holding office.

Performance of functions by officers or servants

14.—The Authority may perform any of its functions through or by any of its officers or servants duly authorised by the Authority in that behalf.

Superannuation of officers and servants of Authority

15.—(1) As soon as may be after the establishment day the Authority shall prepare and submit to the Minister a contributory scheme or schemes for the granting of pensions, gratuities and other allowances on retirement to or in respect of such officers or servants of the Authority as it may think fit.

(2) Every such scheme shall fix the time and conditions of retirement for all persons to or in respect of whom pensions, gratuities or allowances on retirement are payable under the scheme, and different times and conditions may be fixed in respect of different classes of persons.

(3) The Authority may at any time prepare and submit to the Minister a scheme amending a scheme previously submitted and approved of under this section.

(4)(a) The Minister may determine the provisions with respect to pensions, gratuities and other allowances which are to be made pursuant to this section in relation to any of the officers and servants of the Authority who, immediately before the establishment day, were officers and servants of the Minister employed in the broadcasting service.

(b) Any such provision may, if the Minister so thinks proper, have effect as on and from a day, not earlier than the 1st day of January, 1960, before the day of the Minister's determination.

(c) The provisions determined under this subsection shall be communicated by the Minister to the Authority and the Authority shall include them in the first scheme prepared and submitted under this section.

(d) Where—

(i) a person dies or retires on the ground of ill-health before the 31st day of December, 1961, and while he is an officer or servant of the Minister, and

(ii) such person was, while an officer or servant of the Minister employed in the broadcasting service, informed by the Minister that the first scheme under this section would apply to him if he became an officer or servant of the Authority, then, unless the Minister otherwise directs, the first scheme under this section shall apply to him and there shall be paid to or in respect of him such benefits under the scheme as would have been payable if he had been at the date of his death or retirement a member of the scheme.

(5) A scheme submitted to the Minister under this section shall, if approved of by the Minister with the concurrence of the Minister for Finance, be carried out by the Authority in accordance with its terms.

(6) If any dispute arises as to the claim of any person to, or the amount of, any pension, gratuity or allowance payable in pursuance of a scheme under this section, such dispute shall be submitted to the Minister who shall refer it to the Minister for Finance, whose decision shall be final.

[(6A)(a) In applying paragraph (c) of section 2 of the Perpetual Funds (Registration) Act, 1933, to a scheme under this section, that paragraph shall be construed as if 'other than subparagraphs (b) and (c) of paragraph 6 were added thereto.

(b) Subsection (3) of section 7 of the Perpetual Funds (Registration) Act, 1933, shall in relation to an application under the said section 7 by a trustee of a scheme under this section be construed as if 'other than subparagraphs (b) and (c) of paragraph 6' were inserted after 'the Schedule to this Act' in paragraph (a).

(c) Section 12 (2) of the Perpetual Funds (Registration) Act, 1933, shall in relation to a trustee of a scheme under this section be construed and have effect as if 'other than subparagraphs (b) and (c) of paragraph 6' were inserted after 'the Schedule to this Act'.]

(7) Every scheme submitted and approved of under this section shall be laid before each House of the Oireachtas as soon as may be after it is approved of and if either House, within the next twenty-one days on which that House has sat after the scheme is laid before it, passes a resolution annulling the scheme, the scheme shall be annulled accordingly, but without prejudice to the validity of anything previously done thereunder.

Amendment History

Subsection 6A inserted by s.11 of the Broadcasting Authority (Amendment) Act 1976.

Functions of Authority generally

16.—(1) The Authority shall establish and maintain a national television and sound broadcasting service [and may establish and maintain local broadcasting services] and shall have all such powers as are necessary for or incidental to [those purposes].

(2) In particular and without prejudice to the generality of subsection (1) of this section, the Authority shall have the following powers:

(a) to establish, maintain and operate broadcasting stations and to acquire, install and operate apparatus for wireless telegraphy;

(b) subject to any regulations under the Wireless Telegraphy Act, 1926, which are for the time being in force, to provide for the distribution by means of wired broadcast relay stations of programmes broadcast by the Authority and such other programmes as the Authority may decide;

(c) to originate programmes and procure programmes from any source;

(d) to make contracts, agreements and arrangements incidental or conducive to the objects of the Authority;

(e) to acquire and make use of copyrights, patents, licences, privileges and concessions;

(f) to collect news and information and to subscribe to news services and such other services as may be conducive to the objects of the Authority;

(g) to subscribe to such international associations, and to such educational, musical and dramatic bodies and such other bodies promoting entertainment or culture, as may be conducive to the objects of the Authority;

(h) (*Note*: *Repealed by section 7 of the Broadcasting Authority (Amendment) Act 1966)*

(i) to organise, provide and subsidise concerts and other entertainments in connection with the broadcasting service or for any purpose incidental thereto and, in relation to any such concert or entertainment, to provide or procure accommodation and, if desired, to make charges for admission;

(j) to prepare, publish and distribute, with or without charge, such magazines, books, papers and other printed matter as may seem to the Authority to be conducive or incidental to its objects;

(k) (Note: *Repealed by s.7 of the Broadcasting Authority (Amendment) Act, 1966)*

[(l) to arrange with other broadcasting authorities for the distribution, receipt, exchange and relay of programmes (whether live or recorded);

(m) to compile, publish and distribute, with or without charge, recorded aural and visual material;

(n) subject to the consent of the Minister, to provide services for and on behalf of Ministers of State.]

(3)(a) The powers conferred on the Authority by virtue of paragraphs (a) and (b) of subsection (2) of this section shall not be exercised save under licence issued by the Minister and in accordance with any conditions attached by the Minister to such licences.

(b) During any emergency declared under section 10 of the Act of 1926, the Minister may suspend any licence under this subsection and, while any such suspension continues, the Minister may operate any service which was provided by the Authority under the suspended licence.

(c) A copy of every licence under this subsection shall be laid before each House of the Oireachtas as soon as may be after the issue of the licence.

Amendment History

Paragraphs (h) and (k) of subs.(2) repealed by s.7 of the Broadcasting Authority (Amendment) Act 1966. Paragraphs (l), (m) and (n) of subs.(2) inserted by s.5 of the Broadcasting Authority (Amendment) Act 1966. Paragraph (b) of subs.(2) substituted by s.12 of the Broadcasting Authority (Amendment) Act 1976. The words "subject to the consent of the Minister" in paras (j) and (m) were repealed by s.21 of the Broadcasting Authority (Amendment) Act 1976. Subsection (1) amended by s.3 of the Broadcasting Authority (Amendment) Act 1979.

[General duty of Authority

17.—In performing its functions the Authority shall in its programming—

(a) be responsive to the interests and concerns of the whole community, be mindful of the need for understanding and peace within the whole island of Ireland, ensure that the programmes reflect the varied elements which make up the culture of the people of the whole island of Ireland, and have special regard for the elements which distinguish that culture and in particular for the Irish language,

(b) uphold the democratic values enshrined in the Constitution, especially those relating to rightful liberty of expression, and

(c) have regard to the need for the formation of public awareness and understanding of the values and traditions of countries other than the State, including in particular those of such countries which are members of the European Economic Community].

Amendment History

Section 17 substituted by s.13 of the Broadcasting Authority (Amendment) Act 1976.

Impartiality

18.— [(1) Subject to subsection (1A) of this section, it shall be the duty of the

Authority to ensure that—

(a) all news broadcast by it is reported and presented in an objective and impartial manner and without any expression of the Authority's own views,

(b) the broadcast treatment of current affairs, including matters which are either of public controversy or the subject of current public debate, is fair to all interests concerned and that the broadcast matter is presented in an objective and impartial manner and without any expression of the Authority's own views,

(c) any matter, whether written, aural or visual, and which relates to news or current affairs, including matters which are either of public controversy or the subject of current public debate, which pursuant to section 16 of this Act is published, distributed or sold by the Authority is presented by it in an objective and impartial manner.

Paragraph (b) of this subsection, in so far as it requires the Authority not to express its own views, shall not apply to any broadcast in so far as the broadcast relates to any proposal, being a proposal concerning policy as regards broadcasting, which is of public controversy or the subject of current public debate and which is being considered by the Government or the Minister.

Should it prove impracticable in a single programme to apply paragraph (b) of this subsection, two or more related broadcasts may be considered as a whole; provided that the broadcasts are transmitted within a reasonable period.

(1A) The Authority is hereby prohibited from including in any of its broadcasts or in any matter referred to in paragraph (c) of subsection (1) of this section anything which may reasonably be regarded as being likely to promote, or incite to, crime or as tending to undermine the authority of the State.

(1B) The Authority shall not, in its programmes and in the means employed to make such programmes, unreasonably encroach on the privacy of an individual.]

(2) Nothing in this section shall prevent the Authority from transmitting political party broadcasts.

Amendment History

Subsection 18(1) replaced and subs.(1B) inserted by s.3 of the Broadcasting Authority (Amendment) Act 1976.

[Broadcasting Complaints Commission

18A.—(1) Not later than the 31st day of March, 1977, there shall be established by the Government, on the request of the Minister, a body to be known as the Broadcasting Complaints Commission and which is in this Act referred to as the Commission.

(2) The Commission shall consist of a Chairman and not less than two other members who shall be appointed by the Government.

(3) The Minister may out of moneys provided by the Oireachtas, with the consent of the Minister for Finance, in each financial year make a grant or grants to the Commission of such amount or amounts as he considers necessary to enable the Commission to perform its functions.

(4) When appointing a member of the Commission, the Government shall fix his term of office which shall not exceed five years and, subject to subsections (8) and (9) of this section, he shall hold his office on such terms and conditions (other than terms or conditions relating to remuneration or the payment of allowances) as are determined by the Government at the time of his appointment.

(5) A member of the Commission may at any time resign his office by letter addressed to the Government and the resignation shall take effect as on and from the date of receipt of the letter by the Government.

(6) A member of the Commission whose term of office expires by the effluxion of time shall be eligible for re-appointment.

(7) There shall be paid to members of the Commission such remuneration (if any) and allowances (if any) as the Minister, with the consent of the Minister for the Public Service, from time to time determines.

(8) A member of the Commission may be removed from office by the Government for stated reasons, if, and only if, resolutions are passed by each House of the Oireachtas calling for his removal.

(9) Where a member of the Commission is nominated as a member of Seanad Éireann or for election to either House of the Oireachtas, he shall, upon accepting such nomination, cease to be a member of the Commission.

(10)(a) A person who is for the time being entitled under the Standing Orders of either House of the Oireachtas to sit therein shall, while so entitled, be disqualified from becoming a member of the Commission.

(b) A member of the Authority or an officer or servant of the Authority shall be disqualified from becoming or being a member of the Commission.

(11)The quorum for a meeting of the Commission shall be two or such higher number as the Commission may, if it thinks fit, from time to time by resolution determine.

(12)Subject to the provisions of this Act, the Commission shall regulate its procedure and business.

(13)The Minister for the Public Service shall assign to the Commission such officers and servants as in his opinion are necessary to enable it to perform its functions.

Functions of Commission

18B.—(1) Subject to the provisions of this section, the Commission may investigate and decide any of the following complaints—

(a) a complaint that in broadcasting news given by it and specified in the complaint, the Authority did not comply with one or more of the requirements of section 18 (1) of this Act (inserted by section 3 of the Broadcasting Authority (Amendment) Act, 1976),

(b) a complaint that in broadcasting a programme so specified, the Authority either did not comply with one or more of the said requirements or were in breach of the prohibition contained in section 18 (1A) off this Act (inserted by the said section 3),

(c) a complaint that by broadcasting matter so specified, the Authority failed to comply with the requirements of section 31 (1) of this Act (inserted by section 16 of the Broadcasting Authority (Amendment) Act, 1976) as regards an order made under the said section 31 (1) and so specified,

(d) a complaint that on an occasion so specified, there was an encroachment by the Authority contrary to section 18 (1B) of this Act (inserted by the said section 3),

(e) a complaint that an advertisement so specified contravened a code drawn up by the Authority governing standards and practice in broadcast advertising or prohibiting either certain methods of advertising in broadcasting or the broadcast in particular circumstances of advertising.

(f) a complaint that the Authority failed to comply with the requirements of subsection (1) or subsection (1A) of section 18 of this Act (inserted by the said section 3) in relation to a matter so specified which is a matter mentioned in paragraph (c) of the said subsection (1).

[(g) a complaint by a person that on a specified occasion an assertion was made in a broadcast of inaccurate facts or information in relation to that person which constituted an attack on that person's honour or reputation.]

(2) A complaint described in subsection (1) of this section may be made to the Commission by any person in writing but, if the complaint is a complaint other than one described in paragraph (f) of the said subsection (1), it shall only be considered by the Commission if the following provisions are complied with, namely;

(a) prior to its being made to the Commission, the complaint is made to the Authority in writing and is received by the Authority not more than thirty days after—

(i) in case the complaint relates to one broadcast or to two or more unrelated broadcasts, if it relates to one broadcast, the date of the broadcast, or if it relates to two or more such broadcasts, the date of the earlier or earliest, as the case may be, of those broadcasts, and

(ii) in case the complaint relates to two or more related broadcasts of which at least two are made on different dates, the later or latest of those dates,

(b) the complaint is received by the Commission not sooner than thirty days after the day on which it is sent by the complainant to the Authority and is so received not later than—

(i) in case within the period of thirty days beginning on the day on which the complaint is so sent by him, the complainant receives from the Authority a statement in writing of its decision on the complaint, thirty days after the receipt by him of the statement, and

(ii) in any other case, sixty days after the day on which the complaint is sent by the complainant to the Authority.

(3)(a) Subject to subsection (2) of this section, the Commission may, after consultation with the Authority, make rules of procedure as regards complaints described in paragraph (f) of subsection (1) of this section.

(b) Where the Commission makes rules under this section, the Commission shall give public notice of the making of the rules in such manner as the Minister shall approve and the Commission shall make a copy of such rules available to any person on request.

(4) When the Commission proposes to investigate a complaint made under this section, the Commission shall afford to the Authority an opportunity to comment on the complaint.

(5) Where a complaint is made to the Commission and a person employed by the Authority requests, for reasons specified by him, the Commission to afford him an opportunity to comment on the complaint, if, having considered the reasons so specified, the Commission is satisfied that an interest of the person, being an interest which the Commission considers relevant to the person's employment by the Authority, may, because of the complaint, be adversely affected, the Commission shall afford to the person such an opportunity.

(6) When the Commission proposes to consider a complaint described in subsection (1) (e) of this section, the Commission shall afford to the relevant advertiser an opportunity of making to the Commission submissions in relation to the relevant advertisement.

(7) As soon as may be after they decide on a complaint made under this Act, the Commission shall send to the person making the complaint and to the Authority a statement in writing of their decision on the complaint.

(8) In case the Commission decide on a complaint described in subsection (1) (e) of this section, as soon as may be after their decision, the Commission shall, (in addition to complying with the requirement of subsection (7) of this section) send to the person with whom the Authority agreed to broadcast the relevant advertisement .(if he is not the complainant) a statement in writing of their decision.

(9) When the Authority receives a statement of a decision from the Commission pursuant to subsection (7) of this section, the Authority shall, not later than fourteen days after its receipt, inform the Commission in writing whether or not the Commission's decision is accepted by the Authority.

(10)The consideration by the Commission of a complaint made to it under this Act shall be carried out by the Commission in private.

(11)Unless it considers it inappropriate the Commission shall, as soon as may be publish particulars of its decision on a complaint in such manner as it considers suitable and where it considers that the publication should be by the Authority, or should include publication by the Authority, the particulars shall be published by the Authority in such manner as shall be agreed between the Commission and the Authority.

[(11A) Without prejudice to subsection (11) of this section, the Authority shall, unless the Commission considers it inappropriate, broadcast the Commission's decision on every complaint considered by the Commission in which the Commission found in favour, in whole or in part, of the complainant, including any correction of inaccurate facts or information relating to an individual arising from a complaint under subsection (1) (*g*) of this section, at a time and in a manner corresponding to that in which the offending broadcast took place.]

(12)As regards proceedings under this section, the Commission shall not have any power to award to any party costs or expenses.

(13)A person shall not act as a member of the Commission in relation to any matter with respect to which he has a material financial or other beneficial interest.

(14)Subsection (1) of this section shall not apply to a complaint which, in the opinion of the Commission, is frivolous or vexatious, nor, unless the Commission considers that there are special reasons for investigating the complaint (which reasons shall be stated by the Commission when giving its decision), shall that subsection apply to a complaint which is withdrawn.

(4) For the purposes of an investigation by the Broadcasting Complaints Commission pursuant to regulations under this section—

(a) the Broadcasting Authority Act, 1960, shall have effect subject to the following modifications—

(i) a reference in sections 18B and 18C (inserted by the Broadcasting Authority (Amendment) Act, 1976), other than in section 18B (1) (e), to the Authority shall be construed as a reference to the sound broadcasting contractor concerned;

(ii) a reference in section 18B (7) (as so inserted) to the Authority shall be construed as referring to the sound broadcasting contractor concerned and to the Commission established by this Act;

(iii) a reference in section 18B (as so inserted) to section 18 (1), section 18 (1A) or section 18 (1B) of the Broadcasting Authority Act, 1960, shall be construed as a reference to section 9;

(iv) a reference in section 18B (as so inserted) to a complaint that an advertisement contravened a code drawn up by Radio Telefís Éireann governing standards in broadcast advertising, or prohibiting either certain methods of advertising in broadcasting or a broadcast in particular circumstances of advertising, shall be construed as a reference to section 10 (2);

(v) a reference in section 18B (as so inserted) to section 31 (1) of the Broadcasting Authority Act, 1960, shall be construed as a reference to section 12.

(3) A reference in the said section 18B to a code shall be construed as including a reference to a code in force under section 4 of this Act.

Amendment History

References in ss.18B and 18C (Radio and Television Act 1988—s. 11, below) are redefined as a non-textual amendment for s.11(4) of the Radio and Television Act 1988. Paragraph (g) in s.18B(1) inserted by s.8(1) of the Broadcasting Act 1990. Section 18B(11A) inserted by s.8(2) of the Broadcasting Act 1990. "A reference in section 18B to a code shall be construed as including a reference to a code in force under section 4 of the Broadcasting Act 1990"—non-textual amendment.

Reports of Commission

18C.—(1) As soon as may be after the end of each year, the Commission shall make to the Minister a report of its activities during that year and, subject to subsection (2) of this section, the report shall contain such statements (if any) as the Commission thinks fit giving particulars of decisions made by it pursuant to this Act, and copies of the report shall, as soon as may be, be laid before both Houses of the Oireachtas.

(2) In case the Authority pursuant to section 18 (9) of this Act informs the Commission that it does not accept a decision of the Commission, the Commission's report for the year in which the Commission was so informed shall contain a statement giving particulars of the decision.]

Amendment History

Sections 18A, 18B and 18C inserted by s.4 of the Broadcasting Authority (Amendment) Act 1976. References in sections 18B and 18C (Radio and Television Act 1988—s.11, heading above) are redefined as a non-textual amendment for s.11(4) of the Radio and Television Act 1988. Section 11(4) of the Radio and Television Act 1988 states that for the purposes of an investigation by the Broadcasting Complaints Commission pursuant to regulations under this section—

(a) the Broadcasting Authority Act, 1960, shall have effect subject to the following modifications—

(i) a reference in sections 18B and 18C (inserted by the Broadcasting Authority (Amendment) Act, 1976), other than in section 18B (1) (e), to the Authority shall be construed as a reference to the sound broadcasting contractor concerned;

(ii) a reference in section 18B (7) (as so inserted) to the Authority shall be construed as referring to the sound broadcasting contractor concerned and to the Commission established by this Act;

(iii) a reference in section 18B (as so inserted) to section 18 (1), section 18 (1A) or section 18 (1B) of the Broadcasting Authority Act, 1960, shall be construed as a reference to section 9;

(iv) a reference in section 18B (as so inserted) to a complaint that an advertisement contravened a code drawn up by Radio Telefís Éireann governing standards in broadcast advertising, or prohibiting either certain methods of advertising in broadcasting or a broadcast in particular circumstances of advertising, shall be construed as a reference to section 10 (2);

(v) a reference in section 18B (as so inserted) to section 31 (1) of the Broadcasting Authority Act, 1960, shall be construed as a reference to section 12.

(b) Section 6 of the Broadcasting Authority (Amendment) Act, 1976, shall have effect as if a reference therein to the Authority were a reference to the sound broadcasting contractor concerned.

[Approval of total time per year for broadcasting

19.—The total number of hours per year of broadcasting by the Authority in providing—

(a) its television service.

(b) its sound broadcasting service, shall neither exceed a maximum nor be less than a minimum fixed by the Authority, with the approval of the Minister, for that service.]

Amendment History

Section 19 substituted by s.14 of the Broadcasting Authority (Amendment) Act 1976.

Advertisements

20.—(1) The Authority may broadcast advertisements, may fix charges and conditions for such broadcasts and, in fixing the charges, may provide for different circumstances and for additional special charges to be made in special cases.

(2) The Authority may reject any advertisement presented for broadcast in whole or in part.

(3) *(Repealed by s.19 of the Broadcasting Act 1990)*

(4) The Authority shall not accept any advertisement which is directed towards any religious or political end or has any relation to any industrial dispute.

(5)(a) In acting pursuant to this section, the Authority shall have regard to the special position of Irish advertisers and may fix reduced charges and preferential conditions for advertisements from them which are Irish advertisements.

(b) For the purposes of the foregoing paragraph, each of the following advertisers shall be an Irish advertiser:

(i) an advertiser who advertises articles, being articles with respect to which he satisfies the Authority that they are made, produced or manufactured wholly or substantially within the State,

(ii) an advertiser who advertises services, provided that he satisfies the Authority either that the services are provided wholly or substantially within the State or that his sole or principal place of business as a person providing those services is situate within the State,

(iii) an advertiser who advertises activities other than services, being activities with respect to which he satisfies the Authority that they are conducted wholly or substantially within the State, and an advertisement by reference to which an advertiser is an Irish advertiser shall be an Irish advertisement.

(6) Charges and conditions referred to in subsection (1) or subsection (5) of this section may be fixed subject to variations benefiting advertisers who use the Irish language in their advertisements.

(7) A power under this section to fix charges and conditions shall be construed as including a power to cancel or vary any charges or conditions fixed under such power and, where charges or conditions are cancelled, to fix other charges or conditions in lieu of those cancelled.

(8) In this section references to advertisements shall be construed as including references to advertising matter in sponsored programmes, that is to say, programmes supplied for advertising purposes by or on behalf of an advertiser.

Amendment History

Section 20(3) repealed by s.19 of the Broadcasting Act 1990.

Advice to Authority

21.— [(1) For the purpose of enabling the Authority to have advice in performing its functions, the Authority may, with the consent of the Minister, from time to time appoint advisory committees or advisers.

(2)(a) A committee under this section shall consist of so many members (not being less than three) as the Authority considers proper.

(b) A member of a committee under this section shall, unless he previously dies or resigns, retain his membership for the period determined by the Authority when appointing him and no longer, but shall be eligible for re-appointment.

(c) A committee under this section shall meet whenever summoned by the Authority.

(3)(a) An adviser under this section shall, unless he previously dies or resigns, continue as adviser for the period determined by the Authority when appointing him and no longer, but shall be eligible for re-appointment.

(b) An adviser under this section shall advise the Authority whenever requested by the Authority.]

(4) The Authority and the Director-General shall have regard to, but shall not be bound by, the advice of any committee or adviser under this section.

(5) The Authority may pay to a member of any committee under this section or an adviser under this section such amounts in respect of expenses as the Authority considers reasonable.

Amendment History

Subsections (1)–(3) substituted by s.5 of the Broadcasting Authority (Amendment) Act 1976.

Annual amounts to be paid to Authority by Minister

22.—(1) Subject to subsection (2) of this section, the Minister, with the approval of the Minister for Finance, may, in respect of each of the five consecutive financial years beginning with that in which the establishment day occurs, pay to the Authority out of moneys provided by the Oireachtas—

(a) an amount equal to the total of the receipts in that year in respect of broadcasting licence fees less—

(i) any expenses certified by the Minister as having been incurred by him in that year in relation to the collection of those fees, and

(ii) any expenses certified by the Minister as having been incurred by him in that year in respect of the performance of his functions under sections 12 and 12A of the Act of 1926 in relation to interfering with or injuriously affecting wireless telegraphy apparatus for receiving only, and

(b) such further amount as the Minister considers reasonable.

(2) The total of the amounts paid pursuant to paragraph (b) of subsection (1) of this section shall not exceed five hundred thousand pounds.

Repayable advances

23.—(1) The Minister for Finance may make advances to the Authority for capital purposes (including working capital purposes).

(2) Advances under this section—

(a) shall be made out of the Central Fund or the growing produce thereof,

(b) [shall not exceed twenty-five million pounds in the aggregate,]

(c) shall be made on the recommendation of the Minister,

(d) shall be made on such term and conditions as to repayment as the Minister for Finance thinks proper.

Amendment History

Section 23(2)(b) amended by s.2 of the Broadcasting Authority (Amendment) Act 1979.

(3) The Minister for Finance may, for the purpose of providing for the advance of sums out of the Central Fund under this section, borrow on the security of the Central Fund or the growing produce thereof any sums required for that purpose, and, for the purposes of such borrowing, he may create and issue securities bearing such rate of interest and subject to such conditions as to repayment, redemption or any other matter as he thinks fit, and shall pay all moneys so borrowed into the Exchequer.

(4) The principal of and interest on all securities issued under this section shall

be charged on and payable out of the Central Fund or the growing produce thereof.

General duty of Authority with respect to its revenue

24.—It shall be the duty of the Authority so to conduct its affairs as to secure that its revenue becomes at the earliest possible date, and thereafter continues, at least sufficient—

(a) to meet all sums properly chargeable to current account, and

(b) to make suitable provision with respect to capital expenditure.

Accounts and audits

25.—(1) The Authority shall keep in such form as shall be approved by the Minister, after consultation with the Minister for Finance, all proper and usual accounts of all moneys received or expended by it, including an income and expenditure account and a balance sheet, and, in particular, shall keep in such form as aforesaid all such special accounts as the Minister on his own motion, or at the request of the Minister for Finance, shall from time to time direct.

[(1A) (*note: repealed by s.19 of the Broadcasting Act 1990)*

(1B) (*note: repealed by s.19 of the Broadcasting Act 1990)*

(2) (*note: repealed by s.7 of the Broadcasting Authority (Amendment) Act 1966)*

(3) (*note: repealed by s.7 of the Broadcasting Authority (Amendment) Act 1966)*

(4) (*note: repealed by s.7 of the Broadcasting Authority (Amendment) Act 1966)*

(5) The Minister shall cause the documents furnished to him under this section to be laid before each House of the Oireachtas.

Amendment History

Subsections (1A) and (1B) inserted by s.6 of the Broadcasting Authority (Amendment) Act 1966. Subsections (1A) and (1B) repealed by s.19 of the Broadcasting Act 1990. Subsections (2)–(4) repealed by s.7 of the Broadcasting Authority (Amendment) Act 1966.

Annual report and information to the Minister

26.—(1) The Authority shall, in each year, at such date as the Minister may direct, make a report to the Minister of its proceedings under this Act during the preceding year, and the Minister shall cause copies of the report to be laid before each House of the Oireachtas.

(2) Whenever the Minister so directs, the annual report shall also include information on such particular aspects of the Authority's proceedings under this Act as the Minister may specify.

(3) The Authority shall submit to the Minister such information regarding the performance of its functions as he may from time to time require.

Borrowing powers for general purposes

27.—(1) The Authority may, with the consent of the Minister for Finance and the Minister, borrow money [(including money in a currency other than the currency of the State)] by means of the creation of stock or other forms of security to be issued, transferred, dealt with and redeemed in such manner and on such terms and conditions as the Authority with the consents aforesaid, may determine.

(2) The borrowing powers conferred by this section on the Authority may be exercised for any purpose arising in the performance of its functions, but there may be attached to consent to borrow the condition that the moneys shall be utilised only for the purpose of a programme of capital works approved of by the Minister.

(3) The terms upon which moneys are borrowed under this section may include provisions charging the moneys and interest thereon upon all property of whatsoever kind for the time being vested in the Authority or upon any particular property of the Authority and provisions establishing the priority of such charges amongst themselves and in relation to charges in respect of advances made to the Authority out of the Central Fund and such terms may provide that any charge in respect of moneys so borrowed may rank before or equally with charges in respect of such advances.

Amendment History

Section 27(1) amended by s.10 of the Broadcasting Authority (Amendment) Act 1976.

[Temporary borrowing

28.—(1) The Authority may, with the consent of the Minister, borrow temporarily by arrangement with bankers such sums (including sums in currency other than the currency of the State) as it may require for the purpose of providing for current expenditure, provided that borrowing by the Authority under this subsection of sums in currency other than the currency of the State shall also require the consent of the Minister for Finance.

(2) The Authority may, other than for the purpose of providing for current expenditure, with the consent of the Minister, which consent shall only be given if he is satisfied that the circumstances are exceptional, borrow temporarily by arrangement with bankers such sums (in the currency of the State) as it may require for the purpose mentioned in section 27 (2) of this Act.]

Amendment History

Section 28 substituted by s.15 of the Broadcasting Authority (Amendment) Act 1976.

Investment by Authority

29.—The Authority may invest any of its funds in any manner in which a trustee is empowered by law to invest trust funds.

Acquisition and disposal of land

30.—(1) The Authority may acquire by agreement any land or any easement, wayleave or other right in respect of land.

(2)(a) The Authority may acquire land compulsorily for the purpose of providing a site for, or approaches to, any broadcasting station, being a station intended to be used solely for transmitting, repeating or relaying.

(b) The Authority may acquire compulsorily any easement, wayleave or other right in respect of land if it is to be acquired in relation to a site for any broadcasting station, being a station intended to be used solely for transmitting, repeating or relaying.

(3) The Authority may dispose of any land vested in it which it no longer requires.

(4) The provisions of the First Schedule to this Act shall apply to the exercise by the Authority of its powers under subsection (2) of this section.

Directions by Minister

31.— [(1) Where the Minister is of the opinion that the broadcasting of a particular matter or any matter of a particular class would be likely to promote, or incite to, crime or would tend to undermine the authority of the State, he may by order direct the Authority to refrain from broadcasting the matter or any matter of the particular class, and the Authority shall comply with the order.

(1A) An order under subsection (1) of this section shall remain in force for such period not exceeding twelve months as is specified in the order and the period for which the order is to remain in force may be extended or further extended by an order made by the Minister or by a resolution passed by both Houses of the Oireachtas providing for its extension; provided that the period for which an order under the said subsection (1) is extended or further extended by an order or resolution under this subsection shall not exceed a period of twelve months.

(1B) Every order made by the Minister under this section shall be laid before each House of the Oireachtas as soon as may be after it is made and, if a resolution annulling the order is passed by either such House within the next twenty-one days on which that House has sat after the order is laid before it, the order shall be annulled accordingly but without prejudice to its validity prior to the annulment.]

(2) The Minister may direct the Authority in writing to allocate broadcasting time for any announcements by or on behalf of any Minister of State in connection with the functions of that Minister of State, and the Authority shall comply with the direction.

Amendment History

Subsection 1 substituted and subss.(1A) and (1B) inserted by s.16 of the Broadcasting Authority (Amendment) Act 1976. Section 12 of the Radio and Television Act 1988 inserted here for context, which states that every direction given to Radio Telefís Éireann pursuant to s.31(1) of the Broadcasting Authority Act 1960, by the Minister which is in force on the commencement of this Act or which is given by him after such commencement, shall, for so long as the direction remains in force, apply to a sound broadcasting service provided pursuant to a sound broadcasting contract and shall be complied with by a sound broadcasting contractor as if the direction were given to him, and the said s.31(1) shall be construed and have effect accordingly.

Transfer of property and liabilities

32.—(1) All property (excluding land and any benefit or interest referred to in Part III of the Second Schedule to this Act) and all rights (including rights under licences and assignments in copyright) held or enjoyed immediately before the establishment day by the Minister in connection with his functions under Part II of the Act of 1926 shall, by virtue of this subsection, become transferred to the Authority on the establishment day, and accordingly—

(a) that property shall, on the establishment day, vest in the Authority, and

(b) those rights shall, on and after the establishment day, be enjoyed by the Authority.

(2) On the establishment day, the lands described in Part I of the Second Schedule to this Act shall, by virtue of this subsection, vest in the Authority for all the interest therein which immediately before the establishment day was vested in the Minister for Finance.

(3) On the establishment day the lands described in Part II of the Second Schedule to this Act shall, by virtue of this subsection, vest in the Authority for all the interest therein which immediately before the establishment day was vested in the Commissioners.

(4) On the establishment day any benefit or interest specified in Part III of the Second Schedule to this Act shall, by virtue of this subsection, vest in the Authority.

(5)(a) On the establishment day the lands described in Part IV of the Second Schedule to this Act shall, by virtue of this subsection, vest, in the Authority for all the interest therein which immediately before the establishment day was vested in the Commissioners.

(b) The Registrar of Titles shall, at the request of the Authority made on or after the establishment day, cause the Authority to be registered under the Registry of Title Act, 1891 (1891, c. 66.), as owner of the lands described in Part IV of the Second Schedule to this Act.

(c) No fees shall be payable in respect of any proceedings in the Land Registry under this subsection.

(6) Subsections (2), (3) and (5) of this section shall, for the purposes of section 6 of the Conveyancing Act, 1881 (1881, c. 41.), have effect as conveyances of land.

(7)(a) In this subsection, "the Agreement" means the Agreement made on the 30th day of October, 1957, between the City of Cork Vocational Education Committee of the first part, the Minister for Finance of the second part, the Minister of the third part and the Commissioners of the fourth part, whereby it was (amongst other things) agreed that when the Broadcasting Station therein referred to shall have been duly completed, the said Committee shall by deed grant to the Commissioners a lease of the said Broadcasting Station for a term of 150 years from the 25th day of March, 1952.

(b) If the Lease referred to in Clause 5 of the Agreement is not executed before the establishment day:—

(i) the benefit of the Commissioners under the said Clause 5 shall, on the establishment day, vest, by virtue of this paragraph, in the Authority,

(ii) the references to the Minister in Clause (2) of the part of the Schedule to the Agreement which is headed "Covenants by the Lessors" shall, on and after the establishment day, have effect as references to the Authority.

(c) If the Lease referred to in Clause 5 of the Agreement is executed before the establishment day—

(i) the lessee's interest under the said Lease shall, on the establishment day, vest, by virtue of this paragraph, in the Authority,

(ii) the provisions inserted in the said Lease in pursuance of Clause (2) of the part of the Schedule to the Agreement which is headed "Covenants by the Lessor" shall, on and after the establishment day, have effect as if for the references to the Minister there were substituted references to the Authority.

(8)(a) In this subsection—

"the Agreement" means the Agreement for Sale made on the 28th day of September, 1959, between the Right Honourable Mervyn Patrick 9th Viscount Powerscourt of the one part and the Commissioners of the other part whereby it was agreed (amongst other things) that the said Viscount Powerscourt should sell and the Commissioners purchase the lands therein described as "All That part of the townland of Kippure East Barony of Talbotstown Lower containing fifteen acres two roods and twelve perches and part of the townland of Powerscourt Mountain Barony of Rathdown containing two acres one rood twenty-eight perches statute measure or thereabouts both situate in the County of Wicklow and shown outlined in red on the map annexed hereto" together with the right of way specified therein and the easements referred to in clause 16 thereof.

(b) If the conveyance of the lands the subject of the Agreement is not executed before the establishment day—

(i) the benefit of the Commissioners under the Agreement shall, on the establishment day, vest, by virtue of this paragraph, in the Authority,

(ii) the references to the Commissioners in clauses 15 and 16 of the Agreement shall, on and after the establishment day, have effect as references to the Authority.

(c) If the conveyance of the lands the subject of the Agreement is executed before the establishment day,

(i) the interests of the Commissioners in the said lands shall, on the establishment day, vest, by virtue of this paragraph, in the Authority,

(ii) the provisions inserted in the said conveyance in pursuance of clauses 15 and 16 of the Agreement shall, on and after the establishment day, have effect as if for the references to the Commissioners there were substituted references to the Authority,

(iii) subparagraph (i) of this paragraph shall, for the purposes of section 6 of the Conveyancing Act, 1881 (1881, c. 41), have effect as a conveyance of land.

(9) Every debt and other liability (including unliquidated liabilities arising from torts or breaches of contract) which, immediately before the establishment day is owing and unpaid or has been incurred and is undischarged by the Minister or the Commissioners and is so owing or has been incurred in relation to broadcasting (including the proposed television service) shall, on the establishment day, become and be the debt or liability of the Authority and shall be paid or discharged by and may be recovered from and enforced against the Authority accordingly.

(10)The Minister for Finance shall, as soon as may be after the establishment day, certify the sums which in his opinion, represent the value of the property and rights, transferred by the preceding subsections of this section, together with the cost of development of any such property.

(11)Every sum certified under subsection (10) of this section shall be a debt due by the Authority to the Minister for Finance and the debt shall be discharged at such time or times, in such manner and upon such terms as the Minister for Finance, after consultation with the Minister, determines.

(12)(*note: repealed by s.197 of the Finance Act 1999*)

Amendment History

Section 32(12) repealed by s.197 of the Finance Act 1999.

Preservation of contracts and continuance of legal proceedings

33.—(1) Every contract which was entered into in relation to broadcasting (including the proposed television service) and is in force immediately before the establishment day between the Minister or the Commissioners and any person shall continue in force on and after the establishment day, but shall be construed and have effect as if the Authority were substituted therein for the Minister or the Commissioners (as the case may be), and every such contract shall be enforceable by or against the Authority accordingly.

(2) Where, immediately before the establishment day, any legal proceedings (other than a prosecution) are pending to which the Minister is a party and the proceedings have reference to broadcasting, the name of the Authority shall be substituted in the proceedings for that of the Minister, and the proceedings shall not abate by reason of such substitution.

Amendment of Act of 1926

34.—The Act of 1926 is hereby amended as follows:

(a) the Minister shall not, on or after the establishment day, exercise any of the powers conferred on him by Part II;

(b) (*note: amendments applied*)

(c) (*note: amendments applied*)

(d) (*note: amendments applied*)

(e) (*note: amendments applied*)

(f) (*note: amendments applied*)

Expenses of Minister

35.—The expenses incurred by the Minister in the administration of this Act shall, to such extent as may be sanctioned by the Minister for Finance, be paid out of moneys provided by the Oireachtas.

Short title

36.—This Act may be cited as the Broadcasting Authority Act, 1960.

FIRST SCHEDULE

PROVISIONS RELATING TO COMPULSORY ACQUISITION.

Entry on land, etc., before conveyance.

1.(1) At any time before conveyance or ascertainment of price, the Authority may, subject to this paragraph, enter on and take possession of the land to be acquired or exercise the right to be acquired.

(2) Where the Authority exercises any power under the foregoing subparagraph, it shall be liable to pay, to the occupier of the land which is to be acquired or in respect of which the right is to be exercised, interest on the amount of the price payable to such occupier at the rate of five per cent. per annum from the date of entry until payment of the price.

(3) The Authority shall not—

(a) enter on or take possession of any land under this paragraph without giving to the occupier at least three months' previous notice in writing of its intention so to do, or

(b) exercise any right under this paragraph without giving to the occupier of the land in respect of which the right is to be exercised at least three months' previous notice in writing of its intention so to do.

(4) A notice under this paragraph may be served on any person by sending it by registered post in an envelope addressed to him at his usual or last known address.

(5) Where, for any reason, the envelope cannot be so addressed, it may be addressed to the person for whom it is intended in either or both of the following ways:

(a) by the description "the occupier" without stating his name,

(b) at the land to which the notice relates.

Deposit of maps, plans, etc.

2.(1) Not later than one month before entering on land or exercising any right under the foregoing paragraph, the Authority shall cause maps, plans, and books of reference to be deposited in accordance with this paragraph.

(2) The maps and plans shall be sufficient in quantity and character to show on adequate scales the land or right proposed to be acquired.

(3) The books of reference shall contain the names of the owners or reputed owners, lessees or reputed lessees, and occupiers of the land which is proposed to be acquired or in respect of which the right is proposed to be exercised.

(4) The maps, plans, and books of reference shall be deposited at the head office of the Authority and at such other places as the Authority considers suitable and shall remain so deposited for at least three months and shall, while so deposited, be open to inspection by any person, free of charge, between the hours of ten o'clock in the morning and four o'clock in the afternoon on every, day except Saturdays, Sundays and bank holidays.

(5) As soon as may be after the deposit of any maps, plans, or books of reference, the Authority shall give public notice of the deposit by advertisement published twice in each of two or more daily newspapers and in such other newspapers as the Authority considers suitable.

(6) The public notice shall state that the maps, plans, or books of reference to which it relates are open to public inspection in accordance with this paragraph and shall state the times and places at which they may be inspected.

Assessment of price.

3.(1) The amount of the price to be paid by the Authority for any land acquired to the several persons entitled thereto or having estates or interests therein, or for any right acquired to the several persons entitled to or having estates or interests in the land in respect of which the right is exercised, shall, in default of agreement, be fixed under and in accordance with the Acquisition of Land (Assessment of Compensation) Act, 1919.

(2) Sections 69 to 83 of the Lands Clauses Consolidation Act, 1845 (as adapted or amended by or under any subsequent Act) shall apply to the said price and to the conveyance to the Authority of the land or right acquired, and for the purpose of the application the Authority shall be deemed to be the promoters of the undertaking.

Time for claims for price

4. All claims for the price of any land or right acquired shall be made within one year after the land or right is first entered on or exercised by the Authority.

Powers and duties where acquired land is subject to a land purchase annuity, etc.

5.(1) In this paragraph, "public authority" means the Irish Land Commission or the Commissioners.

(2) Where land acquired by the Authority is subject, either alone or in conjunction

with other land, to a land purchase annuity, payment in lieu of rent or other annual sum (not being merely rent under a contract of tenancy) payable to a public authority, the Authority shall, as from the date on which it enters on and takes possession of the land so acquired—

(a) become and be liable for the payment to the public authority of such annual sum, or such portion thereof as shall be apportioned by the public authority on such land, as if the land had been transferred to the Authority by the owner thereof on that date, and

(b) be entitled, if the Authority so thinks fit, to redeem the annual sum or such portion thereof as aforesaid, and

(c) be obliged, if required by the public authority to do so, to redeem such annual sum or such portion thereof as aforesaid.

Section 32 (2), (3) (4) and (5).

SECOND SCHEDULE

LANDS, ETC. TRANSFERRED TO AUTHORITY

PART I

The lands demised by an Indenture of Lease dated the 31st day of January, 1883, made between Samuel H. Bolton of the one part and the Right Honourable Henry Fawcett, then Postmaster General, of the other part and therein described as "All that and those the plot or parcel of ground on the Grove Estate being part of the Lands of St. Supulchre situate in the Township of Rathmines Parish of St. Kevin's and county of Dublin bounded on the North and West by other premises in possession of the said Samuel H. Bolton on the East by Rathmines Road and on the South in an oblique direction by premises occupied by Mr. Henry E. Flavelle known as No. 155 Rathmines Road measuring on the North side one hundred feet on the West ten feet on the East seventy two feet and on the South side in an oblique direction one hundred and eight feet be the same more or less and which said premises are more particularly delineated on the map thereof drawn in red colour upon these presents together with the rights, members and appurtenances thereto belonging."

PART II

The lands (in this Part of this Schedule referred to as the originally demised lands) demised by an Indenture of Lease dated the 7th day of December, 1908, and made between the Right Honourable Sidney Earl of Pembroke and Montgomery of the one part and Vincent Joseph Kelly and Anna Teresa Kelly of the other part and therein described as "All that and those parts of the lands of Priesthouse and Simmonscourt situate in the Parish of St. Mary's Donnybrook Barony of Rathdown and County of Dublin containing twenty eight acres one rood and eleven perches Statute Measure more or less bounded on the South West by Stillorgan Road on the North West by holdings of A. K. McEntire and other Lessees and J. Semple Lessee on the North East partly by lands in the Lessor's hands and partly by the holding of W. Graham, and Company Limited Lessees and partly by the holding of the Very Reverend L. Healy and others Lessees on the South East by Nutley Lane and on the South by a plot in lessor's hands with the messuages offices and buildings thereon now known as "Montrose" which premises are shown on the plan annexed to these presents and thereon edged red " which said lands are as to part thereof the subject of an Indenture of Sub-Lease dated the 4th day of January, 1938, made between the said Vincent Joseph Kelly of the one part and the Right Honourable the Lord Mayor Aldermen and Burgesses of Dublin, and are as to another part thereof the subject of an Indenture of Assignment dated the 18th day of April, 1946, and made between Joseph Bartholomew Shortt and John Marshall Dudley of the one part and the Reverend Thomas Maguire, the Reverend James Finucane, the Reverend Andrew Egan and the Reverend Vincent Dinan of the other part, being the lands therein described as "All that the piece or plot of ground containing 4.62 acres Statute Measure edged blue on the map hereunto annexed being part of the lands of Priesthouse in the Barony of Rathdown and City of Dublin", and are as to another part thereof on which a telephone exchange has been erected, bounded on the South East by Nutley Lane on the South West by Stillorgan Road on the North East and North West by other parts of the demised premises and measuring approximately 200 feet on the South East 163 feet on the South West 216 feet on the North East and 206 feet on the North West subject to the right of the Minister to use and occupy the same free of rent for the purpose of a telephone exchange, except that part of the originally demised lands which is comprised in an Indenture of Assignment dated the 22nd day of October, 1954, and made between University College, Dublin of the one part and the Electricity Supply Board of the other part and is therein described as "All that part of the lands of Priesthouse and Simmonscourt situate in the Parish of Saint Mary's Donnybrook in the Barony of Rathdown and City of Dublin delineated on the map annexed hereto thereon edged with red."

PART III

Any benefit or interest of the Commissioners in respect of an option conferred by an Agreement for sale dated the 29th day of March, 1946, and made between Joseph Bartholomew Shortt and John Marshall Dudley of the one part and the Reverend Thomas Maguire, the Reverend James Finucane, the Reverend Andrew Egan and the Reverend Vincent Dinan of the other part, to take a lease of the plot coloured blue on the map attached to the said Agreement for sale.

PART IV

1891, c. 66.

The lands comprised at Entries Nos. 1, 2 and 7 in Folio 9654 County of Westmeath in the Register of Freeholders maintained under the Registration of Title Act, 1891. section 34.

THIRD SCHEDULE

SUBSECTION AND SECTIONS INSERTED IN WIRELESS TELEGRAPHY ACT, 1926.

PART I (*note: amendments applied*)

PART II (*note: amendments applied*)

BROADCASTING AUTHORITY (AMENDMENT) ACT 1964

Note

All provisions of this Act have been completely applied. No part of this Act remains in force and only appears here for reference.

ARRANGEMENT OF SECTIONS

AN ACT TO INCREASE THE LIMIT ON THE ADVANCES FOR CAPITAL PURPOSES WHICH MAY BE MADE TO RADIO ÉIREANN.

[3RD MARCH, 1964.]

BE IT ENACTED BY THE OIREACHTAS AS FOLLOWS:—

Increase of limit on advances

1.—Paragraph (b) of subsection (2) of section 23 of the Broadcasting Authority Act, 1960, is hereby amended by the substitution of "three million pounds" for "two million pounds".

Short title and collective citation

2.—(1) This Act may be cited as the Broadcasting Authority (Amendment) Act, 1964.

(2) The Broadcasting Authority Act, 1960, and this Act may be cited together as the Broadcasting Authority Acts, 1960 and 1964.

BROADCASTING AUTHORITY (AMENDMENT) ACT 1966

(No. 7 of 1966)

ARRANGEMENT OF SECTIONS

AN ACT TO AMEND AND EXTEND THE BROADCASTING AUTHORITY ACTS, 1960 AND 1964.

[8TH MARCH, 1966.]

BE IT ENACTED BY THE OIREACHTAS AS FOLLOWS:—

Principal Act

1.—In this Act "the Principal Act" means the Broadcasting Authority Act, 1960.

Annual amounts to be paid to Authority by Minister

2.—The Minister, with the approval of the Minister for Finance, may, in respect of each of the five consecutive financial years beginning with that ending on the 31st day of March, 1966, pay to the Authority out of moneys provided by the Oireachtas an amount equal to the total of the receipts in that year in respect of broadcasting licence fees less—

(a) any expenses certified by the Minister as having been incurred by him in that year in relation to the collection of those fees, and

(b) any expenses certified by the Minister as having been incurred by him in that year in respect of the performance of his functions under sections 12 and 12A of the Act of 1926 in relation to interfering with or injuriously affecting wireless telegraphy apparatus for receiving only.

Amendment History

Section 2 is amended by s.1 of the Broadcasting Authority (Amendment) Act 1971. Section 2 is further amended by s.2 of the Broadcasting Authority

(Amendment) Act 1973 and s.1 of the Broadcasting Authority (Amendment) Act 1974, which states that s.2 of the Broadcasting Authority (Amendment) Act 1966 (as amended by the Broadcasting Authority (Amendment) Act 1971 and the Broadcasting Authority (Amendment) Act 1973), shall have effect in relation to the financial period ending on December 31, 1974, and the financial year ending on December 31, 1975 respectively, and accordingly the reference in that section (as so amended) to nine consecutive financial years shall be construed as a reference to 11 consecutive financial years.

Change of corporate of Authority

3.—The corporate name of the Authority is hereby changed from "Radio Éireann" to "Radio Telefís Éireann".

Amendment of section 12 of Principal Act

4.—(*note: amendments applied to the Broadcasting Authority Act 1960*)

Amendment of section 16 of Principal Act

5.—(*note: amendments applied to the Broadcasting Authority Act 1960*)

Amendment of section 25 of Principal Act

6.—(*note: amendments applied to the Broadcasting Authority Act 1960 and subsequently* repealed *by s.19 of the Broadcasting Act 1990)*

Minor amendment and repeals

7.—(*note: amendments applied to the Broadcasting Authority Act 1960*)

Short title, construction and collective citation

8.—(1) This Act may be cited as the Broadcasting Authority (Amendment) Act, 1966.

(2) The Broadcasting Authority Acts, 1960 and 1964, and Act shall be construed together as one Act and may be cited together as the Broadcasting Authority Acts, 1960 to 1966.

BROADCASTING AUTHORITY (AMENDMENT) ACT 1971

(No. 2 of 1971)

Note

All provisions of this Act have been completely applied. No part of this Act remains in force and only appears here for reference.

ARRANGEMENT OF SECTIONS

AN ACT TO AMEND AND EXTEND THE BROADCASTING AUTHORITY ACTS, 1960 TO 1966.

[3RD MARCH, 1971.]

BE IT ENACTED BY THE OIREACHTAS AS FOLLOWS:

Amendment of section 2 of Broadcasting Authority (Amendment) Act, 1966.

1.—Section 2 of the Broadcasting Authority (Amendment) Act, 1966, shall have effect in relation to each of the financial years ending on the 31st day of March, 1971, and on the 31st day of March, 1972, respectively, and accordingly the reference in that section to five consecutive financial years shall be construed as a reference to seven consecutive financial years.

Short title, construction and collective citation.

2.—(1) This Act may be cited as the Broadcasting Authority (Amendment) Act, 1971.

(2) The Broadcasting Authority Acts, 1960 to 1966, and this Act shall be construed together as one Act and may be cited together as the Broadcasting Authority

BROADCASTING AUTHORITY (AMENDMENT) ACT 1973

(No. 1 of 1973)

Note

All provisions of this Act have been completely applied. No part of this act remains in force and only appears here for reference.

ARRANGEMENT OF SECTIONS

AN ACT TO AMEND AND EXTEND THE BROADCASTING AUTHORITY ACTS, 1960 TO 1971.

[30TH MARCH, 1973]

BE IT ENACTED BY THE OIREACHTAS AS FOLLOWS:

Increase of limit on advances

1.—Section 23 (2) (b) of the Broadcasting Authority Act, 1960, is hereby amended by the substitution for "three million pounds" (inserted by the Broadcasting Authority (Amendment) Act, 1964) of "four million pounds".

Amendment of section 2 of Broadcasting Authority (Amendment) Act, 1966

2.—Section 2 of the Broadcasting Authority (Amendment) Act, 1966 (as amended by the Broadcasting Authority (Amendment) Act, 1971), shall have effect in relation to each of the financial years ending on the 31st day of March, 1973, and on the 31st day of March, 1974, respectively, and accordingly the reference in that section (as so amended) to seven consecutive financial years shall be construed as a reference to nine consecutive financial years.

Short title, construction and collective citation

3.—(1) This Act may be cited as the Broadcasting Authority (Amendment) Act, 1973.

(2) The Broadcasting Authority Acts, 1960 to 1971, and this Act shall be construed together as one Act and may be cited together as the Broadcasting Authority Acts, 1960 to 1973.

BROADCASTING AUTHORITY (AMENDMENT) ACT 1974

(No. 33 of 1974)

Note

All provisions of this Act have been completely applied. No part of this act remains in force and only appears here for reference.

AN ACT TO AMEND AND EXTEND THE BROADCASTING AUTHORITY ACTS, 1960 to 1973.

[24TH DECEMBER, 1974)

BE IT ENACTED BY THE OIREACHTAS AS FOLLOWS:

Amendment of section 2 of Broadcasting Authority (Amendment) Act, 1966

1.—Section 2 of the Broadcasting Authority (Amendment) Act, 1966 (as amended by the Broadcasting Authority (Amendment) Act, 1971, and the Broadcasting Authority (Amendment) Act, 1973), shall have effect in relation to the financial period ending on the 31st day of December, 1974, and the financial year ending on the 31st day of December, 1975, respectively, and accordingly the reference in that section (as so amended) to nine consecutive financial years shall be construed as a reference to eleven consecutive financial years.

Short title, construction and collective citation

2.—(1) This Act may be cited as the Broadcasting Authority (Amendment) Act, 1974.

(2) The Broadcasting Authority Acts, 1960 to 1973, and this Act shall be construed together as one Act and may be cited together as the Broadcasting Authority Acts, 1960 to 1974.

BROADCASTING AUTHORITY (AMENDMENT) ACT 1976

(No. 37 of 1976)

ARRANGEMENT OF SECTIONS

AN ACT TO AMEND THE BROADCASTING AUTHORITY ACTS, 1960 TO 1974, TO AMEND THE WIRELESS TELEGRAPHY ACT, 1926, AND TO PROVIDE FOR OTHER MATTERS CONNECTED WITH THE FOREGOING.

[21st December, 1976]

BE IT ENACTED BY THE OIREACHTAS AS FOLLOWS:

Definitions

1.—In this Act—

"the Act of 1926" means the Wireless Telegraphy Act, 1926;

"the Principal Act" means the Broadcasting Authority Act, 1960.

Removal of member of Authority

2.—A member of the Authority may be removed by the Government from office for stated reasons, if, and only if, resolutions are passed by both Houses of the Oireachtas calling for his removal.

Impartiality

3.—(Amendments to section 18 of the Broadcasting Authority Act, 1960 applied)

Broadcasting Complaints Commission

4.—(Sections 18A, 18B and 18C inserted in the Broadcasting Authority Act, 1960)

Advice to Authority

5.—(Amendments to section 21 of the Broadcasting Authority Act, 1960 applied)

Authority to record every broadcast

6.—(1) It shall be the duty of the Authority, by means of its own facilities and in a manner approved of for the purposes of this section by the Commission, to record for those purposes every broadcast made by the Authority; provided that as regards a television broadcast the Authority shall be regarded as complying with the requirements of this section if it records in sound only the broadcast.

(2) Recordings made in compliance with subsection (1) of this section shall be retained by the Authority for at least one hundred and eighty days or for such other period as shall be agreed by the Authority and the Commission, and when a complaint is being investigated by the Commission, the recording of the broadcast to which the complaint relates, together with the recording, made and being retained pursuant to this section, of any other broadcast which in the opinion of the Commission is relevant to that broadcast, shall be supplied by the Authority to the Commission on a request made by the Commission at any time during such period.

(3) The making or retaining of a recording in compliance with subsection (1) of this section shall not be a contravention of section 2 or section 3 of the Performers' Protection Act, 1968, or an infringement of copyright, and nothing contained in the Copyright Act, 1963, shall be construed as prohibiting or restricting the making of such a recording.

Amendment History

References in s.6 shall have effect as if a reference therein to the Authority were a reference to the sound broadcasting contractor concerned. as amended by s.11(4)(b) of the Radio and Television Act 1988.

Assignment of additional functions to Authority

7.—(1) The Minister may, with the consent of the Minister for Finance and the Minister for the Public Service, by order assign to the Authority such functions in respect of the carrying out of subsidiary activities (in addition to the functions conferred on it by section 16 of the Principal Act, as amended by section 5 of the Broadcasting Authority (Amendment) Act, 1966, and by section 12 of this Act) as the Minister thinks proper and specifies in the order, and any such order may contain such ancillary provisions as the Minister thinks necessary or expedient for giving full effect to the order.

(2) The Minister may by order amend or revoke an order under this section (including an order under this subsection).

(3) When an order is proposed to be made under this section, a draft thereof shall be laid before both Houses of the Oireachtas and, if a resolution disapproving of the draft is passed by either such House within the next subsequent twenty-one days on which it has sat after the draft is laid before it, the order shall not be made.

Annual amounts to be paid to Authority by Minister

8.—The Minister, with the approval of the Minister for Finance, may pay to the Authority out of moneys provided by the Oireachtas—

(a) in respect of each financial year after the financial year ending on the 31st day of December, 1975, an amount equal to the total of the receipts in that year in respect of broadcasting licence fees less—

(i) any expenses certified by the Minister as having been incurred by him in that year in relation to the collection of those fees,

(ii) any expenses certified by the Minister as having been incurred by him in that year in respect of the performance of his functions under sections 12 or 12A of the Act of 1926 in relation to interfering with or injuriously affecting wireless telegraphy apparatus for receiving only, and

(iii) the amount of a grant or grants made by the Minister under section 18A of the Principal Act (inserted by section 4 of this Act), and

(b) in respect of each financial year after the financial year ending on the 31st day of March, 1974, an amount equal to the total of the receipts in that year in respect of wired broadcast relay licence fees less any expenses certified by the Minister as having been incurred by him in that year in relation to the collection of those fees.

Increase of limit on repayable advances

9.—(*note: amendment to s.23(2)(b) of the Broadcasting Authority Act 1960 applied*)

Extension of borrowing powers of Authority

10.—(*note: amendment to s.27(1) of the Broadcasting Authority Act 1960 applied*)

Amendment of section 15 of Principal Act

11.—(*note: amendment to s.15 of the Broadcasting Authority Act 1960 applied*)

Amendment of section 16 of Principal Act

12.—(*note: amendment to s.16 of the Broadcasting Authority Act 1960 applied*)

Amendment of section 17 of Principal Act

13.—(*note: amendment to s.17 of the Broadcasting Authority Act 1960 applied*)

Amendment of sections 19 and 20 of Principal Act

14.—(*note: amendment to ss.19 and 20 of the Broadcasting Authority Act 1960 applied. This section was repealed by s.19 of the Broadcasting and Wireless Telegraphy Act 1988*).]

Amendment of section 28 of Principal Act]

15.—(*note: amendment to s.28 of the Broadcasting Authority Act 1960 applied*)

Amendment of section 31 of Principal Act

16.—(*note: amendment to s.31 of the Broadcasting Authority Act 1960 applied*)

Regulation of local programmes for distribution on cable systems

17.—(*note: s.3A inserted into the Wireless Telegraphy Act 1926*)

Amendment of section 2 of Act of 1926

18.—(*note: amendments to s.2 of the Wireless Telegraphy Act 1926 applied)*

Amendment of section 12A of Act of 1926

19.—(*note: amendments to s.12A of the Wireless Telegraphy Act 1926 applied*)

Application of sections 7, 8, 10 and 12 of Act of 1926 in relation to certain apparatus

20.—(*note: non-textual amendments to ss.7, 8, 10 and 12 of the Wireless Telegraphy Act 1926 applied*)

Repeals

21.—(*note: repeals applied*)

Short title, construction and collective citation

22.—(1) This Act may be cited as the Broadcasting Authority (Amendment) Act, 1976.

(2) The Broadcasting Authority Acts, 1960 to 1974, and this Act shall be construed together as one Act and may he cited together as the Broadcasting Authority Acts, 1960 to 1976.

BROADCASTING AUTHORITY (AMENDMENT) ACT 1979

(No. 36 of 1979)

ARRANGEMENT OF SECTIONS

AN ACT TO AMEND AND EXTEND THE BROADCASTING AUTHORITY ACTS, 1960 TO 1976.

[19TH DECEMBER, 1979]

BE IT ENACTED BY THE OIREACHTAS AS FOLLOWS:

Principal Act

1.—In this Act "the Principal Act" means the Broadcasting Authority Act, 1960.

Increase of limit on repayable advances

2.—(*note: amendments to s.23(2)(b) of the Broadcasting Authority Act 1960 applied*)

Local broadcasting

3.—(*note: amendments to s.16(1) of the Broadcasting Authority Act 1960 applied*)

Nomination of officer or servant of Authority for membership of or election to either House of Oireachtas

4.—(1) Where a person who is an officer or servant of the Authority is nominated as a member of Seanad Éireann or for election to either House of the Oireachtas, he shall stand seconded from employment by the Authority and shall not be paid by, or be entitled to receive from, the Authority any remuneration or allowance—

(a) in case he is nominated as a member of Seanad Éireann, in respect of the period commencing on his acceptance of the nomination and ending when he ceases to be a member of that House,

(b) in case he is nominated for election to either House, in respect of the period commencing on his acceptance of the nomination and ending when he ceases to be a member of that House or fails to be elected or withdraws his candidature, as the case may be.

(2) A person who is for the time being entitled under the Standing Orders of either House of the Oireachtas to sit therein shall, while so entitled, be disqualified from becoming an officer or servant of the Authority.

Short title, construction and collective citation

5.—(1) This Act may be cited as the Broadcasting Authority (Amendment) Act, 1979.

(2) The Broadcasting Authority Acts, 1960 to 1976, and this Act shall be construed together as one Act and may be cited together as the Broadcasting Authority Acts, 1960 to 1979.

ACTS REFERRED TO

Broadcasting Authority Act, 1960	1960, No. 10
Broadcasting Authority (Amendment) Act, 1976	1976, No. 37

RADIO AND TELEVISION ACT 1988

(No. 20 of 1988)

ARRANGEMENT OF SECTIONS

Broadcasting Authority Act, 1960	1960, No.10
Broadcasting Authority (Amendment) Act, 1976	1976, No.37
Broadcasting Authority Acts, 1960 to 1979	
Companies Act, 1963	1963, No.33
Wireless Telegraphy Act, 1926	1926, No. 45
Wireless Telegraphy Acts, 1926 to 1972	
Performers Protection Act., 1968	1968, No.19
European Assembly Elections Act, 1977	1977, No.30
European Assembly Elections Act, 1984	1984, No.6

AN ACT TO PROVIDE FOR THE ESTABLISHMENT OF AN INDEPENDENT RADIO AND TELEVISION COMMISSION HAVING THE FUNCTION OF ENTERING INTO CONTRACTS FOR THE PROVISION OF SOUND BROADCASTING SERVICES AND A TELEVISION PROGRAMME SERVICE ADDITIONAL TO SERVICES PROVIDED BY RADIO TELEFÍS ÉIREANN; TO AMEND THE WIRELESS TELEGRAPHY ACT, 1926; AND TO PROVIDE FOR OTHER MATTERS CONNECTED WITH THE MATTERS AFORESAID.

[3RD JULY, 1988]

BE IT ENACTED BY THE OIREACHTAS AS FOLLOWS:

PART I

PRELIMINARY

Short Title

1.—This Act may be cited as the Radio and Television Act, 1988.

Interpretation

2.—(1) In this Act—

"apparatus for wireless telegraphy" has the meaning specified in the Wireless Telegraphy Act, 1926;

"broadcast" means the transmission, relaying or distribution by wireless telegraphy of communications, sounds, signs, visual images or signals, intended for direct reception by the general public whether such communications, sounds, signs, visual images or signals are actually received or not;

"the Commission" means the Commission established by Part II;

"company" has the meaning assigned to it by the Companies Act, 1963;

"the Minister" means the Minister for Communications;

"sound broadcasting service" means a broadcasting service which transmits, relays or distributes, by wireless telegraphy, communications, sounds, signs or signals intended for direct reception by the general public whether such communications, sounds, signs or signals are actually received or not;

"television programme service" means a service which comprises a compilation of audio-visual programme material of any description and is transmitted or relayed by means of wireless telegraphy directly or indirectly for reception by the general public.

(2) A reference in this Act to a section is a reference to a section of this Act, unless it is indicated that a reference to some other enactment is intended.

(3) A reference in this Act to a subsection or to a paragraph or to a subparagraph is a reference to the subsection, paragraph or subparagraph of the provision in which the reference occurs, unless it is indicated that a reference to some other provision is intended.

(4) A reference in this Act to any enactment shall be construed as a reference to that enactment as amended by any subsequent enactment (including this Act).

PART II

THE INDEPENDENT RADIO AND TELEVISION COMMISSION

Establishment of Commission

3.—(1) There shall stand established, on such day as the Minister by order appoints, a body to be known as An Coimisiún Um Raidio agus Telefís Neamhspleách-The Independent Radio and Television Commission.

(2) The Commission shall be a body corporate with perpetual succession and power to sue and be sued in its corporate name and to acquire, hold and dispose of land.

(3) The provisions of the Schedule to this Act shall apply to the Commission.

Functions of Commission

4.—(1) It shall be the function of the Commission to arrange, in accordance with the provisions of this Act, for the provision of sound broadcasting services (including a national sound broadcasting service) and one television programme service additional to any broadcasting services provided by Radio Telefís Éireann pursuant to the Broadcasting Authority Acts, 1960 to 1979.

(2)(a) The Commission shall enter into contracts (in this Act referred to as "sound broadcasting contracts") with persons (in this Act referred to as "sound broadcasting contractors") under which the sound broadcasting contractors have, subject to the provisions of this Act, the right and duty to establish, maintain and operate sound broad casting transmitters serving the areas specified in the sound broadcasting contract and to provide, as the sound broad casting contract may specify, a sound broadcasting service.

(b) The Commission shall also enter into a contract (in this Act referred to as a "television programme service contract") with a person or persons (in this Act referred to as a "television programme service contractor") who shall have the right and duty to provide a television programme service.

(3) The Commission shall not authorise a sound broadcasting contractor to operate a sound broadcasting transmitter and provide a sound broadcasting service pursuant to a sound broadcasting contract unless and until the Minister has issued pursuant to this subsection to the Commission a licence in respect of the sound broadcasting transmitter to which the contract relates.

(4) Any licence issued under subsection (3) shall be valid only for such period of time as a sound broadcasting contract between the Commission and a sound broadcasting contractor is extant.

(5) Every sound broadcasting contract shall contain a condition requiring the sound broadcasting contractor concerned to establish, maintain and operate the sound broadcasting transmitter concerned in accordance with such terms and conditions as the Minister sees fit to attach to the licence referred to in subsection (3), (including any variations made thereto in accordance with the provisions of section 7 of this Act) and so long as the terms and conditions are complied with, the contract shall have the effect of conveying the benefits of the licence to the sound broadcasting contractor and any such transmitter so established, maintained and operated shall be deemed to be licensed for the purposes of section 3 of the Wireless Telegraphy Act, 1926.

(6) Every licence issued by the Minister to the Commission under subsection (3) shall be open to inspection by members of the public at the Commission's registered offices.

(7) It shall be the duty of the Commission to ensure that every sound broadcasting contractor and the television programme service contractor complies with the provisions of this Act.

(8) The Commission shall have all such powers as are necessary for or incidental to the performance of its functions under this Act including, in particular, the power to require sound broadcasting contractors and the television programme service contractor to enter into financial bonds with the Commission and to direct a contractor to record any or all of the programmes broadcast by him in the case of a sound broadcasting contract or provided by him in the case of a television programme service contract and to retain such recordings for a period of 30 days after the recording is made and to submit the recordings to the Commission, if the Commission so requires.

(9) The making of a recording by a contractor pursuant to a direction of the Commission pursuant to subsection (8) and the use by the Commission of any such

recording exclusively for the purposes of its functions under this Act shall not constitute—

(a) an infringement of the copyright in any work, sound recording or cinematograph film, or

(b) an offence under any of the provisions of the Performers Protection Act, 1968.

(10)Without prejudice to the generality of subsection (8), the Commission shall have power—

(a) to make such contracts, agreements and arrangements and do all such other things as are incidental or conducive to the objects of the Commission;

(b) to acquire and make use of copyrights, patents, licences, privileges and concessions;

(c) to compile, prepare, publish and distribute, with or without charge, such magazines, books and other printed material and such aural and visual material as may seem to the Commission to be incidental or conducive to its objectives;

(d) subject to the consent of the Minister, to arrange for the provision of services with or without charge for and on behalf of any Minister of the Government by a sound broadcasting contractor or the television programme service contractor;

(e) to require sound broadcasting contractors and the television programme service contractor to co-operate with the Garda Síochána, local authorities and health boards in the dissemination of relevant information to the public in the event of major emergencies.

(11)During the continuance of any emergency declared under section 10 of the Wireless Telegraphy Act, 1926, the Minister may suspend any licence issued under subsection (3) and, while any such suspension continues, the Minister may. operate any service which was provided under the suspended licence or require such service to be operated as he directs.

PART III

SOUND BROADCASTING SERVICES

Applications for sound broadcasting contracts

5.—(1) In order to secure the orderly development of sound broadcasting services and, having regard to the availability of radio frequencies for sound broadcasting, to allow for the establishment of a diversity of services in an area catering for a wide range of tastes including those of minority interests, the Commission shall as soon as may be after it has been established and may thereafter from time to time by notice published in at least one national newspaper, invite expressions of interest in the securing of contracts for sound broadcasting services under this Act. Such expressions of interest shall indicate in general terms the type of service that would be provided and shall not be regarded as an application for a sound broadcasting contract.

(2) The Commission shall make a report of its findings under subsection (1) to

the Minister who, having considered the report and after consultation with the Commission, shall specify the area (which area may consist of the whole or any part of the State) in relation to which applications for a sound broadcasting contract are to be invited and the Commission shall comply with such direction.

(3) The Minister, having regard to the report furnished by the Commission under subsection (2) and having regard to the availability of radio frequencies for sound broadcasting, may limit the number of areas which he may specify under that subsection.

(4) The Commission shall, subject to the provisions of this Act, invite applications for a sound broadcasting contract for the provision of a sound broadcasting service in each area specified by the Minister under subsection (2) and, subject to the provisions of this Act, may enter into such contracts.

(5) Where the Commission invites applications for a sound broadcasting contract for the provision of a sound broadcasting service it shall by public notice specify the area in relation to which the sound broadcasting service is to be provided pursuant to such contract and by such notice shall invite persons interested in providing such a service to apply for such contract.

(6) Having regard to the findings of the Commission under subsection (1) the Commission may, in considering applications for the award of a sound broadcasting contract, place greater emphasis on one or more of the criteria specified in section 6 (2) of this Act and whenever it is the Commission's intention to so do it shall specify such intention to each person who has indicated his intention of being an applicant for a contract.

(7) Every notice under subsection (5) shall—

(a) be published in at least one national newspaper, and where appropriate, in one local newspaper circulating in the area to be served;

(b) specify the procedure to be followed in order to make an application;

(c) specify any other matters which appear to the Commission to be necessary or relevant.

Determination of applications for award of sound broadcasting contracts

6.—(1) The Commission shall, in accordance with the provisions of this Act, consider every application for a sound broadcasting contract received by it pursuant to a notice under section 5 (5) for the purpose of determining the most suitable applicant, if any, to be awarded a sound broadcasting contract.

(2) In the consideration of applications received by it and in determining the most suitable applicant to be awarded a sound broadcasting contract, the Commission shall have regard to—

(a) the character of the applicant or, if the applicant is a body corporate, the character of the body and its directors, manager, secretary or other similar officer and its members and the persons entitled to the beneficial ownership of its shares;

(b) the adequacy of the expertise and experience and of the financial resources that will be available to each applicant and the extent to which the application accords with good economic principles;

(c) the quality, range and type of the programmes proposed to be provided by each applicant or, if there is only one applicant, by that applicant;

(d) the quantity, quality, range and type of programmes in the Irish language and the extent of programmes relating to Irish culture proposed to be provided;

(e) the extent to which the applicant will create within the proposed sound broadcasting service new opportunities for Irish talent in music, drama and entertainment;

(f) the desirability of having a diversity of services in the area specified in the notice under section 5 (5) catering for a wide range of tastes including those of minority interests;

(g) the desirability of allowing any person, or group of persons, to have control of, or substantial interests in, an undue number of sound broadcasting services in respect of which a sound broadcasting contract has been awarded under this Act;

(h) the desirability of allowing any person, or group of persons, to have control of, or substantial interests in, an undue amount of the communications media in the area specified in the notice under section 5 (5);

(i) the extent to which the service proposed—

(i) serves recognisably local communities and is supported by the various interests in the Community, or

(ii) serves communities of interest, and

(j) any other matters which the Commission considers to be necessary to secure the orderly development of sound broadcasting services.

(3) In considering the suitability of any applicant for the award of a sound broadcasting contract to provide a sound broadcasting service in respect of an area which includes a Gaeltacht area, the Commission shall have particular regard to the preservation as a spoken language of the Irish language.

Variation of licence for sound broadcasting transmitter

7.—(1) The Minister may, if it seems necessary to him so to do for any of the reasons specified in subsection (2), vary any term or condition of a licence issued pursuant to section 4 (3).

(2) The Minister may vary any term or condition of a licence issued pursuant to section 4 (3)-

(a) if it appears to him to be necessary so to do in the interest of good radio frequency management;

(b) for the purpose of giving effect to any international agreement to which the State is a party and which has been ratified by the State and which relates to sound broad casting;

(c) if it appears to him to be in the public interest so to do;

(d) if it appears to him to be necessary for the safety or security of persons or property so to do;

(e) on request from the Commission after consultation with any affected sound broadcasting contractor;

(f) on request from the Commission on behalf of a sound broadcasting contractor.

(3)(a) If the Minister, for any reason specified in paragraph (a), (b) or (c) of subsection (2) proposes to vary, pursuant to this section, any term or condition of a licence issued pursuant to section 4 (3), he shall, by notice in writing, inform the Commission of his intention and of the reasons therefor and the Commission shall, within 7 days of receiving that notification, give notice to the sound broadcasting contractor accordingly.

(b) The sound broadcasting contractor shall have the right to make representations in writing to the Commission in respect of the Minister's intentions, within 21 days after the service of the notice by the Commission.

(c) The Commission shall transmit any such representations to the Minister within a further 7 days and the Minister, having considered the representations, may make such decision thereon as seems to him to be appropriate.

(4)(a) If, having considered the representations (if any) which have been notified to him by the Commission by or on behalf of a sound broadcasting contractor, the Minister decides to vary any term or condition of a licence, he shall, by notice in writing, inform the Commission of his decision.

(b) The Commission shall, within 7 days of receipt of the Minister's decision by notice in writing inform the sound broadcasting contractor of that decision.

(c) On and from the day following service on the contractor of notice of the Minister's decision the licence shall have effect subject to the variation thereof by that decision.

(5) A notice under subsection (3) or (4) may be served on the Commission and by the Commission on a sound broadcasting contractor, by leaving it at, or sending it by prepaid post to, the Commission's address and the sound broadcasting contractor's last known address respectively or if, in the latter case, the sound broadcasting contractor is a company, by leaving it at, or sending it by prepaid post to, the registered office of the company.

Contracts for temporary or institutional sound broadcasting services

8.—(1) The Commission may, in any period of twelve months, enter into a sound broadcasting contract with an applicant therefor for the provision in such area as may be specified in the contract of a sound broadcasting service for a period of not more than fourteen days (whether consecutive days or otherwise) in that period of twelve months.

(2) The Commission may enter into a sound broadcasting contract with an applicant therefor for the provision of a low-power sound broadcasting service which

is intended to serve only such single educational institution, hospital, or other similar establishment as may be specified in the contract.

(3) Section 9 (1) (c) shall not apply to a contract awarded for the provision of a sound broadcasting service under this section.

(4) Sections 5 and 6 shall not apply in the case of a contract applied for, or awarded, for the provision of a sound broadcasting service under this section.

Duty of sound broadcasting contractor in relation to programmes

9.—(1) Every sound broadcasting contractor shall ensure that—

(a) all news broadcast by him is reported and presented in an objective and impartial manner and without any expression of his own views;

(b) the broadcast treatment of current affairs, including matters which are either of public controversy or the subject of current public debate, is fair to all interests concerned and that the broadcast matter is presented in an objective and impartial manner and without any expression of his own views: Provided that should it prove impracticable in relation to a single broadcast to apply this paragraph, two or more related broadcasts may be considered as a whole, if the broadcasts are transmitted within a reasonable period of each other;

(c) a minimum of—

(i) not less than 20 per cent. of the broadcasting time, and

(ii) if the sound broadcasting service is provided for more than 12 hours in any one day, two hours of broadcasting time between 07.00 hours and 19.00 hours, is devoted to the broadcasting of news and current affairs programmes; provided a derogation from this provision is not authorised by the Commission under section 15;

(d) anything which may reasonably be regarded as offending against good taste or decency, or as being likely to promote, or incite to, crime or as tending to undermine the authority of the State, is not broadcast by him;

(e) in programmes broadcast by him, and in the means employed to make such programmes, the privacy of any individual is not unreasonably encroached upon.

(2) Nothing in subsection (1) (a) or (1) (b) shall prevent a sound broadcasting contractor from transmitting political party broadcasts: Provided that a sound broadcasting contractor shall not, in the allocation of time for such broadcasts, give an unfair preference to any political party.

(3) The Commission shall draw up, and may, from time to time as occasion requires, revise a code governing standards and practice (hereinafter referred to as a code of practice) in relation to any matter specified in subsections (1) and (2).

(4) Whenever the Commission draws up pursuant to subsection (3) a code of practice relating to the matter in question every sound broadcasting contractor shall comply with such code and any revision thereof.

Advertisements

10.—(1) Programmes broadcast in a sound broadcasting service provided pursuant to any sound broadcasting contract may include advertisements inserted therein.

(2) The Commission shall draw up, from time to time as it thinks proper, a code governing standards and practice in advertising and every sound broadcasting contractor shall comply with the code in respect of advertisements broadcast by it.

(3) No advertisement shall be broadcast which is directed towards any religious or political end or which has any relation to an industrial dispute.

(4) The total daily times for broadcasting advertisements in a sound broadcasting service provided pursuant to a sound broadcasting contract shall not exceed a maximum of 15 per cent. of the total daily broadcasting time and the maximum time to be given to advertisements in any hour shall not exceed a maximum of ten minutes.

(5) In this section, references to advertisements shall be construed as including references to advertising matter contained in sponsored programmes, that is to say, in programmes supplied for advertising purposes by or on behalf of an advertiser.

(6) It shall be the duty of the Commission to ensure that sound broadcasting contractors comply with the requirements of subsections (2), (3) and (4).

Complaints by public

11.—(1) A sound broadcasting contractor shall give due and adequate consideration to any complaint, which is not of a frivolous or vexatious nature, made by a member of the public in respect of the sound broadcasting service provided by the contractor and shall, whilst his contract is in force, keep due and proper records of all such complaints and of any reply made thereto or of any action taken on foot thereof.

(2) A sound broadcasting contractor shall, if requested by the Commission make available for inspection by the Commission all records kept by him pursuant to subsection (1).

(3) The Minister may, by regulations, direct that complaints made by members of the public in respect of a sound broadcasting service provided under this Act be investigated by the Broadcasting Complaints Commission established by section 18A (inserted by the Broadcasting Authority (Amendment) Act, 1976) of the Broadcasting Authority Act, 1960.

(4) For the purposes of an investigation by the Broadcasting Complaints Commission pursuant to regulations under this section—

(a) the Broadcasting Authority Act, 1960, shall have effect subject to the following modifications—

(i) a reference in sections 18B and 18C (inserted by the Broadcasting Authority (Amendment) Act, 1976), other than in section 18B (1) (e), to the Authority shall be construed as a reference to the sound broadcasting contractor concerned;

(ii) a reference in section 18B (7) (as so inserted) to the Authority shall be construed as referring to the sound broadcasting contractor concerned and to the Commission established by this Act;

(iii) a reference in section 18B (as so inserted) to section 18 (1), section 18 (1A) or section 18 (1B) of the Broadcasting Authority Act, 1960, shall be construed as a reference to section 9;

(iv) a reference in section 18B (as so inserted) to a complaint that an advertisement contravened a code drawn up by Radio Telefís Éireann governing standards in broadcast advertising, or prohibiting either certain methods of advertising in broadcasting or a broadcast in particular circumstances of advertising, shall be construed as a reference to section 10 (2);

(v) a reference in section 18B (as so inserted) to section 31 (1) of the Broadcasting Authority Act, 1960, shall be construed as a reference to section 12.

(b) Section 6 of the Broadcasting Authority (Amendment) Act, 1976, shall have effect as if a reference therein to the Authority were a reference to the sound broadcasting contractor concerned.

Application of orders under section 31 (1) of Broadcasting Authority Act, 1960

12.—Every direction given to Radio Telefís Éireann pursuant to section 31 (1) of the Broadcasting Authority Act, 1960, by the Minister which is in force on the commencement of this Act or which is given by him after such commencement, shall, for so long as the direction remains in force, apply to a sound broadcasting service provided pursuant to a sound broadcasting contract and shall be complied with by a sound broadcasting contractor as if the direction were given to him, and the said section 31(1) shall be construed and have effect accordingly.

Investigation into affairs of sound broadcasting contractor

13.—(1) The Commission may, for any of the reasons in subsection (2) conduct an investigation into the operational, programming, financial, technical or other affairs of a sound broadcasting contractor and the sound broadcasting contractor concerned shall co-operate in any such investigation.

(2) The Commission may conduct, or appoint any other person to conduct, an investigation under this section—

(a) if it has reasonable grounds for believing that the sound broadcasting contractor is not providing a sound broadcasting service in accordance with the terms of his contract; or

(b) if, because of the manner in which the sound broadcasting service is being operated—

(i) there is interference with the working of any apparatus for wireless telegraphy in respect of which a licence has been granted under this or any other Act and is in force, or with any apparatus for wireless telegraphy which is lawfully maintained and worked without such a licence, or

(ii) any apparatus for wireless telegraphy referred to in subparagraph (i) is thereby injuriously affected.

(3) All expenses reasonably incurred in relation to an investigation under this section conducted by the Commission or by any person appointed under subsection (2) shall be borne by the sound broadcasting contractor concerned.

(4)(a) If the Commission considers it necessary or desirable so to do, it may require a sound broadcasting contractor to carry out a market research survey (such market research survey to be carried out by a person approved of by the Commission).

(b) A market research survey carried out pursuant to paragraph (a) shall be of such scope as appears to the Commission to be reasonable, having regard to the extent and nature of the sound broadcasting service being provided by the sound broadcasting contractor.

(c) A market research survey carried out pursuant to a requirement of the Commission under this subsection shall be a survey of the audience reaction to the broadcasting service provided by the sound broadcasting contractor concerned or any particular aspect thereof.

(d) A sound broadcasting contractor shall furnish the Commission with the results of any market research survey carried out in compliance with a requirement of the Commission under this subsection.

Terms and conditions of sound broadcasting contract

14.—(1) Every sound broadcasting contract may contain such terms and conditions as the Commission thinks appropriate and specifies in the contract.

(2) Without prejudice to the generality of subsection (1), the Commission may specify in a sound broadcasting contract all or any of the following terms or conditions:

(a) the period during which the contract shall continue in force;

(b) whether the contract may be renewed and, if so, the manner in which, the terms on which, and the period for which, the contract may be so renewed;

(c) a condition prohibiting the assignment of the contract or of any interest therein;

(d) if the sound broadcasting contractor be a company, a condition prohibiting any alteration in the Memorandum or Articles of Association of the company or in so much of that Memorandum or of those Articles as may be specified or prohibiting any material change in the ownership of the company;

(e) a condition requiring the sound broadcasting contractor to provide the quality, range and type of programmes which he proposed to offer in his application for the award of the contract.

(3) If a sound broadcasting contract does not contain a condition of the type specified in paragraph (c) or (d) of subsection (2), the following provisions shall have effect:

(a) a sound broadcasting contract, or any interest in a sound broadcasting contract, shall not be assignable, nor shall any alteration be made in the Memorandum or Articles of Association of any company which is a sound broadcasting contractor, nor shall there be any material change in the ownership of such a company, without the previous consent in writing of the Commission, and the Commission may, if it considers it reasonable so to do, refuse such consent;

(b) in considering whether to grant its consent to an assignment of a sound broadcasting contract, a change in the Memorandum or Articles of Association of a company which is a sound broadcasting contractor, or a material change in the ownership of such a company, the Commission shall have regard to the criteria specified in section 6 (2) and, where applicable, section 6 (3).

(4) Every sound broadcasting contract shall—

(a) provide that the Commission may, at its discretion, suspend or terminate the contract—

(i) if any false or misleading information was given to the Commission by or on behalf of the sound broadcasting contractor prior to the making of the contract,

(ii) if the sound broadcasting contractor has, in the opinion of the Commission, committed serious or repeated breaches of his obligations under the sound broadcasting contract or under this Act;

(b) provide that a sound broadcasting contractor shall pay to the Commission the fees, shares of profits or royalties specified therein;

(c) provide that the sound broadcasting contractor shall provide such information (including copies of his accounts) which the Commission considers it requires in order to enable it carry out its functions under this Act.

(5) Every sound broadcasting contract shall be open to inspection by members of the public at the Commission's registered office and the Commission shall, on request made by any person and on payment of such sum (if any) as the Commission may reasonably require, furnish to that person a copy of that contract.

Derogation from requirements relating to news and current affairs programming

15.—Notwithstanding section 9(1)(c), the Commission may authorise a derogation from the requirement in question in whole or in part in the case of sound broadcasting services which it contracts to provide in any area to meet specific special interests, provided it is satisfied that there is a reasonable plurality of sources of news and current affairs programming available to the public in question from other sound broadcasting services.

Co-operation with Radio Telefís Éireann in use of broadcasting installation

16.—(1) The Minister may, at the request of the Commission and after consultation with Radio Telefís Éireann, require the latter to co-operate with sound broadcasting contractors in the use of any mast, tower, site or other installation or facility needed in connection with the provision of transmission facilities for sound broadcasting services to be established under this Act.

(2) A sound broadcasting contractor shall make to Radio Telefís Éireann such

periodical or other payments in respect of any facilities provided in pursuance of subsection (1) as the Minister, after consultation with Radio Telefís Éireann and the Commission, directs.

PART IV

TELEVISION PROGRAMME SERVICE

Applications for television programme service contract

17.—The Commission shall, on being directed to do so by the Minister, invite applications for a television programme service contract for the provision of a television programme service which shall be distributed using channel capacity on wired broadcast relay systems and television programme retransmission systems licensed under regulations made under section 6 of the Wireless Telegraphy Act, 1926.

Application of certain provisions of Part III to television programme service contract

18.—(1) The provisions of Part III of this Act, other than sections 7, 8 and 15, relating to the powers, duties, functions, obligations and responsibilities of the Minister, the Commission and sound broadcasting contractors respectively, shall apply with respect to the television programme service contract entered into by the Commission and the television programme service provided under this Part, and any reference in Part III of this Act to a sound broadcasting contractor shall for the purposes of this Part be construed as a reference to the television programme service contractor.

(2) Notwithstanding the generality of subsection (1), section 9 (1) (c) shall not apply in the case of the television programme service provided under the television programme service contract.

(3) The Commission shall ensure that the television programme service provided under this Act shall in its programming—

(a) be responsive to the interests and concerns of the whole community, be mindful of the need for understanding and peace within the whole island of Ireland, ensure that the programmes reflect the varied elements which make up the culture of the people of the whole island of Ireland, and have special regard for the elements which distinguish that culture and in particular for the Irish language;

(b) uphold the democratic values enshrined in the Constitution, especially those relating to rightful liberty of expression;

(c) have regard to the need for the formation of public awareness and understanding of the values and traditions of countries other than the State, including in particular those of such countries which are members of the European Community; and

(d) includes a reasonable proportion of news and current affairs programmes;

and the television programme service contractor shall comply with any requirements of the Commission in respect of such matters.

(4) For the purpose of ensuring compliance with subsection (3) the Commission shall ensure that a reasonable proportion of the programme service—

(a) is produced in the State or in another Member State of the European Communities, and

(b) is devoted to original programme material produced therein by persons other than the contractor, his subsidiary, his parent or existing broadcasting organisations.

PART V

MISCELLANEOUS

Amendment of Wireless Telegraphy Act, 1926

19.—(*note: amendments to s.2 of the Wireless Telegraphy Act 1926 applied*)

Amounts to be paid to Commission by Minister

20.—(1) The Minister, with the approval of the Minister for Finance, may in respect of each of the two consecutive financial years beginning with that in which the establishment day occurs, pay to the Commission such amount as he considers reasonable in respect of its initial expenses.

(2) The total of the amounts paid pursuant to subsection (1) shall not exceed £500,000.

(3) The amounts paid to the Commission pursuant to subsection (1) in respect of a year to which that subsection relates shall be deducted from the receipts in that year in respect of wired broadcast relay licence fees and section 8 (b) of the Broadcasting Authority (Amendment) Act, 1976, which provides for payment of money out of such receipts to Radio Telefís Éireann, shall be modified accordingly.

Expenses

21.—The expenses incurred by the Minister in the administration of this Act shall, to such extent as may be sanctioned by the Minister for Finance, be paid out of moneys provided by the Oireachtas.

SCHEDULE

Membership of Commission

1. (1) The members of the Commission shall be appointed by the Government and shall be not less than seven nor more than ten in number.

(2) The period of office of a member of the Commission shall be such period, not exceeding five years, as the Government may determine when appointing him.

(3) A member of the Commission whose term of office expires by effluxion of time shall be eligible for reappointment.

(4) A member of the Commission may resign his membership by letter sent to the Government and the resignation shall take effect on and from the date of receipt of the letter.

(5) A person shall not be appointed to be a member of the Commission unless he has had experience of, or shown capacity in, media or commercial affairs, radio communications engineering, trade union affairs, administration or social, cultural, educational or community activities.

Chairman of Commission

2.(1) The Government shall from time to time as occasion requires appoint a member of the Commission to be chairman thereof.

(2) The chairman of the Commission shall, unless he sooner dies, resigns the office of chairman or ceases to be chairman under subparagraph (4) of this paragraph, hold office until the expiration of his period of office as a member of the Commission.

(3) The chairman of the Commission may at any time resign his office as chairman by letter sent to the Government and the resignation shall take effect at the commencement of the meeting of the Commission held next after the Commission has been informed by the Government of the resignation.

(4) Where the chairman of the Commission ceases during his term of office as chairman to be a member of the Commission, he shall also then cease to be chairman of the Commission.

Removal of member of Commission

3. A member of the Commission may be removed from office by the Government for stated reasons, if, but only if, resolutions are passed by both Houses of the Oireachtas calling for his removal.

Remuneration and terms of office of members of Commission

4.(1) A member of the Commission shall be paid out of funds at the disposal of the Commission—

(a) such remuneration as may be fixed from time to time by the Minister, with the consent of the Minister for Finance, and

(b) such amounts in respect of expenses as the Commission, with the approval of the Minister given with the consent of the Minister for Finance, considers reasonable.

(2) Subject to the provisions of this Act, a member of the Commission shall hold office upon and subject to such terms and conditions as may, from time to time, be determined by the Minister, with the consent of the Minister for Finance.

(3) The Minister shall cause a statement in writing specifying the terms of office and the remuneration of the members of the Commission to be laid before both Houses of the Oireachtas.

Disclosure by member of Commission of interest in proposed contract

5. A member of the Commission who has—

(a) any interest in any company or concern with which the Commission proposes to make any contract, or

(b) any interest in any contract which the Commission proposes to make,

shall disclose to the Commission the fact of the interest and the nature thereof, and shall take no part in any deliberation or decision of the Commission relating to the contract, and the disclosure shall be recorded in the minutes of the Commission.

Seal of Commission

6.(1) The Commission shall as soon as may be after its establishment provide itself with a seal.

(2) The seal of the Commission shall be authenticated by the signature of the chairman of the Commission or some other member thereof authorised by the Commission to act in that behalf and the signature of an officer of the Commission authorised by the Commission to act in that behalf.

(3) Judicial notice shall be taken of the seal of the Commission, and every document purporting to be an instrument made by the Commission and to be sealed with the seal (purporting to be authenticated in accordance with this paragraph) of the Commission shall be received in evidence and be deemed to be such instrument without further proof unless the contrary is shown.

Meetings and procedure of Commission

7.(1) The Commission shall hold such and so many meetings as may be necessary for the due fulfilment of its functions.

(2) The Minister may fix the date, time and place of the first meeting of the Commission.

(3) Subject to the provisions of this Act, the Commission shall regulate its procedure by rules made under this subparagraph.

(4) At a meeting of the Commission—

(a) the chairman of the Commission shall, if present, be chairman of the meeting,

(b) if and so long as the chairman is not present or the office of chairman is vacant, the members of the Commission who are present shall choose one of their number to be chairman of the meeting.

(5) Every question at a meeting of the Commission shall be determined by a majority of the votes of the members present and voting on the question, and in the case of an equal division of votes, the chairman of the meeting shall have a second or casting vote.

(6) The Commission may act notwithstanding one or more vacancies among its members.

(7) The quorum for a meeting of the Commission shall be fixed by rules made under subparagraph (3) of this paragraph, but—

(a) it shall not be less than five, and

(b) until it is so fixed, it shall be five.

Officers and servants of commission

8.(1) The Commission shall, with the approval of the Minister, from time to time appoint a person to be the chief executive officer of the Commission, and such person shall be known, and in this Act is referred to, as the chief executive.

(2) The Commission may, as well as appointing the chief executive, appoint so many other persons to be members of the staff of the Commission, and to serve in such grades, as the Commission, with the approval of the Minister, given with the consent of the Minister for Finance, from time to time determines.

(3) The Commission may exercise all or any of its functions through or by such members of its staff as may be duly authorised in that behalf by the Commission.

Conditions of service, remuneration etc., of officers and servants of Commission

9.(1) A member of the staff of the Commission, (including the chief executive) shall hold his office or employment on such terms and conditions as the Commission, with the approval of the Minister given with the consent of the Minister for Finance, may from time to time determine.

(2) There shall be paid by the Commission to its staff (including the chief executive) such remuneration and allowances as the Commission, with the approval of the Minister given with the consent of the Minister for Finance, thinks fit.

(3) In determining the remuneration or allowances to be paid to its staff or the terms or conditions subject to which such staff hold or are to hold their employment, the Commission shall comply with any directive with regard to such remuneration, allowances, terms and conditions which the Minister, with the consent of the Minister for Finance, may give from time to time, to the Commission.

(4) The Commission may at any time remove any member of the staff of the Commission from being a member of its staff.

(5) Notwithstanding the foregoing provisions of this paragraph, the chief executive shall not be removed without the consent of the Minister.

Membership of either House of Oireachtas or of European Parliament

10. (1) Where a member of the Commission is—

(a) nominated as a member of Seanad Éireann, or

(b) nominated as a candidate for election to either House of the Oireachtas or to the European Parliament, or

(c) regarded pursuant to section 15 (inserted by the Act of 1984) of the Act of 1977, as having been elected to the European Parliament to fill a vacancy, he shall thereupon cease to be a member of the Commission.

(2) Where a person employed by the Commission is—

(a) nominated as a member of Seanad Éireann, or

(b) nominated as a candidate for election to either House of the Oireachtas or to the European Parliament, or

(c) regarded pursuant to section 15 (inserted by the Act of 1984) of the Act of 1977 as having been elected to the European Parliament to fill a vacancy, he shall stand seconded from employment by the Commission and shall not be paid by, or entitled to receive from, the Commission any remuneration or allowances—

(i) in case he is nominated as a member of Seanad Éireann or is regarded as having been elected to the European Parliament, in respect of the period commencing on such nomination or election, as the case may be, and ending when he ceases to be a member of Seanad Éireann or the European Parliament,

(ii) in case he is nominated as a candidate for election to either House of the Oireachtas or to the European Parliament, in respect of the period commencing on his nomination and ending when he ceases to be a member of such House or the European Parliament, as the case may be, or withdraws his candidature or fails to be elected, as may be appropriate.

(3) A person who is, for the time being, entitled under the Standing Orders of either House of the Oireachtas to sit therein or who is a member of the European Parliament shall, while he is so entitled or is such a member, be disqualified from becoming a member of the Commission or from employment in any capacity by the Commission.

(4) Without prejudice to the generality of subparagraph (2) of this paragraph, that subparagraph shall be construed as prohibiting the reckoning of a period mentioned in clause (i) or (ii) of that subparagraph, as service with the Commission for the purpose of any pensions, gratuities or other allowances payable on retirement or death.

(5) In this paragraph—

"the Act of 1977" means the European Assembly Elections Act, 1977;

"the Act of 1984" means the European Assembly Elections Act, 1984.

Superannuation of staff of Commission

11.(1) The Commission may prepare a scheme or schemes for the granting of pensions, gratuities and other allowances on retirement or death to or in respect of such members of the staff of the Commission (including the chief executive) as it may think fit and the Commission shall submit any such scheme to the Minister for his approval.

(2) Every such scheme shall fix the time and conditions of retirement for all persons to or in respect of whom pensions, gratuities or allowances on retirement or death are payable under the scheme, and different times and conditions may be fixed in relation to different classes of persons.

(3) The Commission may at any time prepare and submit to the Minister a scheme amending a scheme previously submitted and approved of under this paragraph.

(4) A scheme submitted to the Minister under this paragraph shall provide that if any dispute arises as to the claim of any person to, or the amount of, any pension, gratuity or other allowance payable in pursuance of a scheme under this paragraph, such dispute shall be submitted to the Minister who shall refer it to the Minister for

Finance, whose decision shall be final.

(5) A scheme submitted to the Minister under this paragraph shall, if approved of by the Minister with the consent of the Minister for Finance, be carried out by the Commission in accordance with its terms.

(6) No pension, gratuity or other allowance shall be granted by the Commission on the resignation, retirement or death of a member of the staff of the Commission (including the chief executive) otherwise than in accordance with a scheme under this paragraph.

(7) Every scheme submitted and approved of under this paragraph shall be laid before each House of the Oireachtas as soon as may be after it is approved of and if either House, within the next twenty one days on which that House has sat after the scheme is laid before it, passes a resolution annulling the scheme, the scheme shall be annulled accordingly, but without prejudice to the validity of anything previously done thereunder.

General duty of Commission with respect to its revenue

12.(1) It shall be the duty of the Commission so to conduct its affairs as to secure that its revenue becomes as soon as possible, and thereafter continues to be, at least sufficient to meet its expenses.

(2) Any excess of the revenue of the Commission over its expenditure shall be applied in such manner as the Minister, after consultation with the Commission and with the approval of the Minister for Finance, may direct, and any such direction may require that all, or part as may be specified in the direction, of such excess be paid into the Central Fund.

Temporary borrowings

13. The Commission may, with the approval of the Minister, given with the consent of the Minister for Finance, borrow temporarily by arrangement with bankers such sums (including sums in a currency other than the currency of the State) as it may require for the purpose of providing for current expenditure.

Borrowing powers for general purposes

14.(1) The Commission may, with the approval of the Minister, given with the consent of the Minister for Finance, borrow money (including money in a currency other than the currency of the State) by means of the creation of stock or other forms of security to be issued, transferred, dealt with and redeemed in such manner and on such terms and conditions as the Commission, with the consents aforesaid, may determine.

(2) The borrowing powers conferred by this paragraph on the Commission may, subject to the consent of the Minister, be exercised for any purpose arising in the performance of its functions, but there may be attached to a consent to borrow the condition that the moneys shall be utilised only for the purpose of a programme of capital works approved by the Minister.

(3) The terms upon which moneys are borrowed under this paragraph may include provisions charging the moneys and interest thereon upon all property of whatsoever kind for the time being vested in the Commission or upon any particular property of the Commission and provisions establishing the priority of such charges amongst themselves.

Investment by Commission

15. The Commission may invest any of its funds in any manner in which a trustee is empowered by law to invest trust funds.

Accounts and audits

16. (1) The Commission shall keep in such form as shall be approved by the Minister, after consultation with the Minister for Finance, all proper and usual accounts of all moneys received or expended by it, including an income and expenditure account and a balance sheet.

(2) Accounts kept in pursuance of this paragraph shall be submitted annually by the Commission to the Comptroller and Auditor General for audit at such time as the Minister, with the concurrence of the Minister for Finance, directs.

(3) Immediately after every audit under this paragraph of its accounts, the Commission shall send to the Minister—

(a) a copy of the income and expenditure account and balance sheet as certified by the Comptroller and Auditor General,

(b) a copy of the report of the Comptroller and Auditor General, and

(c) copies of such of the accounts submitted for audit as the Minister may appoint as accounts of which copies are to be furnished to him.

(4) As soon as may be after he has received the documents required to be furnished to him under this paragraph, the Minister shall cause such documents to be laid before each House of the Oireachtas.

Annual report and information to Minister

17.(1) The Commission shall, in each year, at such date as the Minister may direct, make a report to the Minister of its proceedings under this Act during the preceding year, and the Minister shall cause copies of the Report to be laid before each House of the Oireachtas.

(2) Whenever the Minister so directs, the annual report shall also include information on such particular aspects of the Commission's proceedings under this Act as the Minister may specify.

(3) The Commission shall submit to the Minister such information regarding the performance of its functions as the Minister may from time to time require.

BROADCASTING ACT 1990

(No. 24 of 1990)

ARRANGEMENT OF SECTIONS

ACTS REFERRED TO

Broadcasting Authority Act, 1960	1960, No. 10
Broadcasting Authority (Amendment) Act, 1966	1966, No. 7
Broadcasting Authority (Amendment) Act, 1976	1976, No. 37
Broadcasting and Wireless Telegraphy Act, 1988	1988 No. 19
Police (Property) Act, 1897	1897, c. 30

Radio and Television Act, 1988	1988, No. 20
Wireless Telegraphy Act, 1926	1926, No. 45

AN ACT TO MAKE FURTHER PROVISION IN RELATION TO BROADCASTING AND WIRELESS TELEGRAPHY AND FOR THIS PURPOSE TO AMEND THE BROADCASTING AUTHORITY ACTS, 1960 TO 1979, THE RADIO AND TELEVISION ACT, 1988, AND THE WIRELESS TELEGRAPHY ACTS, 1926 TO 1988, AND TO PROVIDE FOR OTHER MATTERS CONNECTED WITH THE MATTER AFORESAID.

[24TH JULY, 1990]

BE IT ENACTED BY THE OIREACHTAS AS FOLLOWS:

Interpretation

1.—(1) In this Act—

"the Act of 1926" means the Wireless Telegraphy Act, 1926;

"the Act of 1966" means the Broadcasting Authority (Amendment) Act, 1966;

"the Act of 1976" means the Broadcasting Authority (Amendment) Act, 1976;

"the Authority" means Radio Telefís Éireann;

"licensee" means the holder of a licence issued by the Minister under the Wireless Telegraphy (Wired Broadcast Relay Licence) Regulations, 1974 (S.I. No. 67 of 1974) or a licence issued by the Minister under the Wireless Telegraphy (Television Programme Retransmission) Regulations, 1989 (S.I. No. 39 of 1989);

"the Minister" means the Minister for Communications;

"owner" has the same meaning as in the Broadcasting and Wireless Telegraphy Act, 1988;

"premises" has the same meaning as in the Broadcasting and Wireless Telegraphy Act, 1988;

"the Principal Act" means the Broadcasting Authority Act, 1960;

"service provider" means the provider of a service specified in an order made under *section* 16.

(2) A reference in this Act to a section is a reference to a section of this Act, unless it is indicated that a reference to some other enactment is intended.

(3) A reference in this Act to a subsection or a paragraph is a reference to the subsection or paragraph of the provision in which the reference occurs unless it is indicated that a reference to some other provision is intended.

Commencement

2 .—This Act shall come into operation on the 1st day of October, 1990.

Advertising broadcasts by Authority

3.—(*note: repealed by s.3 of the Broadcasting Authority (Amendment) Act 1993*)

Codes of practice relating to advertising and other commercial promotions

4.—(1) The Minister shall draw up and may amend, from time to time as he thinks proper, codes governing standards, practice and, and prohibitions in advertising, sponsorship or other forms of commercial promotion in broadcasting services and the Authority, every sound broadcasting contractor and the television programme service contractor shall comply with every such code in relation to its broadcasting services

(2) A code under *subsection (1)* relating to the Authority may provide for the extent to which the Authority's promotion of its own commercial activities within its own broadcasting services is to be treated as advertising for the purposes of *section 3* and a code relating to a sound broadcasting contractor or television programme service contractor may provide for the extent to which that contractor's promotion of its own commercial activities within its own broadcasting services is to be so treated for the purposes of section 10 (4) of the Radio and Television Act, 1988.

(3) The Minister shall consult the Authority and the Independent Radio and Television Commission in drawing up or amending a code under *subsection (1)*.

(4) Pending the drawing up of a code under *subsection (1)* the Authority and the Independent Radio and Television Commission shall continue to apply their codes for the time being in force governing standards, practice and prohibitions in broadcast advertising.

(5) A code drawn up under *subsection (1)*, in relation to the broadcasting services of the Authority, sound broadcasting contractors or the television programme service contractor, shall supersede any existing code under Section 18B(1) (*e*) of The Principal Act (inserted by section 4 of the Act of 1976) or under section 10 (2) of the Radio and Television Act, 1988, in relation to such services.

(6) The references to section 10 (2) (which relates to codes of standards) of the Radio and Television Act, 1988, in section 10 (6) or section 11 (4) (*a*) (iv) of that Act shall be construed as including reference to a code under *subsection (1)* of this section.

Independent productions on Authority's television services

5.—In the period from the commencement of this Act until the 3rd day of October, 1991, the Authority shall ensure that a reasonable proportion of the programme material on its television services is devoted to original programme material produced in the State or in another Member State of the European Communities by persons other than the Authority, its subsidiaries or other broadcasting organisations and that, as far as is practicable, that proportion shall not be less than that broadcast by the Authority in the year 1989.

Television programme service contract

6.—(1) The Independent Radio and Television Commission may, if it considers it appropriate to do so, in addition to the contract entered into under section 4 (2) (*b*) of the Radio and Television Act, 1988, enter into an additional contract with the television programme service contractor under which the television programme service contractor shall have the right and duty, in addition to the transmission systems referred to in section 17 of that Act, to establish, maintain and operate television broadcasting transmitters for the purpose of transmitting the television programme service referred to in section 4 of the said Act of 1988.

(2) Subsections (3) to (6) of section 4 of the said Act of 1988 shall apply with necessary modifications with respect to the provision of any such transmission facilities as they apply in relation to sound broadcasting services.

(3) Section 18 (1) of the said Act of 1988 shall be amended by the deletion of the reference therein to section 7 of that Act.

Accounts and audits

7.—(1) The Authority shall submit annually for audit to such duly qualified auditors as the Authority may appoint all accounts kept for the purposes of the Broadcasting Authority Acts, 1960 to 1979, and this Act.

(2) Immediately after each audit of its accounts, the Authority shall send to the Minister—

(a)a copy of the income and expenditure account and balance sheet as certified by the auditors,

(b) a copy of the auditors' report,

(c)a statement certified by the auditors in respect of the total revenue derived by the Authority from advertising, sponsorship or other forms of commercial promotion in its broadcasts,

(d) copies of such of the accounts submitted for audit as the Minister may appoint as accounts of which copies are to be furnished to him.

Complaints to Broadcasting Complaints Commission regarding broadcasts affecting an individual.

8.—(1) section 18B (1) of the Principal Act (inserted by section 4 of the Act of 1976) is hereby amended by the addition of the following paragraph:

"(Note: amendment applied).

(2) section 18B of the Principal Act is hereby amended by the insertion of a new subsection as follows:

(Note: amendment applied).

(3) A reference in the said section 18B to a code shall be construed as including a reference to a code in force under *section 4* of this Act.

Prohibition on interception of services

9.—(1) No person, other than a duly authorised officer of the Minister, shall, in relation to a service provided by a licensee or a service provider—

(a) intercept the service,

(b) suffer or permit or do any other thing that enables such interception by any person,

(c) possess, manufacture, assemble, import, supply, or offer to supply, any equipment which is designed or adapted to be used for the purpose of enabling such interception by any person, or

(d) publish information with the intention of assisting or enabling any person to intercept such a service.

(2) No person shall—

(a) knowingly instal or attempt to instal or maintain any equipment which is capable of being used or designed or adapted to be used for the purpose of enabling such interception by any person, or

(b) wilfully damage or attempt to damage a system or part of a system operated by a licensee or service provider.

(3) A person who contravenes any provision of *subsection (1)* or *(2)* shall be guilty of an offence.

(4) In this section "intercept" in relation to a service means receive, view, listen to, record by any means or acquire the substance or purport of the service or part thereof supplied by a licensee or service provider without the agreement of the licensee or service provider.

Prohibition on owner of premises where prohibited action or conduct takes place

10.—(1) No person, being the owner of, or in control of, or concerned in the management of, any premises shall knowingly suffer or permit any action or conduct to which *section 9* relates to occur on such premises.

(2) A person who contravenes *subsection (1)* shall be guilty of an offence.

(3) Where in proceedings for an offence under this section it is proved that an offence was committed in or on particular premises and that the defendant was, at the time of the alleged offence, the owner of, or in control or concerned in the management of, the premises then, unless there is sufficient other evidence to raise an issue as to whether the defendant knowingly permitted the offence to have been committed, he shall be treated as having so suffered or permitted the offence to have been committed.

Penalties

11.—(1) A person guilty of an offence under *section 9* or *10* shall be liable:

(a) on summary conviction, to imprisonment for a term not exceeding three months or, at the discretion of the court, to a fine not exceeding £1,000, or

(b) on conviction on indictment, to imprisonment for a term not exceeding two years or, at the discretion of the court, to a fine not exceeding £20,000 or to both such fine and such imprisonment.

(2) Where an offence under *section 9* or *10* which has been committed by a body corporate is proved to have been committed with the consent or connivance of, or to

be attributable to any neglect on the part of, a director, manager, secretary or other similar officer of the body corporate, or any person who was purporting to act in any such capacity, he, as well as the body corporate, shall be guilty of that offence and shall be liable to be proceeded against accordingly.

(3) Notwithstanding section 10 (4) of the Petty Sessions (Ireland) Act, 1851, summary proceedings for an offence under *section 9* or *10* of this Act may be instituted at any time within two years from the time when the offence was committed.

Forfeiture of equipment

12.—(1) On summary conviction or on conviction on indictment for an offence under *section 9 (1) (c)* or *9 (2) (a)* the Court may order the forfeiture to the Minister of any equipment used in the commission of the offence.

(2) The Minister may deal with or dispose of, as he thinks fit, anything so forfeited.

(3) The net proceeds of anything sold by the Minister in pursuance of this section shall be paid into or disposed of for the benefit of the Exchequer in such manner as the Minister for Finance shall direct.

Onus of proof

13.—In proceedings for an offence under *section 9* or *10* it shall not be necessary to negative by evidence the existence of an agreement with a licensee or service provider and accordingly the onus of proving the existence of such an agreement shall be on the defendant.

Search warrants

14.—(1) A Justice of the District Court may, upon the information on oath of a member of the Garda Síochána that there is reasonable ground for believing that an offence under *section* 9 or *10* is taking or has taken place in a specified place, grant to such member of the Garda Síochána a search warrant which shall be expressed and shall operate to authorise the member of the Garda Síochána to whom it is granted to enter, and if need be by force, the place named in the said information and there to search for equipment to which *section 9 (1) (c)* or *9 (2) (a)* relates and to examine all such equipment there found and to seize and take away all or any part of such equipment.

(2)(a) A search warrant granted under this section shall operate to authorise any one or more of the following, namely, any member of the Garda Síochána or any person authorised by the member of the Garda Síochána to whom the warrant is granted to accompany and assist him in the exercise of the powers thereby conferred on him.

(b) The member of the Garda Síochána to whom the warrant is granted may retain anything seized under this section which he believes to be evidence of any offence or suspected offence under *section 9 (1) (c)* or *9 (2) (a)* for use as evidence in proceedings in relation to any such offence, for such period from the date of seizure as is reasonable, or, if proceedings are commenced in which the thing so seized is required for use in evidence, until the conclusion of the proceedings, and the member of the Garda Síochána shall, as soon as may be, deliver any such thing to the person who in his opinion is the owner thereof, and in case the member of the Garda Síochána decides that he is unable to ascertain such person, then, on and from the date of his decision, the Police (Property) Act, 1897, shall apply to the thing so seized.

(3)(a) Any person who by act or omission impedes or obstructs a member of the Garda Síochána or any other person in the exercise of a power conferred by this section shall be guilty of an offence.

(b) Any person who with intent to impede or obstruct a member of the Garda Síochána or any other person in the exercise of a power conferred by this section places, erects, instals, keeps or maintains any thing shall be guilty of an offence and if the impediment or obstruction is continued after conviction, he shall be guilty of a further offence on each day on which it is so continued.

(c) Every person guilty of an offence under this subsection shall be liable on summary conviction to a fine not exceeding £500.

Civil remedies

15.—(1) Where it is alleged by a licensee or service provider that any activity or conduct prohibited by *section 9* is being, has been or is about to be carried on and that, as a result, he has suffered, is suffering or may suffer damage he shall be entitled to seek the following remedies against the person responsible—

(a) an order of the High Court or Circuit Court restraining the person from carrying on or attempting to carry on the activity or conduct complained of;

(b) damages or, at the option of the complainant, an account of profits.

(2) An application to the High Court or Circuit Court for an order referred to in *subsection (1)* shall be by motion and the court, when considering the matter, may make such interim or interlocutory order (if any) as it considers appropriate.

(3) An application to the Circuit Court under *subsection (1)* shall be made to the judge of the Circuit where the activity or conduct is alleged to be or to have been carried on or to be apprehended or where the person alleged to be responsible resides.

Extension of provisions

16.—(1) The Minister may by order, subject to such exceptions as he thinks fit, extend provisions of *sections 9* to *15* (subject to such modifications as he thinks proper) to any class of service transmitted by wireless telegraphy intended by the service provider to he received only by persons paying a fee to the service provider.

(2) This section applies to any class of service, whether transmitted from inside or outside the State, which is transmitted by encrypted programme transmission.

(3) In this section the term “encrypted programme transmission” means a transmission in a form whereby the aural or visual characteristics (or both) are modified or altered for the purpose of preventing the unauthorised reception of such transmission by persons without authorised equipment which is designed to eliminate the effects of such modification or alteration.

(4) The Minister may by order revoke or amend any order made by him under this section.

(5) Where it is proposed to make an order under this section a draft of the order shall be laid before each House of the Oireachtas and the order shall not be made until a resolution approving of the draft has been passed by each House.

Amendment of Act of 1926

17.—(1) For the avoidance of doubt, where it appears appropriate to the Minister, he may, in the interests of the efficient and orderly use of wireless telegraphy, limit the number of licences for any particular class or classes of apparatus for wireless telegraphy granted pursuant to section 5 of the Act of 1926.

(2) (*note: section 2A inserted into the Wireless Telegraphy Act 1926*)

Amendment of Broadcasting and Wireless Telegraphy Act, 1988

18.—(*note: amendments to s.6(4) of the Broadcasting and Wireless Act 1988 applied*)

Repeals

19.—(*note: repeals applied*)

Short title

20.—This Act may be cited as the Broadcasting Act, 1990.

BROADCASTING AUTHORITY (AMENDMENT) ACT 1993

(No. 15 of 1993)

ARRANGEMENT OF SECTIONS

ACTS REFERRED TO

Broadcasting Act, 1990	1990, No. 24
Broadcasting and Wireless Telegraphy Act, 1988	1988, No. 18
Broadcasting Authority Act, 1960	1960, No. 10
Companies Act, 1963	1963, No. 15

AN ACT TO AMEND AND EXTEND THE BROADCASTING AUTHORITY ACTS, 1960 TO 1979, TO REPEAL SECTION 3 of THE BROADCASTING ACT, 1990, AND TO PROVIDE FOR RELATED MATTERS.

[30TH JUNE, 1993]

BE IT ENACTED BY THE OIREACHTAS AS FOLLOWS:

Interpretation

1.—(1) In this Act—

"broadcaster" means a person who provides a television programme service (that is to say a service providing to members of the public images or images and sounds for reception on a television set whether the transmission (by broadcasting or any other means) of the said images or images and sounds is effected by the person or another person on his behalf) in the State or elsewhere;

"the consumer price index number" means the All Items Consumer Price Index Number compiled by the Central Statistics Office and a reference to such a number at a particular date shall be construed as a reference to such a number expressed on the basis that the consumer price index number at mid-November, 1989, is 100;

"holding company" has the same meaning as in the Companies Act, 1963;

"independent television programme" has the meaning assigned to it by section 5 of this Act;

"subsidiary" has the same meaning as in the Companies Act, 1963;

"television set has the same meaning as in section 9 of the Broadcasting and Wireless Telegraphy Act, 1988.

(2) For the purposes of this Act, the making of an independent television programme shall not be regarded as having been commissioned by the Authority unless, before work on the making of the programme commences, the Authority has incurred a legal obligation to pay at least 25 per cent. of the cost of its making.

Advertising broadcasts by Authority

2.—The total daily times for broadcasting advertisements fixed by the Authority and the maximum period so fixed to be given to advertisements in any hour shall be subject to the approval of the Minister.

Repeal of section 3 of broadcasting Act, 1990

3.—(1) Section 3 of the Broadcasting Act, 1990, is hereby repealed.

(2) This section shall be deemed to have come into operation on the 1st day of September, 1992.

Independent television programmes account

4.—(1) The Authority shall keep an account which shall be known as the "independent television programmes account and is in this Act referred to as "the account.

(2)(a) Monies standing to the credit of the account shall be used by the Authority for the purpose of—

(i) commissioning the making of independent television programmes,

(ii) procuring the formulation by persons of proposals for the commissioning by the Authority of the making of programmes as aforesaid,

(iii) assisting the completion of programmes as aforesaid the making of which has not been commissioned by the Authority, and for no other purpose.

(b) The amount of monies that the Authority is required by subsection (3) of this section to pay into the account in a financial year shall be expended, unless it is impracticable to do so, in that financial year.

(c) The Authority shall not in a financial year use for the purposes specified in subparagraphs (ii) and (iii) of paragraph (a) of this subsection more than 10 per cent. of the amount of monies that it is required by subsection (3) of this section to pay into the account in that financial year.

(3) The Authority shall in each financial year mentioned in column (1) of the Table to this section pay into the account, in accordance with subsection (4) of this section, an amount of monies that is not less than the amount of monies mentioned in column (2) of the said Table opposite the mention of the financial year concerned in the said column (1).

(4) The amount of monies required to be paid by subsection (3) of this section into the account in a financial year shall be so paid in such number of instalments as the Authority deems appropriate having regard to its duty under subsection (2) (b) of this section:

Provided that the said amount shall be paid into the account not later than the 30th day of September of the financial year concerned.

(5) If any of the monies paid under subsection (3) of this section into the account in a financial year remains unexpended at the end of that financial year the Minister may, having considered the terms of the report made to him by the Authority under section 6 of this Act in respect of that financial year and such other matters as he deems relevant, authorise the Authority to withdraw the said monies or a specified portion thereof from the account and monies so withdrawn shall thereupon become and be available to the Authority for the purposes generally of its functions under the Broadcasting Authority Acts, 1960 to 1993.

(6) References in this section to the expenditure of monies in the account include references to the incurring of a legal obligation or legal obligations to expend such monies.

(7)(a) The Minister may, having had regard to each of the following matters, namely—

(i) the current and prospective financial liabilities of the Authority,

(ii) the effect (if any) for the time being of the operation of the provisions of this section on—

(I) the employment or recruitment of staff by the Authority,

(II) the performance by the Authority of its functions generally under the Broadcasting Authority Acts, 1960 to 1993,

(III) the employment of persons in the making of independent television programmes,

from time to time by order vary an amount or percentage referred to in column (2) of the Table to this section or the amount referred to in paragraph (i) of the definition of "the appropriate amount" in subsection (8) (a) of this section and for so long as such an order is in force the said Table or the said definition, as the case may be, shall be construed and have effect in accordance with the order.

(b) The Minister may by order revoke an order under this subsection.

(c) Where it is proposed to make an order under this subsection, a draft of the order shall be laid before each House of the Oireachtas and the order shall not be made until a resolution approving of the draft has been passed by each such House.

(8)(a) In the Table to this section—

"the appropriate amount means—

(i) in the case of the financial year 1999, £12,500,000,

(ii) in the case of a subsequent financial year, the said amount as increased by an amount equal to the appropriate percentage of the said amount;

"television programme expenditure" means, in respect of a financial year, the total costs incurred by the Authority in that financial year in making, commissioning the making of, acquiring, preparing, producing, or cooperating in the production of, television programmes.

(b) In this subsection "the appropriate percentage" means the difference between the consumer price index number at mid-August, 1998, and the said number at the mid-August immediately preceding the financial year concerned expressed as a percentage of the first-mentioned number.

(c) If at the second-mentioned date in paragraph (b) of this subsection the consumer price index number stands at a figure that is less than that at which it stood at the first-mentioned date in that paragraph, the definition of "the appropriate amount in this subsection shall have effect as respects the financial year immediately following the second-mentioned date as if "reduced" were substituted for "increased" in that definition.

TABLE

Financial year(1)	Amount of monies to be paid by the Authority into the account (2)
1994	£ 5,000,000
1995	£ 6,500,000
1996	£ 7,500,000
1997	£ 8, 500, 000
1998	£10, 000, 000
Each subsequent financial year:	Whichever of the following amounts is the greater- (i) the appropriate amount, or (ii) 20 per cent. of television programme expenditure in the preceding financial year.

"Independent television programme"

5.—(1) In this Act "independent television programme" means a television programme made by a person who complies with the following conditions, namely—

(a) each of the following matters as respects the said programme is determined by him or by one or more persons on his behalf and over whose activities in respect of the determination of such matters he exercises control, namely—

(i) the persons who are to participate in the said programme,

(ii) the persons who are to be involved in the making of the said programme, and

(iii) the equipment and facilities to be used in the making of the said programme,

(b) he is not a subsidiary of a broadcaster, and

(c) he is not a holding company of a broadcaster.

(2) For the purposes of the definition in subsection (1) of this section, where—

(a) two or more broadcasters hold shares in a body corporate or a holding company of a body corporate, or

(b) each of two or more broadcasters (being shareholders in a body corporate or a holding company of a body corporate) by the exercise of some power exercisable by it without the consent or concurrence of any other person can appoint or remove a holder of a directorship of the body corporate or, as the case may be, the holding company,

then, notwithstanding that the body corporate is not a subsidiary of any of the said broadcasters, the body corporate shall be deemed not to comply with the condition specified in paragraph (b) of the aforesaid definition if—

(i) the total number of shares held by the said broadcasters in the body corporate or, as the case may be, the holding company, or

(ii) the total number of directorships of the body corporate or, as the case may be, the holding company that the aforesaid powers of the said broadcasters may be exercised in respect of, is such that, were the said broadcasters to be regarded as one company, the body corporate would be a subsidiary of it, and

(I) the Authority is one of the said broadcasters, or

(II) there exists a business relationship between the said broadcasters that, in the opinion of the Authority, is of such a kind as is likely to result in the said broadcasters acting in concert with one another in exercising their rights under the said shares or in exercising the said powers.

(3) For the purposes of subsection (2) (b) of this section a broadcaster shall be deemed to have power to appoint to a directorship in relation to which the condition specified in paragraph (a) or (b) of section 155 (2) of the Companies Act, 1963, is satisfied and for this purpose references in the said paragraphs to the other company shall be construed as references to the broadcaster.

Annual report by Authority concerning the commissioning of independent television programmes

6.—As soon as may be, but not later than 3 months, after the end of the financial year 1994 and each subsequent financial year the Authority shall make a report to the Minister of—

(a) its activities during that financial year as. respects commissioning the making of independent television programmes.

(b) the operation by it of the account during that financial year,

(c) such other matters relating to the matters referred to in paragraphs (a) and (b) of this section as the Minister may direct,

and the Minister shall cause copies of the report to be laid before each House of the Oireachtas.

Provision as to membership of the Authority

7.—(1) The Broadcasting Authority Act, 1960, is hereby amended—

(a) in section 4, by the insertion after subsection (1) of the following subsection:

"(1A) (a) Where the number of members of the Authority for the time being is 7, not less than 3 of them shall be men and not less than 3 of them shall be women.

(b) Where the number of members of the Authority for the time being is 8 or 9, not less than 4 of them shall be men and not less than 4 of them shall be women.";

(b) in section 10, by the substitution of the following subsection for subsection (5):

"(5) The Authority may act notwithstanding one or more vacancies among its members (including one or more vacancies that result in subsection (1A) (inserted by the Broadcasting Authority (Amendment) Act, 1993) of section 4 of this Act not being complied with).".

(2) This section shall come into operation on the 1st day of June, 1995, or such earlier day as the Minister may appoint by order.

Short title, collective citation and construction

8.—(1) This Act may be cited as the Broadcasting Authority (Amendment) Act, 1993.

(2) The Broadcasting Authority Acts, 1960 to 1979, and this Act may be cited together as the Broadcasting Authority Acts, 1960 to 1993.

(3) The Broadcasting Authority Acts, 1960 to 1979, and this Act shall be construed together as one.

REFERENDUM ACT 1998

(No. 1 of 1998)

(*Note: The Referendum Act 1998 makes reference to certain broadcasting obligations with regard to advertising during a referendum. The relevant sections of this Act are included below for reference purposes only.*)

Functions of Commission

3.—(1) The Commission shall have, in addition to any functions conferred on it by any other provision of this Act, the following principal functions in relation to the referendum in respect of which it is established:

(a) to prepare—

(i) a statement or statements containing a general explanation of the subject matter of the proposal and of the text thereof in the relevant Bill and any other information relating to those matters that the Commission considers appropriate, and

(ii) a statement or statements having regard to any submissions under section 6 concerning the proposal to which the referendum relates and setting out the arguments for and against the proposal, and the statements shall be fair to all interests concerned;

(b) to publish and distribute such statements in such manner and by such means including the use of television, radio and other electronic media as the Commission considers most likely to bring them to the attention of the electorate and to ensure as far as practicable that the means employed enable those with a sight or hearing disability to read or hear the statements concerned;

(c) to foster and promote and, where appropriate, to facilitate debate or discussion in a manner that is fair to all interests concerned in relation to the proposal aforesaid.

(2) The Commission shall have all such powers as it considers necessary or expedient for the performance of its functions including, but without prejudice to the generality of the foregoing, the following powers:

(a) to prepare, publish and distribute brochures, leaflets, pamphlets and posters, and

(b) to distribute the statements aforesaid to each presidential elector or each household.

(3) If the Commission is established before the passing of the Bill containing the proposal or proposals concerned to amend the Constitution, the Commission shall not publish any statement under this section or incur any expenditure without the consent of the Minister for Finance before such passing.

Advertisements etc., by Commission

5.—(1) Section 20(4) of the Broadcasting Authority Act, 1960, and section 10(3) of the Radio and Television Act, 1988, shall not apply to advertisements broadcast at the request of the Commission in relation to a matter referred to in section 3 concerning the referendum.

(2) The Minister for Arts, Heritage, Gaeltacht and the Islands, if so requested by the Commission following consultation by the Commission with Radio Telefís Éireann ("the Authority") and consideration of any proposals of the Authority for broadcasts in connection with the referendum that it communicates to the Commission, shall direct the Authority in writing to allocate broadcasting time to facilitate the Commission in performing its functions, and the Authority shall comply with a direction under this subsection.

(3) The Minister for Arts, Heritage, Gaeltacht and the Islands, if so requested by the Commission following consultation by the Commission with An Coimisiún Um Radio agus Telefís Neamhspleách — The Independent Radio and Television Commission ("the Independent Commission") and consideration of any proposals of the Independent Commission for broadcasts in connection with the referendum by sound broadcasting contractors or television programme service contractors that it communicates to the Commission, shall direct the Independent Commission in writing to arrange for the provision for and on behalf of the Commission of services (with or without charge) including the allocation of broadcasting time to facilitate the Commission in performing its functions, and the Independent Commission shall comply with a direction under this subsection.

BROADCASTING (MAJOR EVENTS TELEVISION COVERAGE) ACT 1999

(No. 28 of 1999)

ARRANGEMENT OF SECTIONS

ACTS REFERRED TO

European Communities Act, 1972	1972, No. 27
European Communities (Amendment) Act, 1993	1993, No. 25

AN ACT TO PROVIDE FOR TELEVISION COVERAGE OF EVENTS OF MAJOR IMPORTANCE TO SOCIETY, TO GIVE EFFECT TO ARTICLE 3a OF COUNCIL DIRECTIVE NO. 89/552/EEC OF 3 OCTOBER, 1989, AS AMENDED BY COUNCIL DIRECTIVE NO. 97/36/EC OF 30 JUNE, 1997, AND TO PROVIDE FOR OTHER RELATED MATTERS.

[13TH NOVEMBER, 1999]

BE IT ENACTED BY THE OIREACHTAS AS FOLLOWS:

Interpretation

1.—(1) In this Act—

"broadcaster" has the meaning assigned in the Council Directive;

"Council Directive" means Council Directive No. 89/552/EEC of 3 October 1989(1) as amended by Council Directive No. 97/36/EC of 30 June 1997(2);

"EEA Agreement" has the meaning assigned in the European Communities (Amendment) Act, 1993;

"event" means an even of interest to the general public in the European Union, a Member State or in the State or in a significant part of the State that is organised by an event organiser who is legally entitled to sell the broadcasting rights to the event;

"free television service" means television broadcasting service for the reception of which no charge is made by the person providing the service;

"Member State" means a member state of the European Communities (within the meaning of the European Communities Act, 1972) and includes a state that is a contracting state to the EEA Agreement;

"the Minister" means the Minister for Arts, Heritage, Gaeltacht and the Islands;

"near universal coverage" means—

(a) free television service, reception of which is available to at least 95 per cent of the population of the State, or

(b) if at any time fewer than three broadcasters are able to provide the coverage required under paragraph (a), free television service, reception of which is available to at least 90 per cent of the population of the State;

"qualifying broadcaster" means a broadcaster who is deemed under subsection (2) to be a qualifying broadcaster;

"television broadcasting" has the meaning assigned in the Council Directive.

(2) The following broadcasters are deemed to be qualifying broadcasters:

(a) until the 31st day of December, 2001, a broadcaster who provides free television service coverage of a designated event to which at least 85 per cent of the population of the State have access;

(b) on and after the 1st day of January, 2002, a broadcaster who provides near universal coverage of a designated event.

(3) For the purpose of subsection (2), two or more broadcasters who enter into a contract or arrangement to jointly provide near universal coverage of a designated event shall be deemed to be a single broadcaster with respect to that event.

(4) A broadcaster may request the Minister to resolve any dispute as to the extent of free television service being provided by a broadcaster in the State for the purpose of subsection (2) and the definition of "near universal coverage" in subsection (1).(5) The Minister may consult with any technical experts or other persons or bodies he or she considers appropriate before resolving a dispute under subsection (4).

(6) In this Act—

(a) a reference to any enactment shall, unless the context otherwise requires, be construed as a reference to that enactment as amended or extended by or under any subsequent enactment including this Act,

(b) a reference to a section is a reference to a section of this Act unless it is indicated that reference to some other enactment is intended, and

(c) a reference to a subsection, paragraph or subparagraph is a reference to the subsection, paragraph or subparagraph of the provision in which the reference occurs unless it is indicated that reference to some other provision is intended.

Designation of major events

2.—(1) The Minister may by order—

(a) designate events as events of major importance to society for which the right of a qualifying broadcaster to provide coverage on free television services should be provided in the public interest, and

(b) determine whether coverage on free television services of an event designated under paragraph (a) should be available—

(i) on a live, deferred or both live and deferred basis, and

(ii) in whole, in part or both in whole and in part.

(2) The Minister shall have regard to all the circumstances and in particular each of the following criteria in making a designation under subsection (1)(a):

(a) the extent to which the event has a special general resonance for the people of Ireland;

(b) the extent to which the event has a generally recognised distinct cultural importance for the people of Ireland.

(3) In order to determine the extent to which the criteria in subsection (2) have been met, the following factors may be taken into account by the Minister:

(a) whether the event involves participation by a national or non-national team or by Irish persons;

(b) past practice or experience with regard to television coverage of the event or similar events.

(4) The Minister shall consider the following in making the determination under subsection (1)(b):

(a) the nature of the event;

(b) the time within the State at which the event takes place;

(c) practical broadcasting considerations.

(5) The Minister may by order revoke or amend an order under this section.

(6) The Minister shall consult with the Minister for Tourism, Sport and Recreation before making, revoking or amending an order under this section.

(7) Where it is proposed to make, revoke or amend an order under this section, a draft of the order shall be laid before each House of the Oireachtas and the order shall not be made until a resolution approving the draft has been passed by each House.

Consultation

3.—(1) Before making an order under section 2, the Minister shall—

(a) make reasonable efforts to consult with the organisers of the event and with broadcasters who are under the jurisdiction of the State for the purpose of the Council Directive,

(b) publish a notice of the event which the Minister intends to designate under that section in at least one newspaper circulating in the State, and

(c) invite comments on the intended designation from members of the public.

(2) The inability to establish who is the organiser of an event or the failure of the organiser or a broadcaster under the jurisdiction of the State to respond to the Minister's efforts to consult shall not preclude the making of an order under section 2.

Broadcasters' duties with respect to designated events

4.—(1) Where a broadcaster under the jurisdiction of the State who is not a qualifying broadcaster acquires exclusive rights to broadcast a designated event, that broadcaster shall not broadcast the event unless the event has been made available to a qualifying broadcaster, in accordance with the order under section 2, on request and the payment of reasonable market rates by the qualifying broadcaster.

(2) Where a qualifying broadcaster acquires the right to broadcast a designated event (under this section or directly), the qualifying broadcaster shall broadcast the event on a free television service providing near universal coverage in accordance with the order under section 2.

(3) In this section, "designated event" means an event that is designated in an order under section 2.

Broadcasters' duties with respect to Member States events

5.—Where another Member State has designated an event as being of major importance to society in that Member State and the European Commission has communicated the measures taken by that Member State in accordance with Article 3a.2 of the Council Directive, no broadcaster under the jurisdiction of the State who acquires exclusive rights to the designated event shall exercise the exclusive rights in such a way that a substantial portion of the public in that Member State is deprived of the possibility of following the events in accordance with the measures taken.

Civil remedies

6.—(1) Where it is alleged by a broadcaster (the "aggrieved broadcaster") that any activity or conduct prohibited by section 4 or 5 is being, has been or is about to be carried on by one or more other broadcasters (the "other broadcaster"), the aggrieved broadcaster shall be entitled to apply to the High Court for the following remedies against the other broadcaster:

(a) an order restraining the other broadcaster from carrying on or attempting to carry on the activity or conduct prohibited by section 4 or 5;

(b) a declaration that the contract under which the other broadcaster received exclusive rights to the designated event is void;

(c) damages from the other broadcaster;

(d) a direction that the right to provide television coverage of the event shall be offered to the aggrieved broadcaster at reasonable market rates.

(2) An application to the High Court for an order referred to in subsection (1) shall be by motion and the court, when considering the matter, may make such interim or interlocutory order as it considers appropriate.

Reasonable market rates

7.—(1) For the purpose of section 4(1), if broadcasters are unable to agree on what constitutes reasonable market rates with respect to television coverage of an event, either of the broadcasters may apply to the High Court in a summary manner for an order determining reasonable market rates for an event.

(2) An order under subsection (1) may contain such consequential or supplementary provisions as the High Court considers appropriate.

Short title

8.—This Act may be cited as the Broadcasting (Major Events Television Coverage) Act, 1999.

BROADCASTING ACT 2001

(No. 4 of 2001)

ARRANGEMENT OF SECTIONS

PART I

PRELIMINARY AND GENERAL

PART II

SUPPLY AND TRANSMISSION OF PROGRAMME MATERIAL GENERALLY

PART III

STANDARDS IN BROADCASTING

PART IV

PROVISIONS IN RELATION TO THE AUTHORITY

PART V

ADDITIONAL BROADCASTING SERVICES — CABLE, SATELLITE SYSTEMS, ETC.

SECTION

PART VI

TEILIFÍS NA GAEILGE

ACTS REFERRED TO

Broadcasting Act, 1990	1990, No. 24
Broadcasting Authority Act, 1960	1960, No. 10
Broadcasting Authority Acts, 1960 to 1999	
Broadcasting Authority (Amendment) Act, 1976	1976, No. 37
Broadcasting Authority (Amendment) Act, 1979	1979, No. 36
Broadcasting Authority (Amendment) Act, 1993	1993, No. 15
Companies Acts, 1963 to 1999	

Copyright and Related Rights Act, 2000	2000, No. 28
European Parliament Elections Act, 1997	1997, No. 2
Prohibition of Incitement to Hatred Act, 1989	1989, No. 19
Radio and Television Act, 1988	1988, No. 20
Wireless Telegraphy Act, 1926	1926, No. 45
Wireless Telegraphy Acts, 1926 to 1988	

AN ACT TO MAKE FURTHER PROVISION IN RELATION TO BROADCASTING, FOR THAT PURPOSE TO MAKE SEPARATE PROVISION IN RELATION TO THE FOLLOWING DISCRETE ASPECTS OF BROADCASTING, NAMELY, THE SUPPLY OF PROGRAMME MATERIAL FOR THE PURPOSE OF ITS BEING TRANSMITTED AND THE TRANSMISSION OF SUCH MATERIAL THAT IS SO SUPPLIED, TO CONFER ON 2 COMPANIES DESIGNATED BY THE MINISTER FOR ARTS, HERITAGE, GAELTACHT AND THE ISLANDS FOR THAT PURPOSE FUNCTIONS IN RELATION TO SUCH TRANSMISSION AND, AS REGARDS SUCH TRANSMISSION THAT IS EFFECTED BY DIGITAL MEANS, IN RELATION TO THE COMBINATION OF MATERIAL AS AFORESAID AND RELATED AND OTHER DATA IN DIGITAL FORM, TO CONFER ADDITIONAL FUNCTIONS ON THE INDEPENDENT RADIO AND TELEVISION COMMISSION AND RENAME THAT BODY AS COIMISIÚN CRAOLACHÁIN NA hÉIREANN OR, IN THE ENGLISH LANGUAGE, THE BROADCASTING COMMISSION OF IRELAND, TO ESTABLISH A BODY TO BE KNOWN AS TEILIFI´S NA GAEILGE AND TO DEFINE ITS FUNCTIONS, TO AMEND THE BROADCASTING AUTHORITY ACTS, 1960 TO 1993, AND CERTAIN OTHER ENACTMENTS AND TO PROVIDE FOR RELATED MATTERS.

[14TH MARCH, 2001]

BE IT ENACTED BY THE OIREACHTAS AS FOLLOWS:

PART I

PRELIMINARY AND GENERAL

Short title, collective citation, construction and commencement

1.— (1) This Act may be cited as the Broadcasting Act, 2001.

(2) The Broadcasting Authority Acts, 1960 to 1993, and this Act (in so far as it amends those Acts) may be cited together as the Broadcasting Authority Acts, 1960 to 2001.

(3) The Broadcasting Authority Acts, 1960 to 1993, and this Act (in so far as it amends those Acts) shall be construed together as one.

(4) This Act shall come into operation on such day or days as the Minister may appoint by order or orders either generally or with reference to any particular purpose or provision and different days may be so appointed for different purposes or different provisions.

Interpretation

2.—(1) In this Act, unless the context otherwise requires—

"the Act of 1960" means the Broadcasting Authority Act, 1960;

"the Act of 1976" means the Broadcasting Authority (Amendment) Act, 1976;

"the Act of 1988" means the Radio and Television Act, 1988;

"the Authority" means Radio Telefís Éireann;

"broadcaster" means a person who supplies a compilation of programme material for the purpose of its being transmitted or relayed as a broadcasting service (whether that person transmits or relays that material as such a service or not);

"broadcasting service" means a service which comprises a compilation of programme material of any description and which is transmitted or relayed by means of wireless telegraphy, a cable or MMD system or a satellite device, directly or indirectly for reception by the general public, whether that material is actually received or not, but does not include such a service that is provided by means of the Internet;

"cable-MMD content contract" has the meaning assigned to it by section 41;

"cable system" means a wired broadcast relay system;

"the Commission" means the body established by section 3 of the Act of 1988;

"community content contract" has the meaning assigned to it by section 39;

"contract" does not include any contract that comes into being between the multiplex company or the transmission company and another person by virtue of the entering into arrangements by the multiplex company or the transmission company with that person under section 13(1) or 14(1);

"the Council Directive" means Council Directive 89/552/EEC of 3 October 1989(O.J. No. L. 298/23, 17 October 1989) on the co-ordination of certain provisions laid down by law, regulation or administrative action in Member States concerning the pursuit of television broadcasting activities as amended by Directive 97/36/EC of the European Parliament and of the Council of 30 June 1997(O.J. No. L. 202/60, 30 July 1997) ;

"digital content contract" has the meaning assigned to it by section 12;

"digital multiplex licence" has the meaning assigned to it by section 9;

"the Director" means the Director of Telecommunications Regulation;

"DTT licence" has the meaning assigned to it by section 7;

"EEA Agreement" means the Agreement on the European Economic Area signed at Oporto on the 2nd day of May, 1992, as amended for the time being;

"electronic programme guide" has the meaning assigned to it by section 16;

"establishment day" has the meaning assigned to it by section 43;

"excepted person" means a person who is under the jurisdiction of another Member State of the European Union or another Member State of the EEA and, for the purposes of this definition, the provisions of the Council Directive shall apply for the purpose of determining the state (whether it be a Member State of the European Union or of the EEA) under the jurisdiction of which the person falls;

"free-to-air service" means a broadcasting service for the reception of which no charge is made by the person providing the service;

"holder" means—

(a) in relation to a contract entered into under the Act of 1988 or this Act, the person with whom the Commission has entered into the contract,

(b) in relation to a licence granted under this Act or any other enactment, the person to whom the licence has been granted;

"the Internet" means the system commonly known by that name;

"local content contract" has the meaning assigned to it by section 38;

"Member State of the EEA" means a state that is a contracting party to the EEA Agreement;

"the Minister" means the Minister for Arts, Heritage, Gaeltacht and the Islands;

"MMD system" means a multipoint microwave distribution system used for the transmission of broadcasting services on a point to multipoint basis;

"multiplex" has the meaning assigned to it by section 8;

"the multiplex company" has the meaning assigned to it by section 8;

"programme guide contract" has the meaning assigned to it by section 16;

"programme material" means audio-visual material or, where used in the context of a sound broadcasting service, audio material and includes advertisements and material which, when transmitted, will constitute a direct offer to the public for the sale or supply to them of goods or other property (whether real or personal) or services;

"provide a broadcasting service" means to supply a compilation of programme material for the purpose of its being transmitted or relayed as a broadcasting service;

"sound broadcasting contractor" and "sound broadcasting service" have the same meaning as they have in the Act of 1988;

"subscription or pay-per-view basis", in relation to the making available of a broadcasting service, means any basis for making a charge on a person in respect of the reception by him or her of a broadcasting service, and includes the basis of making such a charge by reference to the number of items of programme material viewed by him or her;

"Teilifís na Gaeilge" means the body established by section 44;

"television programme service contract" and "television programme service contractor" have the same meaning as they have in the Act of 1988;

"terrestrial means", in relation to the transmission of a broadcasting service, means any means of transmitting such a service by wireless telegraphy, other than by means of a cable or MMD system (or, where the said expression is used in the context of Northern Ireland, any system analogous to a cable or MMD system) or a satellite device and "digital terrestrial means" shall be construed accordingly;

"transmission" includes, in the case of a cable or MMD system, distribution and "transmit" and "re-transmit" shall be construed accordingly;

"the transmission company" has the meaning assigned to it by section 5.

(2) In this Act—

(a) a reference to a section is a reference to a section of this Act unless it is indicated that reference to some other enactment is intended,

(b) a reference to a subsection or paragraph is a reference to the subsection or paragraph of the provision in which the reference occurs unless it is indicated that reference to some other provision is intended,

(c) a reference to any other enactment shall, unless the context otherwise requires, be construed as a reference to that enactment as amended, extended or adapted by or under subsequent enactments, including this Act.

Repeals

3.—Each enactment specified in the First Schedule to this Act is hereby repealed to the extent specified in the third column of that Schedule.

Expenses

4.—The expenses incurred by the Minister in the administration of this Act shall, to such extent as may be sanctioned by the Minister for Finance, be paid out of moneys provided by the Oireachtas.

PART II

Supply and Transmission of Programme Material Generally

Transmission Company

5.—(1) In this section "the transmission company" means a company formed and registered under the Companies Acts, 1963 to 1999 (whether before or after the commencement of this section), being a company which is designated in writing by the Minister to be the body that shall perform the functions expressed in this Act to be performable by the transmission company.

(2) The Minister shall not designate a company for the purposes aforesaid unless the following conditions as respects the company are satisfied, namely—

(a) the company has been so formed and registered by 2 or more persons (who may include the Authority) each of whom the Minister is of the opinion, having regard to the responsibilities the company will assume under this Act, is a person who is a suitable person to be concerned in such formation and registration,

(b) the name of the company is a name which the Minister considers to be appropriate having regard to the said responsibilities,

(c) the company is a company limited by shares, and

(d) the memorandum of association and articles of association of the company are in such form, consistent with this Act, as is approved of by the Minister, after consultation with the Minister for Public Enterprise.

(3) For the purposes of enabling or facilitating the performance by the transmission company of its functions under section 13, the Authority shall transfer such parts of its real and personal property to the company as the Minister, after consultation with the Authority, determines ought to be the subject of such a transfer.

(4) The principal objects of the transmission company shall be stated in its memorandum of association to be—

(a) to transmit, by analogue means, broadcasting services on behalf of the Authority, Teilifís na Gaeilge and the television programme service contractor, being services that the Authority, Teilifís na Gaeilge and that contractor provide under the Broadcasting Authority Acts, 1960 to 2001, the Act of 1988 or this Act, as the case may be,

(b) to transmit, by digital terrestrial means, programme material and related and other data in a digital form in accordance with arrangements entered into by it under this Act with the multiplex company,

(c) to transmit, by analogue means, sound broadcasting services on behalf of the Authority and sound broadcasting contractors, being services that the Authority and such contractors provide under the Broadcasting Authority Acts, 1960 to 2001, or the Act of 1988, as the case may be, (d) to promote the development of multimedia services, and (e) to promote the development of electronic information services, including those provided by means of the Internet.

(5) The transmission company shall endeavour to ensure, in so far as it is reasonably practicable to do so, that the services provided by it are made available to the whole community in the State.

(6) The Authority shall not, without the consent of the Minister and the Minister

for Finance, transfer to another person all or one or more of any shares it holds in the shareholding of the transmission company.

(7) The Minister may, by order, require the Authority to divest itself of all or one or more of any shares it holds in the shareholding of the transmission company.

(8) Where an order is proposed to be made under subsection (7), a draft of the order shall be laid before each House of the Oireachtas and the order shall not be made until a resolution approving of the draft has been passed by each such House.

(9) Nothing in this section shall prevent or restrict the inclusion among the objects of the transmission company as stated in its memorandum of association of all such objects and powers as are reasonably necessary or proper for or incidental or ancillary to the due attainment of the principal objects aforesaid and are not inconsistent with this Act.

(10)The transmission company shall have power to do anything which appears to it to be requisite, advantageous or incidental to, or which appears to it to facilitate, either directly or indirectly, the performance by it of its functions as specified in this Act or its memorandum of association and is not inconsistent with any enactment for the time being in force.

Authorisation of the exercise of certain powers vested in Authority and transmission company

6.—(1) In this section the "relevant section" means section 16 of the Act of 1960.

(2) Subsection (3)(a) of the relevant section shall be construed as including a prohibition with respect to the transmission company exercising its powers to transmit programme material (other than programme material referred to in section 7(2)) of a like kind to the prohibition which that subsection contains with respect to the Authority exercising the powers referred to in paragraphs (a) and (b) of subsection (2) of the relevant section and, accordingly, the Director may, in accordance with this section, issue licences under subsection (3) of the relevant section to the transmission company as well as to the Authority and attach conditions to any licence so issued to that company.

(3) On such date as the Minister, after consultation with the Minister for Public Enterprise and the Director, specifies for the purpose of this section, the Director shall issue a licence under subsection (3) of the relevant section or the Wireless Telegraphy Acts, 1926 to 1988, or both those enactments as appropriate, to—

(a) the Authority with respect to the operation by it of any apparatus the operation of which requires a licence under either or both of the said enactments and which apparatus has not been the subject of the transfer referred to in section 5(3), and

(b) the transmission company with respect to the operation by it of any apparatus the operation of which requires a licence under either or both of the said enactments and which apparatus has been the subject of the said transfer.

(4) Pending the issuing by the Director of the licences referred to in subsection (3), any licence issued to the Authority under subsection (3) of the relevant section or

the Wireless Telegraphy Acts, 1926 to 1988, and in force immediately before the date specified for the purposes of subsection (3), shall, in so far as any right or obligation arising under it relates to an apparatus which has been the subject of the transfer referred to in section 5(3), operate and have effect as if it had been granted to the transmission company.

(5) Upon the issue by the Director of a licence referred to in subsection (3), any licence issued to the Authority under subsection (3) of the relevant section or the Wireless Telegraphy Acts, 1926 to 1988, (including any licence to which subsection (4) applies) which relates to the same matter as the first-mentioned licence relates to and is in force immediately before the issue of that licence shall stand revoked.

(6) Paragraphs (b) and (c) of subsection (3) of the relevant section shall apply to a licence issued under that subsection to the transmission company as they apply to a licence issued under that subsection to the Authority and, for the purposes of such application, the reference in the said paragraph (b) to the Authority shall be construed as a reference to the transmission company.

Authorisation of transmission company to transmit, by digital terrestrial means, programme material

7.—(1) The Director shall, on a date specified by the Minister, after consultation with the Minister for Public Enterprise, for the purposes of this section, grant to the transmission company, under the Wireless Telegraphy Acts, 1926 to 1988, a licence which shall be known as the "digital terrestrial television licence" and is in this Act referred to as the "DTT licence".

(2) The DTT licence shall be expressed to authorise, and shall operate to authorise, the transmission company to transmit by digital terrestrial means programme material and related and other data in a digital form in accordance with arrangements entered into by it under this Act with the multiplex company.

(3) Without prejudice to any powers he or she may have in that behalf under the Wireless Telegraphy Acts, 1926 to 1988, the Director may attach such conditions to the DTT licence as he or she considers appropriate including conditions specifying requirements to be complied with by the transmission company in respect of the entering into of arrangements under subsection (1) of section 13 or the imposition of charges under subsection (3) of that section and, in particular—

(a) a requirement that, as respects such arrangements that are entered into in similar circumstances by the company with different persons for the transmission of broadcasting services comprising similar kinds of programme material supplied to it by each of those persons, the terms of those arrangements, and the charges imposed in respect of them, are similar,

(b) a requirement that the company, as respects any decision made by it to exercise or not to exercise its power under subsection (3) of section 13, and as respects any consequent exercise by it of that power, otherwise ensures fairness of treatment of the persons concerned, and

(c) a requirement that the transmission company supplies such information to the Director, and adopts such procedures in the performance of its functions under this Act, as the Director specifies, in pursuance of the requirement, for the purpose of enabling the Director to verify that each condition attached to the licence is being complied with.

(4) Nothing in this section shall be construed as preventing the Director from granting under the Wireless Telegraphy Acts, 1926 to 1988, in addition to the DTT licence and whether to the transmission company or any other person, licences authorising the transmission, by digital terrestrial means, of programme material and related and other data in a digital form.

Multiplex company

8.—(1) In this section— "multiplex" means a multiplex referred to in subsection (3);

"the multiplex company" means a company formed and registered under the Companies Acts, 1963 to 1999 (whether before or after the commencement of this section), being a company which is designated in writing by the Minister to be the body that shall perform the functions expressed in this Act to be performable by the multiplex company.

(2) The Minister shall not designate a company for the purposes aforesaid unless the following conditions as respects the company are satisfied, namely—

(a) the company has been so formed and registered by one or more than one person who or each of whom the Minister is of the opinion, having regard to the responsibilities the company will assume under this Act, is a person who is a suitable person to be concerned in such formation and registration,

(b) the name of the company is a name which the Minister considers to be appropriate having regard to the said responsibilities,

(c) the company is a company limited by shares, and

(d) the memorandum of association and articles of association of the company are in such form, consistent with this Act, as is approved of by the Minister, after consultation with the Minister for Public Enterprise.

(3) The principal objects of the multiplex company shall be stated in its memorandum of association to be—

(a) to establish, operate and maintain 6 digital multiplexes, that is to say, 6 electronic systems which combine programme material and related and other data in a digital form for the purposes of that material and data, so combined, being transmitted by the transmission company,

(b) to enter into arrangements, in accordance with the provisions of this Act, with the Authority, Teilifís na Gaeilge, the television programme service contractor and any other person concerned for the transmission of programme material and related and other data in a digital form by the transmission company,

(c) to promote the development of multimedia services, and

(d) to promote the development of electronic information services, including those provided by means of the Internet.

(4) The multiplex company shall endeavour to ensure, in so far as it is reasonably practicable to do so, that the services provided by it are made available to the whole community in the State.

(5) Nothing in this section shall prevent or restrict the inclusion among the objects of the multiplex company as stated in its memorandum of association of all such objects and powers as are reasonably necessary or proper for or incidental or ancillary to the due attainment of the principal objects aforesaid and are not inconsistent with this Act.

(6) The multiplex company shall have power to do anything which appears to it to be requisite, advantageous or incidental to, or which appears to it to facilitate, either directly or indirectly, the performance by it of its functions as specified in this Act or its memorandum of association and is not inconsistent with any enactment for the time being in force.

Authorisation of multiplex company to combine programme material in digital form

9.—(1) The Director shall, on a date specified by the Minister, after consultation with the Minister for Public Enterprise, for the purposes of this section, grant to the multiplex company, under the Wireless Telegraphy Acts, 1926 to 1988, a licence which shall be known, and is in this Act referred to, as the "digital multiplex licence".

(2) The digital multiplex licence shall be expressed to authorise, and shall operate to authorise, the multiplex company to establish, operate and maintain 6 multiplexes.

(3) The Director shall attach to the digital multiplex licence a condition requiring the multiplex company to use the whole or, as the case may be, the part of a multiplex specified in column (2) of the Table to this section solely for the purposes of programme material and related and other data supplied to it by the person who is specified in column (1) of that Table opposite the specification of that whole or that part of a multiplex.

(4) If, on the expiration of the appropriate period, a person specified in column (1) of the Table to this section—

(a) has not supplied any programme material and related and other data to the multiplex company for the purposes of that material and data being combined in a digital form by means of the multiplex or part of the multiplex specified in column (2) of that Table opposite the specification of that person, or

(b) is not supplying programme material and related and other data that is sufficient to exhaust, on a day-to-day basis, the capacity of the said multiplex or part, the designated multiplex company may use—

(i) in a case falling within paragraph (a), the whole of the said multiplex or part,

(ii) in a case falling within paragraph (b), so much of the said multiplex or part as is not being so exhausted, in respect of programme material and related and other data supplied to it by another person or persons under and in accordance with this Act or for the purposes referred to in subsection (9).

(5) In subsection (4) "appropriate period" means the period beginning on the commencement of this section and ending on such day as the Commission, after consultation with the multiplex company and the first-mentioned person in subsection (4), determines to be the day by which in the opinion of the Commission, it would be reasonable to expect that person to be supplying sufficient programme material to that company to exhaust, on a day-to-day basis, the capacity of the multiplex or part referred to in that subsection.

(6) The Director shall attach a condition to the digital multiplex licence requiring the multiplex company, where the Commission, in accordance with a direction given by the Minister under subsection (7) for the time being in force, requests it to do so, to use a multiplex or part of a multiplex solely for the purposes of programme material supplied to it under and in accordance with this Act by a person who provides a broadcasting service in Northern Ireland, being a broadcasting service that is receivable throughout the whole of Northern Ireland and which is provided by terrestrial means.

(7) The Minister may, whenever and so often as he or she considers it appropriate to do so, give a direction to the Commission requiring it to make a request of the multiplex company of the kind referred to in subsection (6) and the Commission shall comply with that direction; such a direction may, subject to subsection (8), be revoked at any time by the Minister and where the direction is so revoked, the multiplex company shall thereupon be relieved of the obligation of having to comply any further with the request concerned of the Commission.

(8) The Minister shall not revoke a direction under subsection (7) otherwise than for stated reasons and then only upon resolutions passed by both Houses of the Oireachtas calling for such revocation.

(9) Subject to subsections (3) and (6), nothing in this section shall be construed as preventing the multiplex company from using one or more of the multiplexes for the purposes of providing electronic information services in accordance with the requirements (if any) imposed by any enactment relating to the provision of services concerned which is for the time being in force.

(10) Without prejudice to any powers he or she may have in that behalf under the Wireless Telegraphy Acts, 1926 to 1988, the Director may attach such conditions to the digital multiplex licence as he or she considers appropriate including conditions specifying requirements to be complied with by the multiplex company in relation to the imposition of charges under section 14(4).

(11) The requirement imposed by a condition referred to in subsection (3) or (6) to use a multiplex or part of a multiplex for the purposes referred to in subsection (3) or (6), as the case may be, may be satisfied by the multiplex company's using, with the consent of the relevant person specified in column (1) of the Table to this section, so much of the capacity of 2 or more of the multiplexes that is equivalent to the capacity of that multiplex or part, and references in this section to the capacity of a multiplex or a part of a multiplex being exhausted or not being exhausted, as the case may be, shall be construed accordingly.

(12)Nothing in this section shall be construed as preventing the Director from granting under the Wireless Telegraphy Acts, 1926 to 1988, in addition to the digital multiplex licence and whether to the multiplex company or any other person, licences authorising the combination, by means of a multiplex other than a multiplex referred to in section 8(3), of programme material and related and other data in a digital form.

TABLE

(1)	(2)
The Authority	One multiplex
Teilifís na Gaeilge	One half of one complex
The television programme service contractor	One half of one multiplex

Alteration of name of Commission

10.—(1) The Commission shall henceforth be known as Coimisiún Craolacháin na hÉireann or, in the English language, the Broadcasting Commission of Ireland and section 3 of the Act of 1988 shall be construed and have effect accordingly.

(2) The Commission shall, as soon as may be after the commencement of this section, provide itself with a new seal under paragraph 6 of the Schedule to the Act of 1988.

Additional functions of Commission

11.—(1) Without prejudice to the functions conferred on it by the Act of 1988 or any other enactment, it shall be a function of the Commission to make arrangements, in accordance with the provisions of this Act, for the provision of broadcasting services in the State additional to those provided by the Authority, Teilifís na Gaeilge, the television programme service contractor and each sound broadcasting contractor.

(2) In performing the function conferred on it by this section or the functions conferred on it by the Act of 1988, the Commission shall endeavour to ensure that the number and categories of broadcasting services made available in the State by virtue of this Act or the Act of 1988 best serve the needs of the people of the island of Ireland, bearing in mind their languages and traditions and their religious, ethical and cultural diversity.

(3) The Commission shall have all such powers as are necessary for or incidental to the performance of its function under this section.

Digital content contracts

12.—(1) Subject to subsection (2), a person shall not supply a compilation of programme material for the purpose of any arrangements to be entered into by him or her under paragraph (a) or (b) of section 14(1) otherwise than under and in accordance with a digital content contract.

(2) Subsection (1) shall not apply to such a supply made by—

(a) an excepted person for the purpose of any such arrangements, or

(b) the Authority, Teilifís na Gaeilge or the television programme service contractor for the purpose of any such arrangements, being arrangements for the transmission by the designated company of a free-to-air service.

(3) The Commission may enter into a contract with a person whereby that other person may supply a compilation of programme material for the purposes referred to in subsection (1), and such a contract shall be known as a "provision of content (digital) contract" and is in this Act referred to as a "digital content contract".

(4) A digital content contract shall include—

(a) a condition requiring the holder of the contract to comply with the codes and rules under section 19 with respect to the programme material supplied in pursuance of the contract, and

(b) a condition authorising the Commission to request the holder of the contract to pay to it, in respect of a failure by the holder to comply with a particular term or condition of the contract, a sum of money (not exceeding an amount that shall be specified in the condition as being the maximum amount that may be so requested to be so paid) and requiring the holder to comply with such a request.

(5) A digital content contract shall include a condition providing that, where any of the programme material supplied in pursuance of the contract—

(a) contravenes Article 22 or 22A of the Council Directive or a provision of the Prohibition of Incitement to Hatred Act, 1989, or

(b) constitutes an incitement to commit an offence, the Commission may, or, if such a supply of programme material has occurred within 6 months of a previous such supply by the same person having occurred, shall, terminate the contract.

Transmission of digital and other broadcasting services by transmission company

13.—(1) The transmission company—

(a) shall, if requested to do so by the body or contractor concerned, enter into arrangements with each of the following, namely, the Authority, Teilifís na Gaeilge and the television programme service contractor whereby the company transmits, by analogue means, free-to-air services comprising compilations of programme material supplied to it by the body or contractor for that purpose,

(b) shall, if requested to do so by the multiplex company, enter into arrangements with that company to transmit, by digital terrestrial means, programme material and related and other data in a digital form,

(c) shall, if requested to do so by the Authority or the contractor concerned, enter into arrangements with the Authority and each sound broadcasting contractor whereby the company transmits, by analogue terrestrial means, a sound broadcasting service comprising a compilation of programme material supplied to it by the Authority or contractor concerned for that purpose.

(2) The transmission company, on being notified by the Commission that the Commission has terminated a television programme service contract or sound broadcasting contract, as the case may be, or that such a contract has expired and has not been renewed, shall forthwith discontinue any arrangements it has entered into under subsection (1) with the former holder of the contract in so far as they relate to the transmission of a broadcasting service or sound broadcasting service, as the case may be, comprising programme material supplied pursuant to that contract.

(3) The transmission company may impose charges on a person in respect of the entering into of arrangements under subsection (1) with that person.

(4) For the avoidance of doubt, nothing in this section shall be construed as preventing the transmission company from providing services other than those referred to in subsection (1) in accordance with the requirements (if any) imposed by any enactment relating to the provision of the services concerned which is for the time being in force.

Arranging by multiplex company for transmission of digital broadcasting services by transmission company

14.—(1) The multiplex company—

(a) shall, if requested to do so by the body or contractor concerned, enter into arrangements with the transmission company for the transmission by that company of freeto-air services, comprising compilations of programme material and related and other data in a digital form, supplied by the Authority, Teilifís na Gaeilge or the television programme service contractor to the multiplex company, being programme material and related and other data that has been combined in such form by the use of the multiplex or part of the multiplex referred to in section 9(3),

(b) may enter into arrangements with the transmission company for the transmission by that company of broadcasting services (including free-to-air services) comprising compilations of programme material and related and other data in a digital form supplied, in accordance with the provisions of this Act, to the multiplex company by any person (including a person referred to in paragraph (a)),

(c) may enter into arrangements with any person whereby the company supplies electronic information services in a digital form for transmission by the transmission company in accordance with the requirements (if any) imposed by any enactment relating to the provision of the services concerned which is for the time being in force.

(2) The multiplex company, on being notified by the Commission that the Commission has terminated a digital content contract or a television programme service contract, as the case may be, or that such a contract has expired and has not been renewed, shall forthwith discontinue any arrangements it has entered into under *subsection (1)* in so far as they relate to the transmission of a broadcasting service

comprising programme material supplied pursuant to that contract.

(3) The multiplex company shall take all reasonable steps to ensure that the number of arrangements for the time being entered into by it under *subsection (1)* and the terms of those arrangements (including as to the periods for which the arrangements are to be in force) are not such as to result in there not being sufficient capacity available on one or more of the multiplexes referred to in *subsection (2)* of *section 9* for the purpose of the company's being able to comply with a request referred to in *subsection (6)* of that section.

(4) The multiplex company may impose charges on a person—

(a) in respect of the entering into by it of arrangements under subsection (1) at the request of or, as the case may be, with that person,

(b) in respect of the reception by the person of a broadcasting service (other than a free-to-air service provided pursuant to an arrangement entered into under subsection (1)(a)) comprising programme material supplied by the multiplex company to the transmission company, and (c) in respect of the provision by it to the person of any apparatus or device enabling the reception by the person of broadcasting services (including free-to-air services) in a digital form.

(5) For the avoidance of doubt, the reference in *subsection (4)* to arrangements entered into under subsection (1) includes a reference to arrangements entered into under that subsection in respect of programme material supplied to the multiplex company by a person providing a broadcasting service in Northern Ireland to whom a direction given by the Minister under *section 9(7)* relates and references in *subsection (4)* to a broadcasting service shall be construed accordingly.

Non-liability of Transmission company and multiplex company for dealing with programme material

15.—For the avoidance of doubt, neither the transmission company nor the multiplex company shall—

(a) be under any duty to ensure that the programme material supplied to it, pursuant to arrangements under *section 13(1) or 14(1)*, complies with the enactments applied to the supply of such material by *section 18* or with the codes and rules under section 19,

(b) be liable in damages for any infringement of copyright, other intellectual property rights or other legal rights of any person by virtue of having accepted a supply of programme material, pursuant to arrangements under *section 13(1)* or *14(1)*, and dealt with the material in the performance of its functions,

(c) be liable in damages for any infringement of copyright, other intellectual property rights or other legal rights of any person by virtue of having accepted a supply of data (other than programme material), pursuant to arrangements under *section 13(1) or 14(1),* and dealt with the data in the performance of its functions, unless in so dealing with the data it has effective control over its content,

(d) be regarded, for the purposes of the law of defamation, malicious falsehood or any other form of civil liability, as having, by virtue of accepting a supply of programme material, pursuant to arrangements under *section 13(1) or 14(1),* and dealing with the material in the performance of its functions, published the material, or

(e) be liable in damages to the holder of a contract referred to in *section 13(2) or 14(2)* for the discontinuance by it in good faith under *section 13(2) or 14(2),* as the case may be, of any arrangements under *section 13(1) or 14(1)* in respect of that contract in circumstances where the contract was not lawfully terminated or had not, in fact, expired or had expired but had, in fact, been renewed at the date of the notification by the Commission under *section 13(2) or 14(2)*.

Electronic programme guides

16.—(1) In this section "electronic programme guide" means any electronic means of providing information to members of the public in relation to the schedule of programme material the subject of any broadcasting service and which electronic means is an integral part of the distribution and reception system by which the broadcasting service is provided.

(2) A person shall not prepare or make available for use by another an electronic programme guide otherwise than under and in accordance with a programme guide contract.

(3) The Commission may enter into a contract with a person whereby that other person may prepare and make available for use by another one or more electronic programme guides and such a contract shall be known as an "electronic programme guide contract" and is in this Act referred to as a "programme guide contract".

(4) A programme guide contract shall include a condition requiring the holder of the contract to comply with guidelines under section 17 with respect to the electronic programme guide or guides prepared by him or her in pursuance of that contract.

(5) A programme guide contract shall include a condition requiring the holder of the contract to ensure that the electronic programme guide or guides prepared in pursuance of it may easily be used by a member of the public to access information in relation to the schedules of programme material the subject of each broadcasting service—

(a) provided in the State by—

(i) the Authority,

(ii) Teilifís na Gaeilge, and

(iii) the television programme service contractor, and

(b) provided in Northern Ireland by any person, being a service that is receivable throughout the whole of Northern Ireland and which is provided by terrestrial means.

(6) An electronic programme guide prepared by a person who is the holder of a contract that has been entered into under any other section of this Act shall not be

designed in such a way as to result in a user of the guide experiencing difficulty in accessing the programme material supplied pursuant to any contract entered into with another person under that or any other section of this Act and which is the subject of a broadcasting service.

(7) If the Commission considers it appropriate to do so in order that members of the public may keep themselves informed of the choice of programme material available for viewing on broadcasting services transmitted by the transmission company pursuant to arrangements under *section 14(1)* and each holder of a licence referred to in *section 37(1)*, it may invite expressions of interest in the securing of a programme guide contract in relation to the electronic programme guide or guides prepared under which the Commission may give a direction under *subsection (9)*.

(8) The Commission may, having examined each of the expressions of interest received on foot of such an invitation, enter into a programme guide contract with the person whose proposals for such electronic programme guide or guides would, in its opinion, best serve the needs of the public.

(9) The Commission may give a direction to—

(a) the multiplex company requiring that company to enter into arrangements with the transmission company for the transmission by the transmission company of the electronic programme guide or guides prepared under the programme guide contract referred to in subsection (8), and

(b) each holder of a licence referred to in section 37(1) requiring him or her to transmit the said guide or guides, and the said company and each such holder shall comply with such a direction.

Guidelines with respect to programme guide contracts

17.—The Commission, after consultation with the Director, shall prepare guidelines with respect to the format in which the information in relation to schedules of programme material provided by electronic programme guides may be presented and the making of the arrangements that are necessary to enable the broadcasters referred to in subsection (5) of section 16 to have access to those guides so that the condition referred to in that subsection of each programme guide contract may be properly implemented in their favour.

Application of certain enactments to digital and other broadcasting services

18.—The following provisions of the Act of 1988, namely—

(a) paragraphs (a), (b), (d) and (e) of subsection (1), and subsection (2), of section 9, and

(b) section 10(3), shall apply to a broadcasting service which consists of a compilation of programme material supplied pursuant to a contract entered into under this Act with the following and any other necessary modifications—

(i) references in those provisions to a sound broadcasting contractor shall be construed as references to the holder of the contract concerned,

(ii) references in those provisions to any thing being broadcast shall be construed as references to the thing being supplied pursuant to a contract entered into under this Act for the purpose of its being transmitted as part of a broadcasting service, and (iii) paragraph (d) of the said *section 9(1)* shall have effect as if the words “as offending against good taste or decency, or” were omitted.

PART III

Standards in Broadcasting

Codes and rules with respect to programme material.

19.—(1) The Commission shall, upon being directed by the Minister to do so and in accordance with the provisions of this section, prepare—

(a) a code specifying standards to be complied with, and rules and practices to be observed, in respect of the taste and decency of programme material, the subject of a broadcasting service or sound broadcasting service, and, in particular, in respect of the portrayal of violence and sexual conduct in such material, and

(b) a code specifying standards to be complied with, and rules and practices to be observed, in respect of advertising, teleshopping material, sponsorship and other forms of commercial promotion employed in any broadcasting service or sound broadcasting service (other than advertising and other activities as aforesaid falling within paragraph (c)), and

(c) a code specifying standards to be complied with, and rules and practices to be observed, in respect of advertising, teleshopping material, sponsorship and other forms of commercial promotion employed in any broadcasting service or sound broadcasting service, being advertising and other activities as aforesaid which relate to matters likely to be of direct or indirect interest to children.

(2) A direction of the Minister under *subsection (1)* shall specify that the Commission shall give priority to the preparation of the code under paragraph (c) of that subsection before the preparation of the other codes under that subsection and the Commission shall give such priority in the preparation of the first-mentioned code accordingly.

(3) The Commission shall, in accordance with subsection (5), make rules with respect to—

(a) the total daily times that shall be allowed for the transmission of advertisements and teleshopping material on a broadcasting service or sound broadcasting service, being a service which consists of a compilation of programme material supplied pursuant to a contract entered into under this Act or the Act of 1988, and

(b) the maximum period that shall be allowed in any given hour for the transmission of advertisements and teleshopping material on such a broadcasting service or sound broadcasting service, and the Commission may make different such rules with respect to different classes of broadcasting service or sound broadcasting service.

(4) The codes under *subsection (1)* and the rules under *subsection (3)* shall, respectively, provide for the matters required to be provided for by Chapters IV and V of the Council Directive.

(5) Before preparing a code or making a rule under this section, the Commission shall make available for inspection by any person who makes a request of it in that behalf a draft of the code it proposes so to prepare or the rule it proposes so to make and shall have regard to any submissions made to it, within such period as it specifies for the purpose, by that person in relation to the draft before it prepares the code or makes the rule concerned.

(6) The Commission shall cause to be published in at least one newspaper circulating in the State notice of the fact that, pursuant to *subsection (5),* a draft referred to in that subsection is available for inspection, of the place at which or the means by which the draft can be inspected and of the period specified by it under that subsection within which submissions may be made to it in relation to the draft.

(7) In preparing a code under *paragraph (c)* of *subsection (1)* the Commission shall, taking into account any relevant instrument made or relevant guidelines issued by any body in which are vested functions in relation to the welfare of children, have regard to—

(a) any research which it considers appropriate (including research under *subsection (8)*) conducted with respect to the effect of activities referred to in that paragraph on children, and

(b) the merits or otherwise and the feasibility of such a code containing a prohibition on a specified class or classes of such activity in so far as those activities relate to children in general or children under a particular age.

(8) The Commission may, for the purpose of performing its functions under *paragraph (c)* of *subsection (1)*, conduct, or cause to be conducted, research with respect to the effect of activities referred to in that paragraph on children.

(9) The Commission shall make to the Minister a report in relation to the performance of its functions under *subsections (1)(c)* and *(8)* not later than 1 year from the date of the giving to it of the direction under *subsection (1)* and the Minister shall, as soon as may be after the receipt by him or her of the report, cause copies of it to be laid before both Houses of the Oireachtas.

(10)The Commission shall, once in each period of 3 years, beginning with the period of 3 years commencing on the date of the preparation of the code, review the effect of the code prepared under *subsection (1)(c)*, and shall prepare a report in relation to that review and furnish the report to the Minister; the Minister shall, as soon as may be after the receipt by him or her of the report, cause copies of it to be laid before both Houses of the Oireachtas.

(11)The Commission shall make rules requiring each broadcaster to take specified steps to promote the understanding and enjoyment by—

(a) persons who are deaf or hard of hearing, and

(b) persons who are blind or partially sighted, of programmes transmitted on any broadcasting service provided by him or her.

(12)Rules under *subsection (11)* may, in respect of any specified period beginning on or after the commencement of this subsection, require a broadcaster to ensure that a specified percentage of programmes transmitted on a broadcasting service provided by him or her in that period employs specified means by which the understanding and enjoyment by persons referred to in *paragraphs (a)* and *(b)* of that subsection of that percentage of programmes may be promoted.

(13)In *subsection (12)* "specified" means specified in, or in accordance with, the rules concerned.

(14)The Commission shall prepare a code specifying standards to be complied with, and rules and practices to be observed, in respect of the provision of a broadcasting service which has, as one of its principal objectives, the promotion of the interests of any organisation.

(15)The Commission shall from time to time as it considers appropriate prepare a code or make rules amending a code or rules prepared or, as the case may be, made under each provision of this section.

(16)The making or preparation of a code or rules under *subsection (15)* shall be subject to the like (if any) consents and conditions as the code or rules that the first-mentioned code or rules is or are amending.

(17)Pending the preparation of the codes *under paragraphs (b)* and *(c)* of *subsection (1)* and the making of rules under subsection (3), the provisions of a code under *section 4* of the *Broadcasting Act, 1990*, which are in force before the repeal by this Act of that *section 4* and which correspond to the matters to which those codes or those rules will relate shall, notwithstanding the repeal of that *section 4*, continue in force and have effect in relation to each class of broadcaster in relation to whom they had effect before that repeal.

(18)In this section "teleshopping material" means material which, when transmitted, will constitute a direct offer to the public for the sale or supply to them of goods or other property (whether real or personal) or services.

Codes or standards with respect to certain types of information

20.—(1) The Commission may co-operate with or give assistance to one or more persons (whether residing or having their principal place of business in the State or elsewhere) in the preparation by that person or those persons of codes or standards with respect to the transmission of information by any electronic means (other than by means of broadcasting), including by means of the Internet.

(2) In this section "codes or standards" does not include codes or standards with respect to any technical aspect of the transmission of information by the means referred to in subsection (1).

Functions of Commission in relation to enforcement of Act

21.—(1) It shall be a function of the Commission to enforce—

(a) the provisions of Parts II, III and V of this Act,

(b) any code or rules prepared or made under this Act, and

(c) the terms and conditions of any contract entered into by it under this Act.

(2) *Subsection (1)* is without prejudice to the functions of the Broadcasting Complaints Commission under *section 24*.

Broadcasting Complaints Commission

22.—(1) In this section "the Commission" means the Broadcasting Complaints Commission.

(2) Notwithstanding the repeal by *section 3* of *section 18A* of the Act of 1960, the Commission shall continue in being.

(3) The Commission shall consist of not less than 7 nor more than 9 members.

(4) The members of the Commission shall be appointed by the Government.

(5) Where the number of members of the Commission for the time being is 7, not less than 3 of them shall be men and not less than 3 of them shall be women.

(6) Where the number of members of the Commission for the time being is 8 or 9, not less than 4 of them shall be men and not less than 4 of them shall be women.

(7) A person who was a member of the Commission immediately before the commencement of this section shall continue in office as such a member for the remainder of the term of office for which he or she was appointed, unless he or she sooner dies or resigns from office.

(8) When appointing a member of the Commission, the Government shall fix his or her term of office which shall not exceed 5 years and, subject to *subsections (12)* and *(13)*, the member shall hold his or her office on such terms and conditions (other than terms or conditions relating to remuneration or the payment of allowances) as are determined by the Government at the time of his or her appointment.

(9) A member of the Commission may at any time resign his or her office by letter addressed to the Government and the resignation shall take effect as on and from the date of receipt of the letter by the Government.

(10)A member of the Commission whose term of office expires by the effluxion of time shall be eligible for re-appointment.

(11)There shall be paid to members of the Commission such remuneration (if any) and allowances (if any) as the Minister, with the consent of the Minister for Finance, from time to time determines.

(12)A member of the Commission may be removed from office by the Government for stated reasons if, and only if, resolutions are passed by each House of the Oireachtas calling for his or her removal.

(13)Where a member of the Commission is—

(a) nominated as a member of Seanad Éireann, or

(b) nominated as a candidate for election to either House of the Oireachtas or to the European Parliament, or

(c) regarded pursuant to Part XIII of the Second Schedule to the European Parliament Elections Act, 1997, as having been elected to the European Parliament, he or she shall thereupon cease to be a member of the Commission.

(14)A person who is, for the time being, entitled under the Standing Orders of either House of the Oireachtas to sit therein or who is a member of the European Parliament shall, while he or she is so entitled or is such a member, be disqualified from becoming a member of the Commission.

(15)A member of the Authority, the Broadcasting Commission of Ireland or Teilifís na Gaeilge or an officer or servant of any such body shall be disqualified from becoming or being a member of the Commission.

(16)The Government shall from time to time as occasion requires appoint a member of the Commission to be chairperson thereof.

(17)The chairperson of the Commission shall, unless he or she sooner dies, resigns the office of chairperson or ceases to be chairperson under *subsection (19)*, hold office until the expiration of his or her period of office as a member of the Commission.

(18)The chairperson of the Commission may at any time resign his or her office as chairperson by letter sent to the Government and the resignation shall take effect at the commencement of the meeting of the Commission held next after the body has been informed by the Government of the resignation.

(19)Where the chairperson of the Commission ceases during his or her term of office as chairperson to be a member of the Commission he or she shall also cease to be chairperson of the Commission.

(20)The Commission may act notwithstanding one or more vacancies among its members (including one or more vacancies that result in *subsection (5)* or *(6)* not being complied with).

(21)The quorum for a meeting of the Commission shall be determined by the Commission under *subsection (22)*, but—

(a) the quorum so determined shall not be less than 5, and

(b) until it is so determined, the quorum shall be 5.

(22)Subject to the provisions of this Act, the Commission shall regulate its procedure and practice.

Services, facilities, etc. for Broadcasting Complaints Commission

23.—(1) The Commission may supply or provide to the Broadcasting Complaints Commission, on such terms or conditions as the first-mentioned Commission may specify, any services (including services of staff), accommodation or facilities required by the second mentioned Commission for the performance of their functions.

(2) Subject to *subsection (3)*, the Commission shall defray the expenses incurred by the Broadcasting Complaints Commission in performing their functions out of moneys paid to the Commission under section 20 (inserted by section 58) of the Act of 1988.

(3) Where in the opinion of the Commission an expense incurred by the

Broadcasting Complaints Commission in performing their functions is of an exceptional nature, the Commission may, in lieu of defraying the whole or a part of that expense out of moneys referred to in *subsection (2)*, defray the whole or a part of the expense out of moneys paid to it under *subsection (4)*.

(4) The Minister, with the consent of the Minister for Finance, may pay to the Commission an amount equal to the amount, or a part thereof, of an expense referred to in *subsection (3)* for the purpose of enabling the Commission to defray the amount of that expense or, as the case may be, that part of it in respect of which that payment is made.

(5) *Section 8* of the Act of 1976 is hereby amended by the substitution of the following subparagraph for subparagraph (iii) of paragraph (a):

"(iii) the amount of any moneys paid in that year to the Broadcasting Commission of Ireland by the Minister under section 23(4) of the Broadcasting Act, 2001, and".

Functions of the Broadcasting Complaints Commission

24.—(1) In this section — "broadcaster" means (in addition to the meaning assigned to that expression by *section 2(1)*) a sound broadcasting contractor; "the Commission" means the Broadcasting Complaints Commission.

(2) Subject to the provisions of this section, the Commission may investigate and decide upon any of the following complaints—

(a) a complaint that in broadcasting news given by it and specified in the complaint, a broadcaster did not comply with one or more of the requirements of section 18(1) (inserted by the Act of 1976) of the Act of 1960 or, as the case may be, of paragraphs (a) and (b) of section 9(1) of the Act of 1988 (including that section or those paragraphs as applied by this Act),

(b) a complaint that in broadcasting a programme specified in the complaint, a broadcaster either did not comply with one or more of the said requirements or was in breach of the prohibition contained in section 18(1A) (inserted by the Act of 1976) of the Act of 1960 or, as the case may be, in paragraph (d) of section 9(1) of the Act of 1988 (including that section or paragraph as applied by this Act),

(c) a complaint that on an occasion specified in the complaint, there was an encroachment by a broadcaster contrary to section 18(1B) (inserted by the Act of 1976) of the Act of 1960 or paragraph (e) of section 9(1) of the Act of 1988 (including that section or paragraph as applied by this Act),

(d) a complaint that on an occasion specified in the complaint a broadcaster failed to comply with a provision of a code under section 19(1)(a),

(e) a complaint that on an occasion specified in the complaint a broadcaster failed to comply with a provision of a code under paragraph (b) or (c) of section 19(1) or of a code under section 4 of the Broadcasting Act, 1990, continued in force under section 19(17),

(f) a complaint by a person that in a broadcast by a broadcaster which is specified in the complaint an assertion was made of inaccurate facts or information in relation to that person which constituted an attack on that person's honour or reputation.

(3) A complaint under subsection (2) shall be in writing and be made to the Commission not more than 30 days after—

(a) in case the complaint relates to one broadcast or to 2 or more unrelated broadcasts—

(i) if it relates to one broadcast, the date of the broadcast, or

(ii) if it relates to 2 or more such broadcasts, the date of the earlier or earliest, as the case may be, of those broadcasts, and

(b) in case the complaint relates to 2 or more related broadcasts of which at least 2 are made on different dates, the later or latest of those dates.

(4) When the Commission propose to investigate a complaint made under this section, the Commission shall afford to the broadcaster to whom the complaint relates (hereafter in this section referred to as "the broadcaster concerned") an opportunity to comment on the complaint.

(5) Where a complaint is made to the Commission and—

(a) a person employed by the broadcaster concerned, or

(b) if the making of any programme, the subject of the complaint, was commissioned by the broadcaster concerned, the person commissioned to make that programme, requests, for reasons specified by him or her, the Commission to afford to him or her an opportunity to comment on the complaint, the Commission shall, having considered the reasons so specified, afford to the person such an opportunity if, but only if, they are satisfied that, as appropriate—

(i) an interest of the person referred to in paragraph (a), being an interest which the Commission consider relevant to the person's employment by the broadcaster concerned, or

(ii) the prospects of the person referred to in paragraph (b) obtaining further commissions in respect of programmes from the broadcaster concerned, may, because of the complaint, be adversely affected.

(6) When the Commission propose to consider a complaint referred to in *subsection (2)(e)*, the Commission shall afford to the relevant advertiser an opportunity of making to the Commission submissions in relation to the relevant advertisement.

(7) As soon as may be after they decide on a complaint made under this section, the Commission shall send to—

(a) the person who made the complaint,

(b) the broadcaster concerned, and

(c) if the complaint is in respect of a broadcast made on a broadcasting service which is not a free-to-air service provided by the Authority or Teilifís na Gaeilge, the Broadcasting Commission of Ireland, a statement in writing of their decision.

(8) In case the Commission decide on a complaint referred to in subsection (2)(e),

as soon as may be after their decision, the Commission shall (in addition to complying with the requirement of subsection (7)) send to the person with whom the broadcaster concerned agreed to broadcast the relevant advertisement (if he or she is not the person who made the complaint) a statement in writing of their decision.

(9) The consideration by the Commission of a complaint made to them under this section shall be carried out by the Commission in private.

(10)Unless they consider it inappropriate to do so, the Commission shall, as soon as may be after the making of the decision, publish particulars of their decision on a complaint in such manner as they consider suitable and, without prejudice to *subsection (11)*, where they consider that the publication should be by the broadcaster concerned, or should include publication by the broadcaster concerned, the particulars shall be published by the broadcaster concerned in such manner as shall be agreed between the Commission and the broadcaster concerned.

(11)Without prejudice to subsection (10), the broadcaster concerned shall, unless the Commission consider it inappropriate for the broadcaster to do so, broadcast the Commission's decision on every complaint considered by the Commission in which the Commission found in favour, in whole or in part, of the person who made the complaint, including, in the case of a complaint under *subsection (2)(f)*, any correction of inaccurate facts or information relating to the individual concerned, at a time and in a manner corresponding to that in which the broadcast to which the complaint relates took place.

(12)As regards proceedings under this section, the Commission shall not have any power to award to any party costs or expenses.

(13)A person shall not act as a member of the Commission in relation to any matter with respect to which he or she has a material financial or other beneficial interest.

(14)*Subsection (2)* shall not apply to a complaint which, in the opinion of the Commission, is frivolous or vexatious, nor, unless the Commission consider that there are special reasons for investigating the complaint (which reasons shall be stated by the Commission when giving their decision), shall that subsection apply to a complaint which is withdrawn.

Annual report of Broadcasting Complaints Commission

25.—As soon as may be, but not later than 6 months, after the end of each year, the Broadcasting Complaints Commission shall make to the Minister a report of their activities during that year and the report shall contain such particulars (if any) as they think fit of decisions made by them pursuant to *section 24* during that year, and the Minister shall, as soon as may be after the receipt by him or her of the report, cause copies of it to be laid before both Houses of the Oireachtas.

Holders of contracts to record programme material

26.—(1) A person who is a holder of a contract entered into under the Act of 1988 or this Act shall, for the purposes of *section 24*, record every item of programme material supplied by him or her under the contract in such manner as stands approved of by the Broadcasting Complaints Commission for the purposes of this section.

(2) A recording made by a person under this section shall be retained by that person for such period as stands determined by the Broadcasting Complaints Commission for the purposes of this section, and when a complaint is being investigated by the Commission under *section 24*, the recording of the broadcast to which the complaint relates, together with the recording, made and being retained pursuant to this section, of any other broadcast which in the opinion of the Commission is relevant to that broadcast, shall be supplied by the person to the Commission on a request made by the Commission at any time during such period.

(3) The making or retaining of a recording in compliance with this section shall not constitute a contravention of any provision of Part III of the Copyright and Related Rights Act, 2000, or an infringement of copyright, and nothing contained in the Copyright and Related Rights Act, 2000, shall be construed as prohibiting or restricting the making of such a recording.

Transitional provision in relation to the Broadcasting Complaints Commission

27.—Notwithstanding the repeal by section 3 of sections 18A to 18C of the Act of 1960, anything commenced but not completed before the commencement of section 3 by the Broadcasting Complaints Commission under the said sections 18A to 18C may be carried on and completed by them after that commencement as if those sections had not been repealed.

PART IV

Provisions in relation to the Authority

Public service character of Authority's national broadcasting service

28.—(1) The national television and sound broadcasting service required to be maintained by the Authority under section 16 of the Act of 1960 shall have the character of a public service, continue to be a free-to-air service and be made available, in so far as it is reasonably practicable, to the whole community on the island of Ireland and the Authority shall have all such powers as are necessary for or incidental to that purpose.

(2) Without prejudice to the generality of *subsection (1)*, the Authority shall ensure that the programme schedules of the broadcasting service referred to in that subsection—

(a) provide a comprehensive range of programmes in the Irish and English languages that reflect the cultural diversity of the whole island of Ireland and include, both on television and radio (and also, where appropriate, any means of transmission referred to in section 16(2)(bbb) (inserted by this Act) of the Act of 1960) programmes that entertain, inform and educate, provide coverage of sporting, religious and cultural activities and cater for the expectations of the community generally as well as members of the community with special or minority interests and which, in every case, respect human dignity,

(b) provide programmes of news and current affairs in the Irish and English languages, including programmes that provide coverage of proceedings in the Houses of the Oireachtas and the European Parliament, and

(c) facilitate or assist contemporary cultural expression and encourage or promote innovation and experimentation in broadcasting.

(3) Subject to subsections (5) to (7), the Minister may, for the purpose of ensuring that the character, as a public service, of the broadcasting service referred to in subsection (1) is maintained, by order modify subsection (2)—

(a) by adding thereto provisions specifying categories of programmes that shall be included in the programme schedules referred to in that subsection, and

(b) by making such other alterations to subsection (2) as are necessary or expedient in consequence of the addition of such provisions.

(4) The Minister may by order amend or revoke an order under this section (including an order under this subsection).

(5) Nothing in subsection (3) or (4) shall be construed as enabling a requirement to be imposed on the Authority with respect to the manner in which any particular programme broadcast on the broadcasting service referred to in subsection (1) is made or the manner in which any decision of an editorial nature relating to the broadcasting of such a programme is made.

(6) Where the Minister proposes to make an order under this section, the Minister shall—

(a) consult with the Authority, the Commission and such other persons as he or she considers appropriate,

(b) publish a notice of his or her intention to make such an order in at least one newspaper circulating in the State,

(c) invite, by means of that notice or such other means as he or she considers appropriate, comments from members of the public in relation to the order proposed to be made, and

(d) publish in such manner as he or she considers appropriate a statement outlining the consultations that have been carried out under paragraph (a) and any comments received by him or her pursuant to the invitation referred to in paragraph (c) and indicating a place at which any document furnished to the Minister by a person referred to in paragraph (a) in the course of consultations under that paragraph or by a member of the public pursuant to the said invitation may be inspected (and such a document shall, accordingly, be made available at that place for inspection at all reasonable times before a draft of the order concerned is laid before the Houses of the Oireachtas under subsection (7)).

(7) Where an order is proposed to be made under this section, a draft of the order shall be laid before each House of the Oireachtas and the order shall not be made until a resolution approving of the draft has been passed by each such House.

(8) The amount paid to the Authority in each financial year under section 8 of the Act of 1976 shall be used by the Authority solely for the purposes of—

(a) providing programmes for the purposes of the programme schedules referred to in subsection (2),

(b) complying with its duty under section 17 of the Act of 1960,

(c) exercising all or any of the powers conferred on it by subsection (2) (other than paragraphs (bb) and (bbb) (inserted by this Act) thereof) of section 16 of the Act of 1960, and

(d) providing, pursuant to its powers under the Broadcasting Authority Acts, 1960 to 2001, any service (other than a broadcasting service) for the benefit of the public.

(9) The Authority may use moneys it obtains from any source, other than under section 8 of the Act of 1976, in whole or in part for any of the purposes referred to in subsection (8).

(10)Without prejudice to sections 25(1) and 26 of the Act of 1960, the Authority shall, as soon as may be after the end of each financial year, make a report to the Minister of the use it has made, with regard to, respectively, the television broadcasting service and the sound broadcasting service referred to in subsection (1), of the moneys paid to it under section 8 of the Act of 1976 in that year for the purpose of the activities, during that year, referred to in paragraphs (a), (b) and (c) of subsection (2) and subsection (8)(d).

(11)The Minister shall cause copies of each report made to him or her under subsection (10) to be laid before each House of the Oireachtas.

(12)Nothing in this section shall be construed as preventing the Authority from including in the programme schedules referred to in subsection (2) programmes made outside the State.

Amendment of section 16(1) of Act of 1960

29.—Subsection (1) (as amended by the Broadcasting Authority (Amendment) Act, 1979) of section 16 of the Act of 1960 is hereby amended by the substitution for "local broadcasting services" of "broadcasting services of a local, community or regional character".

Amendment of section 16(2) of Act of 1960

30.—Subsection (2) of section 16 of the Act of 1960 is hereby amended by the insertion of the following paragraphs after paragraph (b) (inserted by the Act of 1976):

"(bb) to provide, in addition to the broadcasting services referred to in subsection (1) of this section, broadcasting services which are of a special interest to only certain members of the community and which are made available on a subscription or pay-per-view basis (within the meaning of the Broadcasting Act, 2001);

(bbb) to transmit by electronic means (other than by means of broadcasting) such of the programme schedules of the broadcasting services referred to in subsection

(1) of this section or paragraph (bb) of this subsection, with such alterations or adaptations as are appropriate, as it thinks fit;".

Advertising broadcasts by Authority

31.—(1) In the case of a broadcasting service provided by the Authority (not being a broadcasting service which consists of programme material supplied by it pursuant to a contract entered into under this Act), the total daily times for broadcasting advertisements and teleshopping material fixed by the Authority and the maximum period so fixed to be given to advertisements and teleshopping material in any hour shall be subject to the approval of the Minister.

(2) In section 20 of the Act of 1960 references to advertisements shall be construed as including references to teleshopping material (within the meaning of this section).

(3) In this section "teleshopping material" has the same meaning as it has in section 19.

Special accounts under section 25(1) of Act of 1960 and amendment of section 6 of Act of 1976

32.—(1) The function conferred on the Minister by section 25(1) of the Act of 1960 with respect to directing (whether on the Minister's own motion or at the request of the Minister for Finance) the Authority to keep special accounts includes a power (exercisable on the Minister's own motion or at the request of the Minister for Finance) to direct the Authority to keep a special account showing the manner, with regard to, respectively, the television broadcasting service and sound broadcasting service referred to in subsection (1) of section 28, in which the moneys paid to it under section 8 of the Act of 1976 in the year concerned have been appropriated for the purpose of the activities of the Authority, during that year, referred to in paragraphs (a), (b) and (c) of subsection (2) and subsection (8)(d) of section 28.

(2) Section 6 of the Act of 1976 is hereby amended by the deletion in subsection (1) of all the words from "; provided that as regards a television broadcast" to the end of that subsection.

Amendment of Broadcasting Authority (Amendment) Act, 1993

33.—With respect to the financial year 2001 and subsequent financial years, section 4 of the Broadcasting Authority (Amendment) Act, 1993, shall have effect as if—

(a) in subsection (7)(a), "vary the sum referred to in the definition of 'the appropriate amount'" were substituted for "vary an amount or percentage referred to in column (2) of the Table to this section or the amount referred to in paragraph (i) of the definition of 'the appropriate amount'",

(b) in subsection (8)—

(i) the following definition were substituted for the definition of "the appropriate amount" in paragraph (a):

"'the appropriate amount' means the sum of £20,000,000 as increased by an amount equal to the appropriate percentage of the said sum;",

(ii) the definition of "television programme expenditure" in paragraph (a) were deleted, and

(iii) the following paragraph were substituted for paragraph (b):

"(b) In this subsection 'the appropriate percentage' means the difference between the consumer price index number at mid-August, 2000, and the said number at the mid-August immediately preceding the financial year concerned expressed as a percentage of the first-mentioned number.",

and

(c) the following Table were substituted for the Table to the section:

TABLE

Financial Year(1)	Amount of monies to be paid by the Authority into the account(2)
2001 Each subsequent financial year	£20,000,000 The appropriate amount

PART V

ADDITIONAL BROADCASTING SERVICES — CABLE, SATELLITE SYSTEMS, ETC.

Additional Broadcasting services by television programme service contractor

34.—(1) Subject to subsection (3), the television programme service contractor may provide, in addition to any free-to-air service being provided by it immediately before the commencement of this section, such other broadcasting services (whether free-to-air or not) as it considers appropriate, including broadcasting services of a community, local or regional character.

(2) The television programme service contractor may, for the purposes of providing a broadcasting service under *subsection (1)*, enter into arrangements with a holder of a digital content contract whereby that holder provides a compilation of programme material to the contractor for that service.

(3) The television programme service contractor shall not provide any broadcasting service referred to in *subsection (1)* unless the Commission has authorised the provision by the contractor of that service by means of a variation made by it, at the request of the contractor, of the terms and conditions of the television programme service contract (which variation the Commission is hereby authorised to make) and the provision of the service shall be subject to the terms and conditions of that contract as so varied and subsections (1) to (3) of section 18 of the Act of 1988.

Meaning of "independent television programme" in certain contracts

35.—The Commission shall ensure that any contract entered into by it under section 17 of the Act of 1988, any such contract renewed by it under that Act and any other arrangement in writing entered into by it with the holder of such a contract, being in each case a contract or an arrangement entered into or renewed by it after the commencement of this section, contains a term providing that the expression "independent television programme", where used in the contract or arrangement, has the same meaning as it has in the Broadcasting Authority (Amendment) Act, 1993.

Satellite content contracts

36.—(1) A person who is under the jurisdiction of the State (within the meaning of the Council Directive) shall not supply a compilation of programme material for the purpose of its being transmitted as a broadcasting service (whether for reception in the State or elsewhere) by means of a satellite device otherwise than under and in accordance with a satellite content contract.

(2) The Commission may enter into a contract with a person whereby that other person may supply a compilation of programme material for the purposes referred to in *subsection (1)*, and such a contract shall, without prejudice to *subsection (4)*, be known as a "provision of content (satellite) contract" and is in this Act referred to as a "satellite content contract".

(3) A satellite content contract shall include the same kind of conditions as *subsections (4)* and *(5)* of *section 12* provide that a digital content contract shall include.

(4) The Commission may divide the contracts it may enter into under this section into different classes by reference to the different conditions which, in pursuance of its powers under this Act, it may attach to the contracts and may style each such class of contract by the addition of such distinguishing words as it considers appropriate to the name by which *subsection (2)* provides a contract under this section shall be known.

(5) The Commission may, before it enters into a satellite content contract with a person, require that person to pay a fee to it of such amount as it considers appropriate; if that person fails to pay that fee to the Commission, the Commission shall not enter into the contract with him or her.

(6) The fee referred to in *subsection (5)* is in addition to any fee the Commission may charge under section 56 in respect of an application by the person concerned for a satellite content contract.

(7) The amount of any fee paid to the Commission under *subsection(5)* may be used by it for the purpose of defraying the expenses incurred by it in performing its functions generally.

Transmission of broadcasting services by cable or MMD system

37.—(1) A holder of a licence granted by the Director, being a licence that authorises the transmission by means of a cable or MMD system of programme material, shall not transmit, by such means, a broadcasting service unless the programme material, the subject of the broadcasting service, is supplied for such transmission—

(a) by—

(i) the Authority,

(ii) Teilifís na Gaeilge,

(iii) the television programme service contractor,

(iv) the holder of a digital content contract or satellite content contract and the programme material so supplied by him or her is the compilation of programme material authorised by that contract to be supplied by him or her for transmission otherwise as a broadcasting service, or

(v) an excepted person,

or

(b) pursuant to—

(i) a local content contract,

(ii) a community content contract, or

(iii) a cable-MMD content contract.

(2) A person, other than a person referred to in *subparagraph (i)*, *(ii)*, *(iii)* or *(v)* of *subsection (1)(a)* but including a holder of the licence concerned, shall not supply a compilation of programme material for the purpose of its being transmitted as a broadcasting service by means of a cable or MMD system, the subject of a licence referred to in *subsection (1)*, unless—

(a) the material is supplied under and in accordance with a local content contract, a community content contract or a cable-MMD content contract, or

(b) in case the person is the holder of a digital content contract or satellite content contract, the material is the compilation of programme material authorised by that contract to be supplied by him or her for transmission otherwise as a broadcasting service.

(3) A holder of a licence referred to in *subsection (1)* who transmits by the means referred to therein a broadcasting service shall—

(a) if that service was being transmitted by him or her immediately before the commencement of this section, forthwith, after such commencement, notify, in writing, the Commission of the fact that that service is being transmitted by him or her,

(b) if the transmission of that service begins on or after the commencement of this section, forthwith, after that transmission begins, notify, in writing, the Commission of the fact that that service is being transmitted by him or her.

(4) A holder of a licence granted by the Director, being a licence that authorises the re-transmission by means of a cable or MMD system of programme material shall—

(a) in relation to any broadcasting service that is being re-transmitted by him or her, pursuant to that licence, immediately before the commencement of this section, forthwith, after such commencement, notify, in writing, the Commission of the fact that that service is being re-transmitted by him or her,

(b) in relation to any broadcasting service the re-transmission of which, pursuant to that licence, by him or her begins on or after the commencement of this section, forthwith, after that re-transmission begins, notify, in writing, the

Commission of the fact that that service is being re-transmitted by him or her.

(5) The holder of a licence referred to in *subsection (4)*, being a licence that authorises the re-transmission of programme material by means of a cable system, shall re-transmit, by those means—

(a) in case the cable system used by that holder is, in whole or in part, an analogue system, each free-to-air service of an analogue nature provided for the time being by the Authority, Teilifís na Gaeilge and the television programme service contractor and which that body or contractor requests the holder to so re-transmit,

(b) in case the cable system used by that holder is, in whole or in part, a digital system, each free-to-air service of a digital nature provided for the time being by the Authority, Teilifís na Gaeilge and the television programme service contractor and which that body or contractor requests the holder to so re-transmit.

(6) The holder of a licence referred to in *subsection (4)*, being a licence that authorises the re-transmission of programme material by the means of a MMD system, shall re-transmit, by those means—

(a) in case the MMD system used by that holder is, in whole or in part, an analogue system, each free-to-air service of an analogue nature provided for the time being by the television programme service contractor and which that contractor requests the holder to so re-transmit,

(b) in case the MMD system used by that holder is, in whole or in part, a digital system, each free-to-air service of a digital nature provided for the time being by the television programme service contractor and which that contractor requests the holder to so re-transmit.

(7) If a dispute arises between the holder of a licence referred to in *subsection (4)* and the Authority, Telifís na Gaeilge or the television programme service contractor in relation to the placement by the holder, relative to the placement by him or her of another broadcasting service, on the system concerned of a free-to-air service provided by that body or contractor, being a placement made on an analogue cable or MMD system for the purposes of the holder's complying with a request by that body or contractor under *subsection (5)(a)* or *(6)(a)*, as the case may be, the dispute shall be referred to the Commission for its determination and the determination of the Commission in the matter shall be final.

(8) The holder of a licence referred to in *subsection (4)*, being a licence that authorises the re-transmission of programme material by the means of a cable system, shall re-transmit, by those means, each national sound broadcasting service provided for the time being by the Authority and each sound broadcasting contractor and which the Authority or the contractor concerned requests the holder to so retransmit.

(9) The holder of a licence referred to in *subsection (4)* shall not impose a charge in relation to the making available to a person of any service referred to in *subsection (5)*, *(6)* or *(8)* if he or she imposes a charge on that person in relation to the making

available of any other service to that person by means of the cable or MMD system concerned.

(10)Subject to *subsection (11)*, the Commission may require the holder of a licence referred to in subsection (1) to transmit as a broadcasting service, by means of the cable system or, as the case may be, the MMD system concerned, the whole or part of the programme material supplied under one or more specified community content contracts the holders of which are members of the local community that is served by the said system and who request the firstmentioned holder to so transmit the whole or, as the case may be, a part of that programme material.

(11)*Subsection (10)* shall not apply if the system used by the holder of the licence concerned is an analogue MMD system.

(12)A person of whom a requirement is made by the Commission under *subsection (10)* shall comply with that requirement.

(13)The holder of a licence referred to in *subsection (1)* shall not impose a charge in relation to the making available to a person of any service referred to in *subsection (10)*, pursuant to a requirement made of him or her under that subsection, if he or she imposes a charge on that person in relation to the making available of any other service to that person by means of the cable or MMD system concerned.

(14)In this section "re-transmission" means simultaneous, unaltered and unabridged transmission.

Local interest channels

38.—(1) Subject to *subsection (2)*, the Commission may enter into a contract under this section with a person whereby that person may supply a compilation of programme material for the purposes of its being transmitted as a broadcasting service under and in accordance with a licence referred to in *section 37(1)*, and such a contract shall be known as a "provision of local content contract" and is in this Act referred to as a "local content contract".

(2) The Commission shall not enter into such a contract unless it is satisfied that—

(a) either—

(i) the programme material to be supplied pursuant to the contract will be made by the person with whom it proposes to enter into that contract, or

(ii) the making of that programme material will be commissioned by that person, and

(b) a substantial proportion of that programme material will be made in the locality which the cable or MMD system, the subject of the licence concerned referred to in subsection (1), serves or will be of such a character as is likely to make it of special interest to persons living in that locality.

(3) Without prejudice to *subsection (4)*, a local content contract shall include a condition requiring the holder of the contract to comply, in relation to the programme material supplied in pursuance of the contract, with such guidelines as the Commission may from time to time issue for the purposes of this section with respect to the general

character of the programme material that may be supplied in pursuance of local content contracts.

(4) A local content contract shall include a condition requiring the holder of the contract to comply with the codes and rules under section 19 with respect to the programme material supplied in pursuance of the contract.

(5) A local content contract may include one or more of the following conditions, namely—

(a) a condition requiring the holder of the contract not to include in the programme material supplied in pursuance of the contract a specified class or specified classes of advertisement,

(b) a condition requiring the said holder to ensure, as respects that programme material, that a specified proportion of that material supplied for the time being constitutes material that has been made within a specified period ending immediately before that time,

(c) a condition requiring the said holder to ensure, as respects that programme material, that a specified proportion of the financial resources for the time being used for the purpose of funding the provision of that material is used for the purpose of funding the provision of programme material that has been made within a specified period ending immediately before that time.

(6) In deciding whether to enter into a local content contract with a particular person, the Commission shall have regard to whether the entering into of such a contract would operate against the public interest and, in particular, shall have regard to—

(a) the desirability of allowing any person, or group of persons, to have control of, or substantial interests in, an undue amount of the communications media in the locality served by the cable or MMD system proposed to be used to transmit that material, and

(b) the desirability of promoting diversity in the sources of information available to the public and in the opinions expressed in the communications media.

(7) For the purposes of subsection (6), the Commission may require the person referred to in that subsection to furnish to it such information as it specifies with respect to the extent (if any) of—

(a) any interest of a proprietary or financial nature held by him or her in relation to the provision of broadcasting services (including sound broadcasting services) in the State or the publication of any newspaper, magazine or journal in the State, or

(b) the control he or she may exercise in relation to the provision of any such service or the publication of any such newspaper, magazine or journal, and if the person fails to comply with any such requirement, then the Commission shall not enter into a local content contract with him or her.

Community channels

39.—(1) Subject to the provisions of this section, 2 or more members of a local community may supply a compilation of programme material for the purposes of its being transmitted as a broadcasting service under and in accordance with a licence referred to in *section 37(1)*.

(2) Subject to *subsections (3)* and *(4)*, the Commission may enter into a contract with 2 or more members of a local community whereby those members may supply a compilation of programme material for the purposes referred to in *subsection (1)* if it is satisfied that—

(a) those members are representative of the community concerned,

(b) the supply of programme material in pursuance of the contract will be effected with the sole objective of—

(i) specifically addressing the interests of the community concerned, and

(ii) achieving a monetary reward of no greater amount than is reasonably necessary to defray the expenses that will be incurred in effecting that supply, and

(c) there is a reasonable prospect that all such expenses as are likely to be incurred during the period of the contract will be defrayed, and such a contract shall be known as a "provision of community content contract" and is in this Act referred to as a "community content contract".

(3) The Commission shall not enter into a community content contract save after consultation with the person who it appears to the Commission will transmit or, as the case may be, will be the subject of a requirement under *section 37(10)* to transmit, the programme material supplied pursuant to the contract as a broadcasting service.

(4) The Commission shall establish procedures whereby members of local communities are enabled, at regular intervals, to make submissions to the Commission as to what particular contracts ought, in their opinion, to be entered into under this section and what particular terms and conditions ought, in their opinion, to be included in such contracts and requiring the Commission to furnish, on request, to any such members particulars of any proposals formulated, for the time being, by the Commission itself with regard to each of those matters.

(5) Before entering into a community content contract, the Commission shall have regard to any submissions made to it under and in accordance with procedures established under subsection (4) and which appear to it to be of relevance to that contract.

(6) The Commission shall conduct, or arrange with members of the local community concerned for there to be conducted, a survey, which shall be as comprehensive as is practicable, amongst members of that community for the purpose of ascertaining—

(a) the extent to which that community is facilitated in the active participation by it in the compilation and transmission of the programme material supplied pursuant to a community content contract,

(b) the extent to which those members view any broadcasting service on which there is transmitted that programme material, and

(c) the opinion of those members with regard to—

(i) the quality of that programme material, and

(ii) whether that material specifically addresses the interests of their community, and shall have regard to the results of such a survey in deciding, in relation to any community content contract it proposes to enter into with members of that community next after the conduct of that survey, with whom it shall enter into such a contract and the nature of the terms and conditions it may include in that contract.

(7) For the avoidance of doubt, if the holder of a licence referred to in *subsection (1)* of *section 37* is required under *subsection (10)* of that section to transmit as a broadcasting service the programme material supplied pursuant to a community content contract, he or she shall not be—

(a) under any duty to ensure that the material complies with the terms and conditions of that contract or the enactments that apply in respect of the supply of the material by virtue of *section 18*,

(b) regarded, for the purposes of the law of defamation, malicious falsehood or any other form of civil liability as having, by virtue of such transmission, published the material, or

(c) liable in damages, by virtue of such transmission, for any infringement of copyright, other intellectual property rights or other legal rights of any person.

(8) In this section "local community" means the community of a town or other urban or rural area.

Assessment of community needs in respect of broadcasting

40.—The Commission may, on its own initiative or at the request of a community group or organisation, carry out an assessment of the needs of a community in respect of broadcasting and such an assessment shall include an ascertainment of the extent to which production facilities, training and resources are available to the community to enable the community to best serve its interests in respect of those needs.

Commercial cable and MMD system channels

41.—(1) Without prejudice to the means under section 38 or 39 that may enable him or her to make such a supply, a person may supply a compilation of programme material for the purpose of its being transmitted as a broadcasting service by means of a cable or MMD system, the subject of a licence referred to in section 37(1), under and in accordance with a contract entered into by him or her with the Commission under this section, which contract shall be known as "a provision of content (cable-MMD) contract" and is in this Act referred to as a "cable-MMD content contract".

(2) The Commission may enter into a cable-MMD content contract with a person if, but only if, it is satisfied that the entering into that contract will result in the range and diversity of broadcasting services available in the relevant area being increased.

(3) In *subsection (2)* "relevant area" means the area served by the cable or MMD system by which it is proposed that the programme material concerned will be transmitted as a broadcasting service.

(4) Subject to *subsection (5)* but without prejudice to *subsection (6)*, a cable-MMD content contract shall, where appropriate, include a condition that, as respects the programme material supplied pursuant to it, the provisions of the Council Directive in relation to European works (within the meaning of that Directive) shall be complied with.

(5) *Subsection (4)* shall not apply in relation to a cable-MMD content contract the programme material supplied pursuant to which does not contain any advertisements that are to be broadcast in return for payment or for similar consideration.

(6) A cable-MMD content contract shall include the same kind of conditions as *subsections (4)* and *(5)* of *section 12* provide that a digital content contract shall include.

PART VI

Teilifís na Gaeilge

Definition

42.—In this Part "establishment day" means the day appointed by the Minister under *section 43*.

Establishment day

43.—The Minister may by order appoint a day to be the establishment day for the purposes of this Part.

Teilifís na Gaeilge

44.—(1) On the establishment day there shall stand established a body, to be known as Teilifís na Gaeilge, to perform the functions assigned to it by this Act.

(2) Teilifís na Gaeilge shall be a body corporate with perpetual succession and power to sue and be sued in its corporate name and to acquire, hold and dispose of land and other property.

(3) The provisions of the Second Schedule to this Act shall have effect in relation to Teilifís na Gaeilge.

Functions of Teilifís na Gaeilge

45.—(1) Teilifís na Gaeilge shall establish and maintain a national television broadcasting service which shall have the character of a public service and be made available, in so far as it is reasonably practicable, to the whole community on the island of Ireland.

(2) The broadcasting service referred to in *subsection (1)* shall be a free-to-air service.

(3) Teilifís na Gaeilge shall have all such powers as are necessary for or incidental to its function under *subsection (1)*.

(4) Without prejudice to the generality of *subsection (1)*, Teilifís na Gaeilge shall commission the making of programme material, originate programme material and, subject to, and in accordance with, *subsection (5)*, acquire programme material from such sources as it thinks appropriate so as to ensure that the programme schedules of the broadcasting service referred to in *subsection (1)* (and also, where appropriate, any means of transmission referred to in *subsection (8)(c)*)—

(a) provide a comprehensive range of programmes, primarily in the Irish language, that reflect the cultural diversity of the whole island of Ireland and include programmes that entertain, inform and educate, provide coverage of sporting, religious and cultural activities and cater for the expectations of those of all age groups in the community whose preferred spoken language is Irish or who otherwise have an interest in Irish,

(b) provide programmes, primarily in the Irish language, of news and current affairs,

(c) provide coverage of proceedings in the Houses of the Oireachtas and the European Parliament, and

(d) facilitate or assist contemporary cultural expression and encourage or promote innovation and experimentation in broadcasting.

(5) Teilifís na Gaeilge may, for the purpose of complementing the programme material it broadcasts in the Irish language, acquire programme material in other languages; in acquiring such material, Teilifs na Gaeilge shall have regard to the need to maintain the distinctive character of the broadcasting service referred to in *subsection(1)* and to cater for the expectations of audiences who are not generally catered for by other broadcasting services.

(6) Each amount paid to Teilifís na Gaeilge under *section 51* shall be used by it solely for the purposes of performing its function under subsection (1) and exercising the powers conferred on it by this Act with respect to that function.

(7) Teilifís na Gaeilge may use moneys it obtains from any source, other than under section 51, in whole or in part for the purposes referred to in subsection (5).

(8) Without prejudice to the generality of the preceding provisions of this section, Teilifís na Gaeilge shall have the following powers—

(a) to make contracts, agreements and arrangements incidental or conducive to the functions of Teilifís na Gaeilge,

(b) to provide, in addition to the broadcasting service referred to in subsection (1), broadcasting services which are of a special interest to only certain members of the community or which are made available on a subscription or pay-per-view basis,

(c) to transmit by any electronic means (other than by means of broadcasting) such of the programme schedules of the broadcasting services referred to in subsection (1) or paragraph (b), with such alterations or adaptations as are appropriate, as it thinks fit,

(d) to acquire and make use of copyrights, patents, licences, privileges and concessions,

(e) to collect news and information and to subscribe to news services and such other services as may be conducive to the functions of Teilifís na Gaeilge,

(f) to subscribe to such international associations and to such educational, musical and dramatic bodies and such other bodies promoting entertainment or culture as may be conducive to the functions of Teilifís na Gaeilge,

(g) to arrange with other broadcasters for the distribution, receipt, exchange and relay of programme material (whether live or recorded),

(h) to organise, provide and subsidise concerts and other entertainments in connection with the broadcasting service referred to in subsection (1) or for any purpose incidental thereto and, in relation to any such concert or entertainment, to provide or procure accommodation, and, if desired, to make charges for admission,

(i) to prepare, publish and distribute, with or without charge, such magazines, books, papers and other printed matter as may seem to Teilifís na Gaeilge to be conducive or incidental to its functions,

(j) to compile, publish, distribute, sell and exchange recorded aural and visual material in whatsoever form contained (including any form of electronic storage developed after the establishment day).

General duty of Teilifís na Gaeilge

46.—In performing its functions, Teilifís na Gaeilge—

(a) shall use its best endeavours to commission the making of, procure, adapt or originate programme material for the purposes of the broadcasting service referred to in section 45(1) that is responsive to the interests and concerns of the whole community,

(b) shall—

(i) be mindful of the need for understanding and peace within the whole island of Ireland, and

(ii) ensure that the programme material aforesaid reflects the varied elements which make up the culture of the whole island of Ireland and have special regard for the elements which distinguish that culture, and, in particular, the Gaeltachtaí,

(c) shall uphold the democratic values enshrined in the Constitution, especially those relating to rightful liberty of expression, and

(d) shall have regard to the need for the formation of public awareness and understanding of the values and traditions of countries other than the State, including in particular those of the Member States of the European Union.

Supply of programme material by Authority to Teilifís na Gaeilge

47.—The Authority shall provide to Teilifís na Gaeilge programme material in the Irish language of such amounts and at such times as may be agreed between them, being such amounts and such times as, in their opinion, will result in the equivalent of one hour of such programme material being provided daily by the Authority to Teilifís na Gaeilge.

Approval of total time per year for broadcasting by Teilifís na Gaeilge

48.—The total number of hours per year of broadcasting by Teilifís na Gaeilge in providing the television broadcasting service referred to in section 45(1) shall neither exceed a maximum nor be less than a minimum fixed by Teilifís na Gaeilge, with the approval of the Minister, for that service.

Advertising broadcasts by Teilifís na Gaeilge

49.—(1) In the case of a broadcasting service provided by Teilifís na Gaeilge (not being a broadcasting service which consists of programme material supplied by it pursuant to a contract entered into under this Act), the total daily times for broadcasting advertisements and teleshopping material fixed by Teilifís na Gaeilge and the maximum period so fixed to be given to advertisements and teleshopping material in any hour shall be subject to the approval of the Minister.

(2) In this section "teleshopping material" has the same meaning as it has in section 19.

Application of certain enactments to Teilifís na Gaeilge

50.—(1) Section 18 (as amended by the Act of 1976) of the Act of 1960 shall apply to Teilifís na Gaeilge as it applies to the Authority and for the purposes of that application the reference in that section to section 16 of that Act shall be construed as a reference to section 45 of this Act.

(2) Subsections (1), (2) and (4) of section 20, section 21 (as amended by the Act of 1976) and section 31(2) of the Act of 1960 shall apply to Teilifís na Gaeilge as they apply to the Authority and for the purposes of that application the reference in subsection (4) of that section 21 to the Director-General shall be construed as a reference to the chief executive of Teilifís na Gaeilge.

(3) Section 6 (as amended by this Act) of the Act of 1976 shall apply to Teilifís na Gaeilge as it applies to the Authority.

Provision of moneys by Minister to Teilifís na Gaeilge

51.—The Minister, with the consent of the Minister for Finance, may from time to time pay to Teilifís na Gaeilge such an amount as he or she determines to be reasonable for the purposes of defraying the expenses incurred by Teilifís na Gaeilge in performing its functions.

Transitional provisions in relation to Teilifís na Gaeilge

52.—(1) On the establishment day all land which, immediately before that day, was vested in Seirbhísí Theilifís na Gaeilge Teoranta and all rights, powers and privileges relating to or connected with such land shall, without any conveyance or assignment, stand vested in Teilifís na Gaeilge for all the estate or interest for which immediately before the said day it was vested in the said company, but subject to all trusts and equities affecting the land subsisting and capable of being performed.

(2) On the establishment day all property other than land, including choses-in-action, which immediately before that day was the property of Seirbhísí Theilifís na Gaeilge Teoranta shall stand vested in Teilifís na Gaeilge without any assignment.

(3) Every chose-in-action transferred by subsection (2) to Teilifís na Gaeilge may, after the establishment day, be sued on, recovered or enforced by it in its own name and it shall not be necessary for it or Seirbhísí Theilifís na Gaeilge Teoranta to give notice to the person bound by the chose-in-action of the transfer effected by that subsection.

(4) All rights and liabilities of Seirbhísí Theilifís na Gaeilge Teoranta arising by virtue of any contract or commitment (express or implied) entered into by it before the establishment day shall on that day stand transferred to Teilifís na Gaeilge.

(5) Every right and liability transferred by subsection (4) to Teilifís na Gaeilge may, on and after the establishment day, be sued on, recovered or enforced by or against it in its own name and it shall not be necessary for it or Seirbhísí Theilifís na Gaeilge Teoranta to give notice to the person whose right or liability is transferred by that subsection of such transfer.

(6) Any legal proceedings pending immediately before the establishment day to which Seirbhísí Theilifís na Gaeilge Teoranta is a party shall be continued with the substitution in the proceedings for that company of Teilifís na Gaeilge.

(7) Anything commenced but not completed before the establishment day by Seirbhísí Theilifís na Gaeilge Teoranta may be carried on and completed on or after that day by Teilifís na Gaeilge.

(8) Nothing in the preceding provisions of this section shall operate to transfer to Teilifís na Gaeilge any right or liability of Seirbhísí Theilifís na Gaeilge Teoranta under any contract of employment entered into by that company with any person before the establishment day unless that person is designated as a person to be employed by Teilifís na Gaeilge on and after the establishment day in a direction given by the Authority for the purposes of this section (which the Authority is hereby empowered to give).

Construction of references to certain acts of Teilifís na Gaeilge

53.—A reference in a provision of this Act to a free-to-air service being provided by Teilifís na Gaeilge shall, to the extent that that provision falls to be applied at, or by reference to, a time that is prior to the establishment day (including a time that is prior to the passing of this Act), be construed as a reference to such a service being provided by Seirbhísí Theilifís na Gaeilge Teoranta.

PART VII

MISCELLANEOUS

Provisions in relation to certain broadcasting services provided by Authority or Teilifís na Gaeilge

54.—(1) In this section "secondary broadcasting service" means a broadcasting service that is not the national television and sound broadcasting service referred to in *section 16(1)* of the Act of 1960 or the television service referred to in *section 45(1)*.

(2) In relation to any secondary broadcasting services provided by the Authority or Teilifís na Gaeilge—

(a) each such body shall keep, separately from the accounts it keeps in respect of its other activities, such accounts in respect of the provision of those services as it is required by section 25 of the Act of 1960 or, as the case may be, paragraph 17 of the Second Schedule to this Act to keep in respect of the carrying on by it of those other activities,

(b) moneys which it receives in consideration of broadcasting advertisements on any free-to-air service, the provision of which by it commenced before the passing of this Act, or from sponsorship of such a service, shall not be used to defray, in whole or in part, the expenses incurred by it in providing a secondary broadcasting service that is not a free-to-air service or taking any steps in pursuance of arrangements entered into under *subsection (4)* for the purposes of such a service.

(3) The Minister may require the Authority or Teilifís na Gaeilge to prepare, and furnish to him or her, such financial and other statements as he or she may specify indicating the extent to which, in its opinion, the provision by it of any secondary broadcasting services has, in a specified period—

(a) facilitated the provision by it of any free-to-air service, the provision of which commenced before the passing of this Act, or contributed to an improvement in the quality of that service,

(b) in the case of the Authority, facilitated the carrying on by it of any activity, apart from broadcasting, mentioned in section 16 of the Act of 1960, and the Authority or Teilifís na Gaeilge, as the case may be, shall comply with such a requirement.

(4) The Authority and Teilifís na Gaeilge may each, for the purpose of providing a secondary broadcasting service, enter into arrangements with a holder of a digital content contract whereby that holder provides a compilation of programme material to it for that service.

Provisions in relation to contracts generally under Act

55.—(1) Without prejudice to any specific provision of this Act, or of a contract thereunder, in that behalf, the Commission may terminate or suspend for such period as it specifies any contract entered into by it under this Act—

(a) if any false or misleading information was given to the Commission by or on behalf of the holder of the contract before it was entered into, or

(b) if the holder of the contract, has, in the opinion of the Commission, failed on one or more occasions to comply with a term or condition of the contract and the nature of that failure is of such seriousness as, in the opinion of the Commission, warrants the termination or suspension by it of the contract.

(2) A contract terminated or suspended under this or any other provision of this Act, or pursuant to a provision of that contract, shall, in case it is terminated, cease to have effect and, in case it is suspended, cease to have effect for the period for which it is suspended.

(3) A contract under this Act may contain such terms and conditions as the Commission considers appropriate and specifies in the contract.

(4) Without prejudice to the generality of subsection (3) or any other provision of this Act, a contract under this Act may include—

(a) terms or conditions with respect to—

(i) the period during which the contract shall continue in force,

(ii) whether the contract may be renewed and, if so, the manner in which, the terms on which, and the period for which, the contract may be renewed, and

(b) a condition prohibiting the assignment of the contract or any interest therein.

Fees in respect of applications for contracts

56.—The Commission may charge a fee, of such an amount as it considers reasonable, in respect of an application made by a person to the Commission for the entry into, by the Commission with that person, of—

(a) a contract under the Act of 1988, or

(b) a contract under this Act.

Offences

57.—(1) A person who contravenes section 12(1), 16(2), 36(1) or subsection (1), (2), (3), (4), (5), (6), (8), (9), (12) or (13) of section 37 shall be guilty of an offence.
(2) A person guilty of an offence under *subsection (1)* shall be liable—

(a) on summary conviction, to a fine not exceeding £1,500 or imprisonment for a term not exceeding 12 months or both,

(b) on conviction on indictment, to a fine not exceeding £15,000 or imprisonment for a term not exceeding 2 years or both.

Provision of moneys by Minister to Commission

58.—The Act of 1988 is hereby amended by the substitution of the following section for section 20:

"20. Without prejudice to *section 23(4)* or *59(3)* of the *Broadcasting Act, 2001*, the Minister, after consultation with the Commission and with the consent of the Minister for Finance, may from time to time pay to the Commission such an amount as he or she determines to be reasonable for the purposes of defraying the expenses incurred by the Commission in performing its functions.".

Capital grants to sound broadcasting contractors

59.—(1) The Commission shall, as soon as may be after the commencement of this section, prepare a scheme providing for the grant by it of such an amount of moneys, if any, as it considers appropriate to each relevant sound broadcasting contractor for the purposes of defraying capital expenditure incurred by the contractor in connection with the transmission by it of a sound broadcasting service.

(2) A scheme under subsection (1) shall—

(a) provide for the making of applications to the Commission by relevant sound broadcasting contractors for the grant, under the scheme, of moneys to them,

(b) provide that the Commission, in considering any such application, shall have regard to—

(i) any difficulty the applicant has experienced in providing a sound broadcasting service in the area to which his or her sound broadcasting contract relates,

(ii) the financial resources available to the applicant for the purposes of providing such a service,

(iii) the improvement (if any) in the quality of the service concerned that has resulted or, as the case may be, is likely to result by reason of the capital expenditure, the subject of the application, being incurred.

(3) The Minister, with the consent of the Minister for Finance, may pay to the Commission such amounts as he or she determines to be reasonable for the purposes of the making by the Commission of grants of moneys under a scheme under *subsection (1)*.

(4) The aggregate of the amounts paid under *subsection (3)* to the Commission shall not exceed £500,000.

(5) In this section "relevant sound broadcasting contractor" means a sound broadcasting contractor whose sound broadcasting contract authorises the provision of a sound broadcasting service in a specified part only of the State or to a local community that is readily identifiable.

Amendment of section 6 of Act of 1988

60.—Section 6 of the Act of 1988 is hereby amended by the insertion of the following subsections after *subsection (3)*:

"(4) In considering the suitability of an applicant for the award of a sound broadcasting contract, the Commission shall have regard to the overall quality of the performance of the applicant with respect to the provision by him of a sound broadcasting service under any sound broadcasting contract held by him at, or before, the date of the making of the application.

(5) Where the Commission decides to refuse to award a sound broadcasting contract to an applicant therefor, the Commission shall notify the applicant of the reasons for the decision.".

Amendment of section 8 of Act of 1988

61.—Section 8 of the Act of 1988 is hereby amended by the substitution, in *subsection (1)*, of "thirty" for "fourteen".

Amendment of section 15 of Act of 1988

62.—The following section is hereby substituted for section 15 of the Act of 1988: (derogation from requirements relating to news & current affairs programming)

"Notwithstanding section 9(1)(c), the Commission may authorise a derogation from the requirement in question in whole or in part in the case of a sound broadcasting service which a sound broadcasting contractor contracts to provide in any area, but only if it is satisfied that the authorisation of such a derogation would be beneficial to the listeners of sound broadcasting services in that area".

Amendment of section 15 of Act of 1960

63.—Section 15 of the Act of 1960 is hereby amended—

(a) in subsection (3), by the insertion after "amending" of "or revoking",

(b) in subsection (6), by the insertion after "in pursuance of a scheme" of "or schemes", and

(c) by the insertion after subsection (6A) (inserted by the Act of 1976) of the following subsection:

"(6B) No pension, gratuity or other allowance shall be granted by the Authority on the resignation, retirement or death of an officer or servant of the Authority (including the Director-General) otherwise than in accordance with a scheme under this section or, if the Minister, with the consent of the Minister for Finance, sanctions the granting of such a pension, gratuity or allowance, in accordance with that sanction.".

Amendment of Schedule to Act of 1988

64.—Paragraph 11 of the Schedule to the Act of 1988 is hereby amended—

(a) in subparagraph (3), by the insertion after "amending" of "or revoking", and

(b) in subparagraph (6), by the insertion after "under this paragraph" of "or, if the Minister, with the consent of the Minister for Finance, sanctions the granting of such a pension, gratuity or allowance, in accordance with that sanction".

Religious Advertising

65.—Nothing in section 20(4) of the Act of 1960 or section 10(3) of the Act of 1988 (including either of those sections as applied by this Act) shall be construed as preventing the broadcasting of a notice of the fact—

(a) that a particular religious newspaper, magazine or periodical is available for sale or supply, or

(b) that any event or ceremony associated with any particular religion will take place,

if the contents of the notice do not address the issue of the merits or otherwise of adhering to any religious faith or belief or of becoming a member of any religion or religious organisation.

FIRST SCHEDULE

Enactments Repealed

Number and Year(1)	Short Title(2)	Extent of Repeal(3)
No. 10 of 1960	Broadcasting Authority Act, 1960	Sections 18A, 18B, 18C and 19; Subsections (1), (1A) & 1(b) of section 31.
No. 20 of 1988	Radio & Television Act 1988	Subss.(3) & (4) of section 11; Sections 12 & 14(4)(b)
No. 24 of 1990	Broadcasting Act 1990	Section 4
No. 15 of 1993	Broadcasting Authority (Amendment) Act 1993	Section 2

SECOND SCHEDULE

Provisions in relation to Teilifís na Gaeilge

1. In this Schedule "the body" means Teilifís na Gaeilge.

2.(1) The body shall consist of not less than 7 nor more than 9 members.

(2) The members of the body shall be appointed by the Government.

(3) Where the number of members of the body for the time being is 7, not less than 3 of them shall be men and not less than 3 of them shall be women.

(4) Where the number of members of the body for the time being is 8 or 9, not less than 4 of them shall be men and not less than 4 of them shall be women.

(5) The period of office of a member of the body shall be such period, not exceeding 5 years, as the Government may determine when appointing him or her.

(6) A member of the body whose term of office expires by effluxion of time shall be eligible for reappointment.

(7) A member of the body may resign his or her membership by letter sent to the Government and the resignation shall take effect on and from the date of receipt of the letter.

(8) A person shall not be appointed to be a member of the body unless—

(a) he or she has experience of or shown capacity in—

(i) media or commercial affairs,
(ii) radio communications engineering,
(iii) trade union affairs,
(iv) administration, or
(v) social, cultural, educational or community activities or Gaeltacht affairs,

and

(b) he or she is able to speak and write proficiently in the Irish language.

3(1) The Government shall from time to time as occasion requires appoint a member of the body to be chairperson thereof.

(2) The chairperson of the body shall, unless he or she sooner dies, resigns the office of chairperson or ceases to be chairperson under subparagraph (4) of this paragraph, hold office until the expiration of his or her period of office as a member of the body.

(3) The chairperson of the body may at any time resign his or her office as chairperson by letter sent to the Government and the resignation shall take effect at the commencement of the meeting of the body held next after the body has been informed by the Government of the resignation.

(4) Where the chairperson of the body ceases during his or her term of office as chairperson to be a member of the body, he or she shall also then cease to be chairperson of the body.

4.A member of the body may be removed from office by the Government for stated reasons, if, but only if, resolutions are passed by both Houses of the Oireachtas calling for his or her removal.

5.(1) A member of the body shall be paid out of funds at the disposal of the body—

(a) such remuneration as may be fixed from time to time by the Minister, with the consent of the Minister for Finance, and

(b) such amounts in respect of expenses as the body, with the approval of the Minister given with the consent of the Minister for Finance, considers reasonable.

(2) Subject to the provisions of this Schedule, a member of the body shall hold office upon and subject to such terms and conditions as may, from time to time, be determined by the Minister, with the consent of the Minister for Finance.

(3) The Minister shall cause a statement in writing specifying the terms of office and the remuneration of the members of the body to be laid before both Houses of the Oireachtas.

6. A member of the body who has—

(a) any interest in any company or concern with which the body proposes to enter into any contract, or

(b) any interest in any contract which the body proposes to enter into, shall disclose to the body the fact of the interest and the nature thereof, and shall take no part in any deliberation or decision of the body relating to the contract, and the disclosure shall be recorded in the minutes of the body.

7.(1) The body shall as soon as may be after its establishment provide itself with a seal.

(2) The seal of the body shall be authenticated by the signature of the chairperson of the body or some other member thereof authorised by the body to act in that behalf and the signature of an officer of the body authorised by the body to act in that behalf.

(3) Judicial notice shall be taken of the seal of the body, and every document purporting to be an instrument made by the body and to be sealed with the seal (purporting to be authenticated in accordance with this paragraph) of the body shall be received in evidence and be deemed to be such instrument without further proof unless the contrary is shown.

8. (1) The body shall hold such and so many meetings as may be necessary for the due fulfilment of its functions.

(2) The Minister may fix the date, time and place of the first meeting of the body.

(3) Subject to the provisions of this Schedule, the body shall regulate its procedure by rules made under this subparagraph.

(4) At a meeting of the body—

(a) the chairperson of the body shall, if present, be chairperson of the meeting,

(b) if and so long as the chairperson is not present or the office of chairperson is vacant, the members of the body who are present shall choose one of their number to be chairperson of the meeting.

(5) Every question at a meeting of the body shall be determined by a majority of the votes of the members present and voting on the question, and in the case of an equal division of votes, the chairperson of the meeting shall have a second or casting vote.

(6) The body may act notwithstanding one or more vacancies among its members (including one or more vacancies that result in subparagraph (3) or (4) of paragraph 2 not being complied with).

(7) The quorum for a meeting of the body shall be fixed by rules made under subparagraph (3) of this paragraph, but—

(a) it shall not be less than five, and

(b) until it is so fixed, it shall be five.

9.(1) The body shall, with the approval of the Minister, from time to time appoint a person to be the chief executive officer of the body, and such person shall be known, and in this Act is referred to, as the "chief executive".

(2) The body may, as well as appointing the chief executive, appoint so many other persons to be members of the staff of the body as the body, with the approval of the Minister, given with the consent of the Minister for Finance, from time to time determines.

(3) The body may perform all or any of its functions through or by such members of its staff as may be duly authorised in that behalf by it.

10.(1) A member of the staff of the body (including the chief executive) shall hold his or her office or employment on such terms and conditions as the body, with the approval of the Minister given with the consent of the Minister for Finance, may from time to time determine.

(2) There shall be paid by the body to its staff (including the chief executive) such remuneration and allowances as the body, with the approval of the Minister given with the consent of the Minister for Finance, thinks fit.

(3) In determining the remuneration or allowances to be paid to its staff or the terms or conditions subject to which such staff hold or are to hold their employment, the body shall comply with any directive with regard to such remuneration, allowances, terms and conditions which the Minister, with the consent of the Minister for Finance, may give, from time to time, to the body.

(4) The body may at any time remove any member of the staff of the body from being a member of its staff.

(5) Notwithstanding the foregoing provisions of this paragraph, the chief executive shall not be removed without the consent of the Minister.

11.(1) Where a member of the body is—

(a) nominated as a member of Seanad Eireann, or

(b) nominated as a candidate for election to either House of the Oireachtas or to the European Parliament, or

(c) regarded pursuant to Part XIII of the Second Schedule to the European Parliament Elections Act, 1997, as having been elected to the European Parliament, he or she shall thereupon cease to be a member of the body.

(2) Where a person employed by the body is—

(a) nominated as a member of Seanad Eireann, or

(b) nominated as a candidate for election to either House of the Oireachtas or to the European Parliament, or

(c) regarded pursuant to the said Part XIII as having been elected to the European Parliament, he or she shall stand seconded from employment by the body and shall not be paid by, or entitled to receive from, the body any remuneration or allowances—

(i) in case he or she is nominated as a member of Seanad Eireann or is regarded as having been elected to the European Parliament, in respect of the period commencing on such nomination or election, as the case may be, and ending when he or she ceases to be a member of Seanad Eireann or the European Parliament,

(ii) in case he or she is nominated as a candidate for election to either House of the Oireachtas or to the European Parliament, in respect of the period commencing on his or her nomination and ending when he or she ceases to be a member of such House or the European Parliament, as the case may be, or withdraws his or her candidature or fails to be elected, as may be appropriate.

(3) A person who is, for the time being, entitled under the Standing Orders of either House of the Oireachtas to sit therein or who is a member of the European Parliament shall, while he or she is so entitled or is such a member, be disqualified from becoming a member of the body or from employment in any capacity by the body.

(4) Without prejudice to the generality of subparagraph (2) of this paragraph, that subparagraph shall be construed as prohibiting the reckoning of a period mentioned in clause (i) or (ii) of that subparagraph as service with the body for the purpose of any pensions, gratuities or other allowances payable on retirement or death.

12.(1) The body may prepare a scheme or schemes for the granting of pensions, gratuities and other allowances on retirement or death to or in respect of such members of the staff of the body (including the chief executive) as it may think fit and the body shall submit any such scheme to the Minister for his or her approval.

(2) Every such scheme shall fix the time and conditions of retirement for all persons to or in respect of whom pensions, gratuities or allowances on retirement or death are payable under the scheme, and different times and conditions may be fixed in relation to different classes of persons.

(3) The body may at any time prepare and submit to the Minister a scheme amending or revoking a scheme previously submitted and approved of under this paragraph.

(4) If any dispute arises as to the claim of any person to, or the amount of, any pension, gratuity or other allowance payable in pursuance of a scheme or schemes under this paragraph, such dispute shall be submitted to the Minister who shall refer it to the Minister for Finance, whose decision shall be final.

(5) A scheme submitted to the Minister under this paragraph shall, if approved of by the Minister with the consent of the Minister for Finance, be carried out by the body in accordance with its terms.

(6) No pension, gratuity or other allowance shall be granted by the body on the resignation, retirement or death of a member of the staff of the body (including the chief executive) otherwise than in accordance with a scheme under this paragraph or, if the Minister, with the consent of the Minister for Finance, sanctions the granting of such a pension, gratuity or allowance, in accordance with that sanction.

(7) Every scheme submitted and approved under this paragraph shall be laid before each House of the Oireachtas as soon as may be after it is approved of and if a resolution annulling the scheme is passed by either such House within the next 21 days on which that House has sat after the scheme is laid before it, the scheme shall be annulled accordingly, but without prejudice to the validity of anything previously done thereunder.

13. It shall be the duty of the body so to conduct its affairs as to ensure that its expenses can be met from its revenues.

14. The body may, with the approval of the Minister, given with the consent of the Minister for Finance, borrow temporarily by arrangement with bankers such sums (including sums in a currency other than the currency of the State) as it may require for the purpose of providing for current expenditure.

15.(1) The body may, with the approval of the Minister, given with the consent of the Minister for Finance, borrow money (including money in a currency other than the currency of the State) by means of the creation of stock or other forms of security to be issued, transferred, dealt with and redeemed in such manner and on such terms and conditions as the body, with the consents aforesaid, may determine.

(2) The borrowing powers conferred by this paragraph on the body may, subject to the consent of the Minister, be exercised for any purpose arising in the performance of its functions, but there may be attached to a consent to borrow the condition that the moneys shall be utilised only for the purpose of a programme of capital works approved by the Minister.

(3) The terms upon which moneys are borrowed under this paragraph may include provisions charging the moneys and interest thereon upon all property of whatsoever kind for the time being vested in the body or upon any particular property of the body and provisions establishing the priority of such charges amongst themselves.

16. The body may invest any of its funds in any manner in which a trustee is empowered by law to invest trust funds.

17.(1) The body shall keep in such form as shall be approved by the Minister, after consultation with the Minister for Finance, all proper and usual accounts of all moneys received or expended by it, including an income and expenditure account and a balance sheet.

(2) Accounts kept in pursuance of this paragraph shall be submitted annually by the body to the Comptroller and Auditor General for audit at such time as the Minister, with the concurrence of the Minister for Finance, directs.

(3) Immediately after every audit under this paragraph of its accounts, the body shall send to the Minister—

(a) a copy of the income and expenditure account and balance sheet as certified by the Comptroller and Auditor General,

(b) a copy of the report of the Comptroller and Auditor General,

and

(c) copies of such of the accounts submitted for audit as the Minister may appoint as accounts of which copies are to be furnished to him or her.

(4) As soon as may be after he or she has received the documents required to be furnished to him or her under this paragraph, the Minister shall cause such documents to be laid before each House of the Oireachtas.

18.(1) The body shall, in each year, at such date as the Minister may direct, make a report to the Minister of its proceedings under this Act during the preceding year, and the Minister shall cause copies of the report to be laid before each House of the Oireachtas.

(2) Whenever the Minister so directs, the annual report shall also include information on such particular aspects of the body's proceedings under this Act as the Minister may specify.

(3) The body shall submit to the Minister such information regarding the performance of its functions as the Minister may from time to time require.

COMMUNICATIONS REGULATIONS ACT 2002

(No. 20 of 2002)

SECTION INCLUDED IN THIS VOLUME

Transfer of functions

9.—(1) On the establishment day there is transferred to the Commission the functions of the Director by or under—

(a) each of the provisions mentioned in column (3) of Part 1 of Schedule 1 of the enactments mentioned in column (2) of that Part opposite the mention of that provision, and

(b) each of the statutory instruments mentioned in Part 2 of Schedule 1.

(2) On the establishment day there is transferred to the Commission the functions of the Minister under section 20 (except in so far as it relates to television sets) of the Broadcasting and Wireless Telegraphy Act, 1988.

(3) Reference—

(a) in section 8 of the Wireless Telegraphy Act, 1926, and

(b) in section 9(1) of the Broadcasting Act, 1990,

to an officer of the Minister shall, from the establishment day, be construed as reference to an officer of the Commission.

(4) Reference in a transferred function to the Director or the Minister (construed by virtue of section 4 of the Act of 1996 as a reference to the Director) shall, from the establishment day, be construed as a reference to the Commission.

BROADCASTING (MAJOR EVENTS TELEVISION COVERAGE) (AMENDMENT) ACT 2003

(No. 13 of 2003)

ARRANGEMENT OF SECTIONS

ACTS REFERRED TO

Broadcasting (Major Events Television Coverage) Act 1999	1999, No. 28
Companies Acts 1963 to 2001	

AN ACT TO GIVE FURTHER EFFECT TO ARTICLE 3A OF COUNCIL DIRECTIVE NO. 89/552/EEC OF 3 OCTOBER 1989 AS AMENDED BY DIRECTIVE NO. 97/36/EC OF THE EUROPEAN PARLIAMENT AND OF THE COUNCIL OF 30 JUNE 1997; TO REGULATE IN THE COMMON GOOD AND FOR THE PURPOSES OF THAT DIRECTIVE THE SALE AND EXERCISE OF RIGHTS TO EVENTS DESIGNATED UNDER SECTION 2 OF THE BROADCASTING (MAJOR EVENTS TELEVISION COVERAGE) ACT 1999, AND TO REGULATE THE EXERCISE BY BROADCASTERS OF EXCLUSIVE BROADCASTING RIGHTS THAT THEY MAY HAVE PURCHASED, TO ENSURE FOR THE PURPOSE OF THAT DIRECTIVE THAT A SUBSTANTIAL PORTION OF THE PUBLIC IS NOT DEPRIVED OF THE POSSIBILITY OF FOLLOWING EVENTS LIVE OR ON A DEFERRED BASIS ON FREE TELEVISION SERVICES WHICH EVENTS ARE REGARDED BY THE MINISTER FOR COMMUNICATIONS, MARINE AND NATURAL RESOURCES AS BEING OF MAJOR IMPORTANCE TO SOCIETY AND TO AVOID SPECULATIVE RIGHTS PURCHASES OF EVENTS DESIGNATED BY THE

MINISTER FOR COMMUNICATIONS, MARINE AND NATURAL RESOURCES UNDER THE SAID SECTION 2; AND FOR THAT PURPOSE TO AMEND THE BROADCASTING (MAJOR EVENTS TELEVISION COVERAGE) ACT 1999; AND TO PROVIDE FOR CONNECTED MATTERS.

[22ND APRIL, 2003]

BE IT ENACTED BY THE OIREACHTAS AS FOLLOWS:

Interpretation

1.—(1) In this Act—

"broadcaster", "free television service" and "qualifying broadcaster" have the meanings assigned to them, respectively, by section 1 of the Principal Act;

"Council Directive" means Council Directive No. 89/552/EEC of 3 October 1989[1] as amended by Directive No. 97/36/EC of the European Parliament and of the Council of 30 June 1997[2];

"designated event" means an event designated under section 2 of the Principal Act;

"designation order" means an order under section 2 of the Principal Act;

"event" has the meaning assigned to it by section 1 of the Principal Act and includes the whole event or where part of it has already taken place the remainder;

"event organiser" means the person who is legally entitled to sell the rights to the event;

"Principal Act" means the Broadcasting (Major Events Television Coverage) Act 1999;

"rights" in relation to the broadcast of a designated event, means the exclusive or non-exclusive rights to broadcast the event.

(2) In this Act—

(a) a reference to any enactment shall, unless the context otherwise requires, be construed as a reference to that enactment as amended or extended by or under any subsequent enactment including this Act,

(b) a reference to a section is a reference to a section of this Act, unless it is indicated that reference to some other enactment is intended, and

(c) a reference to a subsection, paragraph or subparagraph is a reference to the subsection, paragraph or subparagraph of the provision in which the reference occurs, unless it is indicated that reference to some other provision is intended.

Application

2.—This Act applies to a designated event which is designated, before or after the passing of this Act, under section 2 of the Principal Act, whether or not any agreement or arrangement has been entered into between the event organiser and a broadcaster in respect of the acquisition by the broadcaster of rights to the event, and where such an agreement or arrangement has been entered into before the passing of this Act, in respect of those rights, it was entered into after the publication of the Council Directive concerning an event which takes place after 13 November 1999 (being the date Article 3a of the Council Directive was given effect to by the Principal Act).

"Minister"

3.—Section 1(1) of the Principal Act is amended by substituting for the definition of "the Minister" the following definition:

" 'Minister' means Minister for Communications, Marine and Natural Resources;".

Qualifying broadcaster may apply to High Court to obtain rights from event organiser to provide coverage of designated event on free television services in State, etc.

4.—(1) Where an event has been designated under section 2 of the Principal Act, and if within 56 days, or such other lesser or greater period which the Minister directs, before the event or a part of it takes place the event organiser has not made an agreement or arrangement with a qualifying broadcaster to enable it to provide coverage on free television services in the State of the event or part of it, as determined under section 2(1)(b) of the Principal Act in the designation order which designated the event—

(a) subject to subsection (3), a qualifying broadcaster may apply to the High Court in a summary manner for an order directing the event organiser to give rights to the qualifying broadcaster to provide such coverage and upon such terms as are fixed by the High Court, including the fixing of reasonable market rates, in respect of the acquisition of the rights, or

(b) within that period a qualifying broadcaster has not so applied, the event organiser may apply to the High Court in a summary manner to request the High Court to invite qualifying broadcasters to make such an application.

(2) Subject to subsection (3), the High Court may, on application to it under subsection (1) by a qualifying broadcaster, direct the event organiser, upon such terms as to the Court appears just and proper, to give to the qualifying broadcaster rights to provide coverage of the designated event or part of it on free television services, as determined under section 2(1)(b) of the Principal Act in the designation order which designated the event, notwithstanding that all of the terms for the acquisition of the rights to provide coverage under subsection (1), have not yet been fixed by it, including the fixing of reasonable market rates.

(3) Subsection (1) does not apply where an event organiser decides, prior to the making of an application under subsection (1), not to allow coverage of an event or a part of it, as determined under section 2(1)(b) of the Principal Act in the designation order designating the event, on any television service provided by a broadcaster. Where an event organiser has so decided, the event organiser must notify, as soon as possible, the Minister.

(4) The High Court in fixing the terms under subsection (1) may, in arriving at a computation of reasonable market rates, to be paid by a qualifying broadcaster for the acquisition of the rights under that subsection, refer the computation of the rates to an

arbitrator appointed by the High Court. The arbitrator shall report to the Court and the parties, by way of issuing an award, setting out the amount that he or she decides are reasonable market rates.

(5) An arbitration under subsection (4) shall be conducted in accordance with such procedures as are determined by the Court referring the computation of the rates to the arbitrator. The Court may, in determining such procedures, give such directions as it considers just and proper for the processing of the arbitration, including fixing the period within which the award of the arbitrator is to be issued.

(6) Where in an application under subsection (1) -

(a) the High Court has fixed the reasonable market rates, or an arbitrator has issued an award under subsection (4), and prior to the High Court making a final order in respect of the application, or

(b) in the circumstances referred to in subsection (2), the High Court indicates that it will fix the reasonable market rates for coverage of the event after the event has taken place, and prior to the event taking place, the qualifying broadcaster may withdraw the application. The High Court may in these circumstances, having regard to the intention of the broadcaster making the application, award such costs to such party or parties to the application as it considers appropriate.

(7) The High Court may, either of its own motion or on application to it by an arbitrator appointed under subsection (4), give, from time to time, such directions in connection with the arbitration as it considers just and proper.

(8) Where more than one qualifying broadcaster applies under subsection (1) for rights to provide coverage of a designated event or part of it, and the High Court has fixed under this section the terms upon which a qualifying broadcaster may obtain the rights, the event organiser may choose to which qualifying broadcaster it gives the rights.

(9) Where there is an existing contract in respect of an event or part of it between the event organiser and another broadcaster, who is not a qualifying broadcaster, the High Court in an application to it under subsection (1) shall decide to whom and in which proportions monies in respect of the reasonable market rates, fixed under this section in respect of the acquisition of rights to the event or part of it, should be paid.

(10) The High Court may, if it considers it necessary, for the purposes of exercising its powers under this section, adjust an existing agreement or arrangement, in respect of rights to a designated event or a part of it, between the event organiser and a broadcaster, who is not a qualifying broadcaster.

(11) Without prejudice to subsection (2), when considering any matter under this section, the High Court may make such interim or interlocutory order as it considers appropriate.

Arbitration in respect of reasonable market rates where event organiser is willing to sell broadcasting rights to designated event to qualifying broadcaster

5.—(1) Where an event organiser is willing to sell rights enabling a qualifying broadcaster to provide coverage on free television services in the State of a designated event or a part of it, as determined under section 2(1)(b) of the Principal Act in the designation order which designated the event, but the qualifying broadcaster and the event organiser have not agreed the amount to be paid in respect of the acquisition of the rights, the following provisions of this section apply.

(2) The qualifying broadcaster or the event organiser may request the other to agree to the appointment of an arbitrator for the purposes of fixing reasonable market rates for the acquisition of the rights referred to in subsection (1). In default of agreement, on the appointment of an arbitrator by the parties, the Minister may appoint an arbitrator, who he or she considers to be suitably qualified in this regard, within 21 days of being notified by either party of such default.

(3) An arbitrator appointed under subsection (2) shall issue his or her award, in writing, which, subject to subsection (4), shall be a provisional award. The arbitrator shall notify the parties concerned of the award.

(4) An award issued under subsection (3) is not binding on the qualifying broadcaster concerned unless, within the period of 21 days from the date of issuing of the award of the arbitrator under subsection (3), the qualifying broadcaster has notified the event organiser concerned of the qualifying broadcaster's acceptance of the award.

Criteria for determining reasonable market rates.

6.—In determining that which constitutes reasonable market rates or terms for the purposes of this Act and the Principal Act, the High Court or an arbitrator shall have regard to, inter alia -

(a) previous fees (if any) for the event or similar events,

(b) time of day for live coverage of the event,

(c) the period for which rights are offered,

(d) the revenue potential associated with the live or deferred coverage of the event,

(e) the purposes of Article 3a of the Council Directive and the rights conferred on Member States of the European Communities to regulate the exercise of broadcasting rights, and

(f) such other matters as may appear to be relevant.

Obligation to give copy of agreement or arrangement to broadcasting rights to Minister

7.—(1) The Minister may, where he or she considers it is in the public interest, direct an event organiser who has entered into an agreement or arrangement with a broadcaster in respect of the broadcasting rights to a designated event to give to the Minister, at the Department of Communications, Marine and Natural Resources, within such period specified in the direction, a copy of the agreement or arrangement.

(2) Where an agreement or arrangement referred to in subsection (1) is not in

writing, the event organiser must, upon receiving a direction of the Minister, notify the Minister of the agreement or arrangement and set out all its terms and conditions.

Service of directions and notification

8.—(1) Where a direction or notification is required under this Act to be given to a person, it shall be in writing, addressed to the person and given to the person in one of the following ways -

(a) by delivering it to the person,

(b) by leaving it at the address at which the person ordinarily carries on business,

(c) by sending it by post in a pre-paid registered letter addressed to the person at the address at which the person ordinarily carries on business,

(d) if an address for the service of directions or notifications has been furnished by the person, by leaving it at, or sending it by pre-paid registered post addressed to the person at that address,

(e) in any case where the person giving the direction or notification considers that the immediate giving of it is required, by sending it, by means of a facsimile machine, to a device or facility for the reception of facsimiles located at the address at which the person ordinarily carries on business or, if an address for the service of directions or notifications has been furnished by the person, that address, provided that the sender's facsimile machine generates a message confirming successful transmission of the total number of pages of the direction or notification and it is also given in one of the ways referred to in any of the preceding paragraphs.

(2) For the purposes of this section—

(a) a company registered under the Companies Acts 1963 to 2001 is deemed to carry on business at its registered office, and every other body corporate and unincorporated body is deemed to carry on business at its principal office or place of business, and

(b) the Minister is deemed to carry on business at the Department of Communications, Marine and Natural Resources.

Review of designated events

9.—(1) Subject to subsection (2), the Minister shall review, from time to time, designated events and the designation of events under section 2 of the Principal Act.

(2) A review under subsection (1) shall be—

(a) in the case of the first review, not later than 3 years after the passing of this Act, and

(b) in the case of any subsequent review, not later than 3 years after the preceding review.

Short title, collective citation and construction

10.—(1) This Act may be cited as the Broadcasting (Major Events Television Coverage) (Amendment) Act 2003.

(2) The Broadcasting (Major Events Television Coverage) Act 1999 and this Act may be cited together as the Broadcasting (Major Events Television Coverage) Acts 1999 and 2003 and shall be construed together as one.

BROADCASTING (FUNDING) ACT 2003

(No. 43 of 2003)

ARRANGEMENT OF SECTIONS

ACTS REFERRED TO

Broadcasting Act 2001	2001, No. 4
Broadcasting Authority Act 1960	1960, No. 10
Broadcasting Authority (Amendment) Act 1976	1976, No. 37
Radio and Television Act 1988	1988, No. 20
Wireless Telegraphy Act 1926	1926, No. 45
Wireless Telegraphy Act 1972	1972, No. 5

AN ACT TO PROVIDE THAT THE BROADCASTING COMMISSION OF IRELAND PREPARE A SCHEME OR SCHEMES FOR THE FUNDING OF GRANTS TO SUPPORT CERTAIN TELEVISION AND RADIO PROGRAMMES AND PROJECTS OUT OF AN AMOUNT OF 5 PER CENT OF NET RECEIPTS FOR TELEVISION LICENCE FEES, TO OUTLINE THE OBJECTIVES OF A SCHEME AND TO PROVIDE FOR RELATED MATTERS.

[23RD DECEMBER, 2003]

BE IT ENACTED BY THE OIREACHTAS AS FOLLOWS:

Interpretation

1.—(1) In this Act—

"Act of 1926" means Wireless Telegraphy Act 1926;

"Act of 1988" means Radio and Television Act 1988;

"Act of 2001" means Broadcasting Act 2001;

"Commission" means Broadcasting Commission of Ireland;

"free television service" means a television broadcasting service for the reception of which no charge is made by the person providing the service, and reception of which is available to at least 90 per cent of the population of the State;

"Minister" means Minister for Communications, Marine and Natural Resources;

"MMD system" has the meaning given to it in section 2 of the Act of 2001;

"programme material" means audio-visual or audio material, including advertising and similar material, which was broadcast in whole or in part or was recorded for broadcast, and includes stills and photographs produced from such material or in the context of the recording of such material;

"scheme" means a scheme prepared under section 2.

(2) In this Act—

(a) a reference to a section is a reference to a section of this Act, unless it is indicated that a reference to some other enactment is intended,

(b) a reference to a subsection or paragraph is a reference to a subsection or paragraph of the provision in which the reference occurs, unless it is indicated that a reference to some other provision is intended, and

(c) a reference to any enactment shall be construed as a reference to that enactment as amended, adapted or extended by or under any subsequent enactment including this Act.

Broadcasting Funding Scheme

2.—(1) The Commission shall prepare and submit to the Minister for his or her approval a scheme or a number of schemes for the granting of funds to support all or any of the following—

(a) new television or radio programmes on Irish culture, heritage and experience, including -

(i) history (including history relating to particular areas, groups or aspects of experience, activity or influence),

(ii) historical buildings,

(iii) the natural environment,

(iv) folk, rural and vernacular heritage,

(v) traditional and contemporary arts,

(vi) the Irish language, and

(vii) the Irish experience in European and international contexts,

(b) new television or radio programmes to improve adult literacy,

(c) programmes under paragraphs (a) and (b) in the Irish language, and

(d) the development of archiving of programme material produced in the State.

(2) A scheme—

(a) may only fund television programmes under subsection (1) which are broadcast—

(i) on a free television service which provides near universal coverage in the State, or

(ii) on a cable or MMD system as part of a community content contract under section 39 of the Act of 2001, and which, other than in the case of programmes for children or educational programmes, are broadcast during peak viewing times,

(b) may only fund radio programmes under subsection (1) which are carried on sound broadcasting services (within the meaning of section 2 of the Act of 1988) licensed by the Commission or operated by Radio Telefis Eireann and which, other than in the case of programmes for children or educational programmes, are broadcast during peak listening times,

(c) may provide funding for projects relating to matters such as research, needs assessments, analyses, feasibility studies and pilot projects in relation to subsection (1)(d), including such projects undertaken by or on behalf of the Minister, and

(d) may not provide funding for programmes which are produced primarily for news or current affairs.

(3) A scheme may provide—

(a) for the making of applications by persons for funding under a scheme,

(b) general terms and conditions of funding, or

(c) that funding in a particular year will be directed at—

(i) particular classes of television or radio programmes referred to in subsection (1) including but not limited to programmes of a specified nature or subject matter, or broadcast by means of a particular medium (including media of a local or regional nature such as local or community television or radio), or

(ii) particular classes of projects referred to in subsection (1)(d).

(4) The Commission may attach to any particular funding under a scheme such particular terms or conditions as it considers appropriate in the circumstances.

(5) The Commission, in preparing a scheme, shall have regard to the understanding and enjoyment of television programmes under the scheme by persons who are deaf or hard of hearing.

(6) A scheme submitted by the Commission to the Minister under subsection (1) may be amended or revoked by the Commission.

(7) The Minister may direct the Commission—

(a) to prepare and submit to him or her a scheme relating to any matter in subsection (1), or

(b) to amend or revoke a scheme.

The Commission shall comply with a direction under this section.

(8) Any amendment or revocation of a scheme under subsection (6) or (7) shall be submitted by the Commission to the Minister for his or her approval.

(9) A scheme shall, if approved of by the Minister, be—

(a) published (including publication by electronic means capable of being read in legible form), and

(b) carried out in accordance with its terms, by the Commission.

(10)(a) A scheme shall be laid before each House of the Oireachtas by the Minister as soon as may be after it is made.

(b) Either House of the Oireachtas may, by resolution passed within 21 sitting days after the day on which a scheme was laid before it in accordance with paragraph (a), annula scheme.

(c) The annulment of the scheme takes effect immediately on the passing of the resolution concerned but does not affect anything that was done under a scheme before the passing of the resolution.

Objectives of the scheme

3.—(1) The objectives of a scheme in relation to programmes referred to in section 2(1)(a) are to—

(a) develop high quality programmes based on Irish culture, heritage and experience,

(b) develop these programmes in the Irish language,

(c) increase the availability of programmes referred to in paragraphs (a) and (b) to audiences in the State,

(d) represent the diversity of Irish culture and heritage,

(e) record oral Irish heritage and aspects of Irish heritage which are disappearing, under threat, or have not been previously recorded, and

(f) develop local and community broadcasting.

(2) The objective of a scheme in relation to the development of archiving of programme material produced in the State referred to in section 2(1)(d) is to develop an integrated approach to the archiving of programme material, including the development of suitable storage processes and formats and the accessing of material by interested parties.

(3) The Commission, in preparing a scheme and in considering applications for funding, shall have regard to the objectives of a scheme.

Amounts to be paid by Minister to scheme

4.—(1) In this section—

"broadcasting licence fees" has the meaning given to it in section 1(1) (as amended by subsection (4)) of the Broadcasting Authority Act 1960;

"net receipts" in relation to the receipt of broadcasting licence fees, means the total receipts less any expenses in respect of those receipts certified by the Minister as having been incurred by him or her in that year in relation to the collection of the fees.

(2) The Minister, with the approval of the Minister for Finance, may pay to the Commission out of moneys provided by the Oireachtas for the purposes of grants under a scheme and any administration of or reasonable expenses relating to a scheme, in respect of each financial year, after the financial year ending on 31 December 2002, an amount being equal to 5 per cent of net receipts in that year in respect of broadcasting licence fees.

(3) Section 8(a) (as amended by section 23(5) of the Act of 2001) of the Broadcasting Authority (Amendment) Act 1976 is amended by inserting after subparagraph (i) the following:

"(ia) any amount paid under section 4(2) of the Broadcasting (Funding) Act 2003,".

(4) Section 1(1) of the Broadcasting Authority Act 1960 is amended by substituting for the definition of "broadcasting licence fee" the following:

> " 'broadcasting licence fee' means a fee paid on a licence granted under section 5 of the Act of 1926 in respect of a television set (within the meaning of section 1 of the Wireless Telegraphy Act 1972);".

Review of scheme

5.—(1) The Commission shall review the operation, effectiveness and impact of a scheme not later than 3 years from the date on which it comes into operation, and every 3 years thereafter, or at such other time as may be requested by the Minister, and make a written report to the Minister on the review.

(2) A copy of a report under subsection (1) shall be laid by the Minister before each House of the Oireachtas, as soon as may be, after it has been made to him or her.

(3) The Minister shall publish (including publication by electronic means capable of being read in legible form) a report made to him or her under subsection (1).

Details of scheme to be included in accounts and reports to Commission

6.—(1) The accounts of the Commission kept under paragraph 16 of the Schedule to the Act of 1988 shall include a special account of any scheme.

(2) A report of the Commission under paragraph 17 of the Schedule to the Act of 1988 shall include details of any scheme.

Winding-up and dissolution of scheme

7.—(1) The Minister may, with the consent of the Minister for Finance, direct the Commission to wind-up, where there is only one scheme, the scheme or, where there is more than one scheme, all schemes and to pay to the Minister any monies remaining in respect of the scheme or schemes. The Minister shall pay to Radio Telefis Eireann any such monies paid to him or her.

(2) Where the Minister directs that the scheme or all schemes, as the case may be, be wound up in accordance with subsection (1), he or she shall upon being satisfied that the scheme has or the schemes have been wound up in accordance with that

subsection, by order (in this section referred to as a "dissolution order") dissolve the scheme or schemes.

(3) Upon the commencement of a dissolution order no further scheme may be made under section 2.

(4)(a) A dissolution order shall be laid before each of the Houses of the Oireachtas as soon as practicable after it is made.

(b) Either House of the Oireachtas may, by resolution passed within 21 sitting days after the day on which an order was laid before it in accordance with paragraph (a), annul the order.

(c) The annulment of a dissolution order takes effect immediately on the passing of the resolution concerned, but does not affect anything that was done under the order before the passing of the resolution.

Expenses

8.—The expenses incurred by the Minister in the administration of this Act shall, to such extent as may be sanctioned by the Minister for Finance, be paid out of moneys provided by the Oireachtas.

Short title

9.—This Act may be cited as the Broadcasting (Funding) Act 2003.

SECTION 3

CENSORSHIP OF FILMS ACT 1923

(No. 23 of 1923)

ARRANGEMENT OF SECTIONS

AN ACT TO PROVIDE FOR THE OFFICIAL CENSORING OF CINEMATOGRAPH PICTURES AND FOR OTHER MATTERS CONNECTED THEREWITH.

[16TH JULY, 1923.]

BE IT ENACTED BY THE OIREACHTAS OF SAORSTAT EIREANN AS FOLLOWS:—

Establishment of office of Official Censor of Films

1.—(1) There shall be established the office of Official Censor of Films.

(2) The Official Censor of Films shall be a corporation sole under that name with perpetual succession and an official seal, and may sue and be sued under that name.

Appointment of Official Censor

2.—(1) The Minister shall as soon as may be after the passing of this Act and thereafter as occasion arises, appoint a fit person to the office of Official Censor, who shall hold office for such time and on such terms as the Minister shall, with the sanction of the Minister for Finance, appoint.

(2) Every person appointed to be Official Censor under this Act shall receive such salary or fees as the Minister for Finance shall determine.

(3) Whenever the Official Censor is temporarily unable to attend to his duties, or his office is vacant, the Minister may appoint a fit person to perform the duties of the Official Censor under this Act, during such inability or vacancy, and every person so appointed shall during his appointment have all the powers of the Official Censor under this Act, and shall receive such remuneration, out of moneys to be provided by the Oireachtas, as the Minister shall, with the sanction of the Minister for Finance, direct.

Establishment of Censorship of Films Appeal Board

3.—(1) There shall be established a Censorship of Films Appeal Board consisting of nine Commissioners of whom one shall be Chairman [one at least shall be a man and one at least shall be a woman.]

(2) The members of the Appeal Board shall hold office for five years from the date of their appointment and shall, at the end of any such term of office, be eligible for re-appointment.

(3) The Minister shall as soon as may be after the passing of this Act and thereafter as occasion arises appoint fit persons to be members of the Appeal Board.

(4) Whenever any vacancy shall occur in the membership of the Appeal Board by reason of the death, becoming disqualified or resignation of a member before the expiration of his term of office, the Minister shall appoint a fit person to fill such vacancy, but the person so appointed shall hold office only for the residue of the term of office of the member whose death, becoming disqualified or resignation occasioned such vacancy.

(5) The Minister shall from time to time as occasion arises nominate one of the members of the Appeal Board to be Chairman thereof.

(6) Four members of the Appeal Board personally present shall form a quorum for the hearing of appeals, and the decision of the majority of the members present shall be the decision of the Appeal Board, save that whenever such majority is less than four, or the members present are equally divided, the [appeal shall be re-heard in the presence of not less than seven members of the Appeal Board, and the decision of the majority of the members present at such re-hearing shall be the decision of the Appeal Board, but if, on such re-hearing, the members present are equally divided, the decision of the Official Censor shall be affirmed.

(7) The Appeal Board may act for all purposes notwithstanding the existence of not more than two vacancies in its membership.

(8) A person shall be disqualified for being a member of the Appeal Board if he has, directly or indirectly, any share or interest in any Company or undertaking, having as its object or one of its objects the exhibition for profit of pictures by means of a cinematograph or similar apparatus, or the production of pictures capable of being so exhibited.

Amendment History

Section 3(1) amended by s.30 of the Video Recordings Act 1989. Section 3(6) amended by s.6 of the Censorship of Films (Amendment) Act 1925, which states that "subs.(6) of s.3 of the Principal Act shall have effect subject to the following modifications, that is to say—

(a) three members of the appeal board personally present shall form a quorum for the hearing of appeals;

(b) an appeal shall be re-heard whenever the majority mentioned in the said sub-section is less than three or the members present are equally divided;

(c) every re-hearing shall be in the presence of not less than five members of the appeal board."

Appointment of officers of Official Censor and of Appeal Board

4.—(1) The Minister shall appoint such persons to be officers of the Official Censor and of the Appeal Board respectively, as subject to the sanction of the Minister for Finance as to number, he may consider necessary for the purposes of this Act, and these officers shall hold office upon such terms and be remunerated at such rates and in such manner as the Minister for Finance may sanction.

(2) The salaries or remuneration of the Official Censor and his officers and of the officers of the Appeal Board, and such other expenses of carrying this Act into effect as may be sanctioned by the Minister for Finance shall be paid out of moneys provided by the Oireachtas.

No picture to be exhibited in public without a certificate

5.—(1) No picture shall be exhibited in public by means of a cinematograph or similar apparatus unless and until the Official Censor has certified that the whole of such picture is fit for exhibition in public.

(2) Every person who exhibits in public by means of a cinematograph or similar apparatus any picture which, or any part of which, has not been certified by the Official Censor to be fit for exhibition in public, and every person who knowingly permits any cinematograph or other apparatus owned or hired by him to be used for the exhibition in public of any such picture as aforesaid, and every person who knowingly permits any building or any and in his possession or occupation to be used for the exhibition in public by any such means as aforesaid of any such picture as aforesaid, shall be guilty of all offence under this Act and shall be liable on summary conviction to a fine not exceeding £50, and in the case of a continuing offence to a further fine not exceeding £5 for each day on which the offence continues.

(3) This Section shall come into operation at the expiration of six months from the passing of this Act, or at such earlier time as the Minister shall appoint.

Restrictions in certificate to be complied with

6.—(1) No picture nor any part of a picture in respect of which the Official Censor has granted a limited certificate shall be exhibited in public by means of a cinematograph or similar apparatus at any place not authorised by such certificate or under any conditions inconsistent with the special conditions specified in such limited certificate or in the presence of any person who is not a member of the class in whose presence such picture is by such certificate authorised to be exhibited.

(2) Every person who exhibits in public by means of a cinematograph or similar apparatus any picture or any part of a picture in respect of which a limited certificate has been granted by the Official Censor under this Act either at any place not authorised by such certificate or under any conditions inconsistent with the special conditions specified in such certificate or in the presence of any person who is not a member of the class in whose presence such picture is by such certificate authorised to be exhibited, and every person who knowingly permits any cinematograph or other apparatus owned or hired by him or any land in his possession or occupation to be used for such exhibition as aforesaid, shall be guilty of an offence under this Act and shall be liable on summary conviction to a fine not exceeding £50, and in the case of a continuing offence to a further fine not exceeding £5 for each day during which the offence continues.

(3) This Section shall come into operation at the expiration of six months from the passing of this Act, or at such earlier time as the Minister shall appoint.

When certificate to be granted by Official Censor

7.—(1) Every person desiring to exhibit in public by means of a cinematograph or similar apparatus any picture which has not been certified by the Official Censor to be fit for exhibition in public may apply to the Official Censor in the prescribed manner for a certificate that such picture is fit for exhibition in public.

(2) Whenever any such application as is mentioned in the fore-going sub-section is made to the Official Censor, he shall certify in the prescribed manner that the picture to which the application relates is fit for exhibition in public, unless he is of opinion that such picture or some part thereof is unfit for general exhibition in public by reason of its being indecent, obscene or blasphemous or because the exhibition thereof in public would tend to inculcate principles contrary to public morality or would be otherwise subversive of public morality.

(3) If the Official Censor is of opinion that any picture in respect of which an application is made to him under this section is not fit for general exhibition in public but is fit for exhibition in public in certain places in Saorstát Éireann or under special conditions or in the presence of certain classes of persons, he shall grant a certificate that such picture is fit for exhibition in public subject to such restrictions and conditions (which shall be expressed on the certificate) in regard to the places at which or the special conditions under which the picture may be exhibited or the classes of persons who may be admitted to an exhibition of the picture as in the opinion of the Official Censor are necessary to prevent the exhibition of the picture in public being subversive of public morality.

(4) Whenever the Official Censor is of opinion that part only of any picture in respect of which an application is made to him under this section is unfit for exhibition in public he shall indicate such part to the person making such application and there upon such person may either (a) separate such part from the picture and surrender it to

the Official Censor, who shall retain it in his possession and grant a certificate for the picture with the omission of such part, or (b) may regard the decision of the Official Censor as a refusal to grant a certificate and may appeal in the prescribed manner to the Appeal Board.

(5) Whenever the Official Censor refuses to grant a certificate under this section he shall record such refusal in the prescribed manner.

Amendment History

Section 2 of the Censorship of Films (Amendment) Act 1970 is applied to s.7.

Right of appeal to the Appeal Board

8.—(1) Any person aggrieved by a decision of the Official Censor refusing to grant a certificate under this Act or attaching any restrictions or conditions to such certificate may appeal in the prescribed manner from such decision to the Appeal Board, and on the hearing of such appeal the Appeal Board may affirm, reverse or vary the decision of the Official Censor.

(2) When notice of an appeal under this section has been given the Official Censor shall furnish to the Appeal Board his reasons in writing for the decision appealed against, and shall furnish on payment of the prescribed fees, copies of such reasons to every person who is entitled to appear and be heard at the hearing of such appeal.

(3) The Appeal Board shall not have power to grant any certificate under this Act, but shall as soon as may be after the hearing of an appeal communicate its decision thereon to the Official Censor and thereupon the Official Censor shall grant or withhold a certificate in accordance with such decision.

(4) The decision of the Appeal Board shall be final.

Amendment History

Section 8 amended non-textually by s.3(3) of the Censorship of Films (Amendment) Act 1925.

Meaning of exhibition of a picture

9.—For the purposes of this Act the exhibition of a picture in respect of which a certificate has been granted by the Official Censor under this Act means the exhibition of such picture by means of a film produced, directly or indirectly, either from the negative from which the film by means of which such picture was exhibited to the Official Censor was produced or from a negative from which the first mentioned negative was itself, directly or indirectly, produced, and the exhibition of a picture by means of a film produced in any other manner shall not for the purposes of this Act be an exhibition of the picture in respect of which such certificate was given.

Amendment of the Cinematograph Act, 1909

10.—(1) It shall not be lawful for the Council of any County, A County Borough or Urban District, or for any Town Commissioners after the passing of this Act to attach to any licence granted under the Cinematograph Act, 1909, any condition or restriction as to the character or nature of the pictures to be exhibited in the premises to which such licence refers.

(2) Every condition or restriction attached before the passing of this Act to a licence granted by the Council of a County, County Borough or Urban District or by any Town Commissioners under the Cinematograph Act, 1909, in relation to the character or nature of the pictures to be exhibited in the premises to which such licence refers, shall, as from the passing of this Act, be void and such licence shall have effect as if such conditions and restrictions were deleted therefrom on the date of the passing of this Act.

Fees to be charged by Official Censor and Appeal Board

11.—(1) There shall be charged in respect of applications to the Official Censor, and the granting or refusal by him of certificates, and in respect of other acts done by him in the execution of his duties under this Act, such fees as the Minister, with the sanction of the Minister for Finance, shall from time to time fix.

(2) There shall also be charged, in respect of appeals to the Appeal Board, and in respect of acts done by the Appeal Board in the execution of its duties under this Act, such fees as the Minister, with the sanction of the Minister for Finance, shall from time to time fix.

(3) The fees to be charged under this section shall be arranged, from time to time, so as to produce as nearly as may be an annual sum sufficient to discharge the salaries and other expenses incidental to the working of this Act.

[(4) Where, pursuant to section 8 (1) of this Act, the Appeal Board either reverses a decision of the Official Censor or varies such a decision by relaxing or removing a restriction or condition attached to a limited certificate, the fee paid in respect of the appeal pursuant to subsection (2) of this section shall be refunded to the appellant concerned.]

Amendment History

Section 11(4) inserted by s.3 of the Censorship of films (amendment) Act 1992.

Minister may make regulations

12.—(1) The Minister for Home Affairs may by order, from time to time, make, and when made vary and revoke regulations for carrying into effect the objects of this Act, and in particular for regulating the conduct of the office of the Official Censor, the making of applications to him, the granting of certificates by him, and the bringing of appeals to the Appeal Board.

(2) Every regulation made by the Minister under this section shall be laid before each House of the Oireachtas as soon as may be after it is made, and if a resolution is passed by each House of the Oireachtas within the next subsequent twenty-one days on which either House has sat annulling such regulation, such regulation shall be annulled accordingly, but without prejudice to the validity of anything previously done under such regulation.

(3) If any such regulation requires a declaration to be made for any purpose, a person who makes such declaration, knowing the same to be untrue in any material particular, shall be guilty of a misdemeanour.

(4) (*note: repealed by s.5 of the Censorship of Films (Amendment) Act 1992*).

Amendment History

Section 12 amended non-textually by s.7 of the Censorship of Films (Amendment) Act 1925. Section 12 amended non-textually by s.3 of the Censorship of Films (Amendment) Act 1930. Subsection 4 repealed by s.5 of the Censorship of Films (Amendment) Act 1992.

Definitions

13.—In this Act whenever the context so admits or requires the expression—
"Official Censor" means the Official Censor of Films appointed under this Act;
The expression "Appeal Board" means the Censorship of Films Appeal Board appointed under this Act;
The expression "limited certificate" means a certificate granted by the Official Censor under this Act containing a condition or restriction as to the places at which, or the special conditions under which or the persons before whom the picture to which such certificate relates may be exhibited, and the expression "general certificate" means any such certificate not containing any such condition or restriction;
The word "picture" includes any optical effect produced by means of a cinematograph or similar apparatus;
The expression "in public" means at any exhibition, show or entertainment to which the public are admitted, whether on payment or otherwise, and includes any exhibition, show or entertainment to which only a particular class of the public specified in a limited certificate are admitted;
The word "Minister" means the Minister for Home Affairs;
The word "prescribed" means prescribed by regulations made under this Act.

Short Title

14.—This Act may be cited as the Censorship of Films Act, 1923.

CENSORSHIP OF FILMS (AMENDMENT) ACT 1925

(No. 21 of 1925)

ARRANGEMENT OF SECTIONS

AN ACT TO PROVIDE FOR THE CONTROL OF PICTORIAL ADVERTISEMENTS OF CINEMATOGRAPH PICTURES AND FOR THAT AND OTHER PURPOSES TO AMEND THE CENSORSHIP OF FILMS ACT, 1923.

[27TH JUNE, 1925.]

BE IT ENACTED BY THE OIREACHTAS OF SAORSTÁT EIREANN AS FOLLOWS:

Definitions

1.—In this Act—

the expression "Principal Act" means the Censorship of Films Act, 1923 (No. 23 of 1923);

the expression "display in public" means display in any street, way, or place, whether enclosed or unenclosed, through or to which the public have an unrestricted right of passage or access or in any place, enclosed or unenclosed to which the public have ,access of right or by permission either generally or at specified times and whether such access is or is not subject to payment or other restriction, and all cognate expressions shall be construed accordingly;

the expression "exploitation sheet" means the document commonly known by that name amongst persons engaged in the trade of exhibiting pictures by means of a cinematograph or other similar apparatus or the making, distribution, or renting of such pictures.

Advertisement by extract from picture

2.—(1) It shall not be lawful for any person to display in public in relation to the exhibition of a picture by means of a cinematograph or other similar apparatus any photographic or other reproduction of any part of such picture unless such including the part thereof so reproduced, has been certified by the Official Censor to be fit for exhibition in public.

(2) Every person who displays in public in contravention of this section any such photographic or other reproduction as aforesaid shall be guilty of an offence under this section and shall be liable on summary conviction thereof to a fine not exceeding fifty pounds and, in the case of a continuing offence, to a further fine not exceeding five pounds for every, day on which the offence continues.

Prohibition of certain advertisements

3.—(1) Every application to the Official Censor for a certificate under the Principal Act shall be accompanied by a copy of the exploitation sheet relating to the picture in respect of which the application is made.

(2) Whenever the Official Censor is of opinion that any pictorial poster, card, handbill, or other pictorial advertisement mentioned in any such exploitation sheet as aforesaid is unfit for display in public by reason of its being indecent, obscene, or blasphemous, or because the display thereof in public would convey suggestions contrary to public morality or would be otherwise subversive of public morality, he shall prohibit the display in public of such pictorial advertisement and shall record such prohibition in the prescribed manner.

(3) Section 8 (which relates to appeals from the Official Censor to the Appeal Board) of the Principal Act shall apply to prohibitions by the Official Censor under this section of the display in public of a pictorial advertisement in like manner in all respects as it applies to the decisions of the official censor mentioned in that section, and every mention or reference contained in the Principal Act of or to appeals to the Appeal Board shall be construed and take effect as including appeals under the said section 8 as applied by this sub-section.

Offences in relation to prohibited advertisements

4.—(1) Every person who shall display or cause to be displayed in public any pictorial poster, card, handbill, or other pictorial advertisement the display of which in public has been prohibited under this Act by the Official Censor shall be guilty of an offence under this section unless he establishes to the satisfaction of the court either that he did not know and could not reasonably have known of such prohibition or that he was informed by the person from whom he obtained the advertisement that no such prohibition existed.

(2) Every person who sells to another person for the purpose of display in public any pictorial poster, card, handbill or other pictorial advertisement the display of which in public has been prohibited under this Act by the Official Censor and does not at the time of the sale inform such other person of such prohibition shall be guilty of an offence under this section.

(3) Every person who is guilty of an offence under this section shall on summary conviction thereof be liable to a fine not exceeding fifty pounds, and in the case of a continuing offence to a further fine of five pounds for every day during which the offence continues.

Prohibition of exhibition of certain certificates

5.—(1) It shall not be lawful for any person to exhibit or cause to be exhibited with or in relation to any picture exhibited by means of a cinematograph or other similar apparatus any certificates (other than a certificate granted by the Official Censor under the Principal Act) purporting to authorise the exhibition of such picture

(2) Every person who exhibits or causes to be exhibited in contravention of this section any such certificate as aforesaid shall be guilty of an offence under this section and shall be liable on summary conviction thereof to a fine not exceeding twenty-five pounds.

Quorum, etc, of appeal board

6.—Sub-section (6) of section 3 of the Principal Act shall have effect subject to the following modifications, that is to say:—

(a) three members of the appeal board personally present shall form a quorum for the hearing of appeals;

(b) an appeal shall be re-heard whenever the majority mentioned in the said sub-section is less than three or the members present are equally divided;

(c) every re-hearing shall be in the presence of not less than five members of the appeal board.

Punishment for contravention of regulations

7.—(1) The Minister for Justice may by regulations made by him under section 12 of the Principal Act do all or any of the following things, that is to say:—

(a) declare the contravention of all or any regulations made under section 12 of the Principal Act to be an offence under such regulations and authorise the trial by courts of summary jurisdiction of persons charged with having committed any such offence;

(b) prescribe the punishments which may be inflicted by courts of summary jurisdiction on persons convicted by such courts of an offence against the said regulations or any of them, so, however, that no punishment so prescribed shall exceed a fine of twenty-five pounds or imprisonment for a term of three months, and that no minimum punishment shall be so prescribed;

(c) regulate the procedure of the appeal board in relation to the bearing of appeals.

(2) The several provisions of section 12 of the Principal Act in relation to regulations made thereunder shall apply to regulations made under that section by virtue of this section.

Short title, construction and citation

8.—(1) This Act may be cited as the Censorship of Films (Amendment) Act, 1925.

(2) This Act shall be construed as one with the Principal Act, and that Act and this Act may be cited to,-other as the Censorship of Films Acts, 1923 and 1925.

CENSORSHIP OF FILMS (AMENDMENT) ACT 1930

(No. 23 of 1930)

ARRANGEMENT OF SECTIONS

AN ACT TO EXTEND THE CENSORSHIP OF FILMS ACTS, 1923 AND 1925, TO VOCAL OR OTHER SOUNDS PRODUCED BY MECHANICAL MEANS AS AN ACCOMPANIMENT TO AND IN SYNCHRONISATION WITH CINEMATOGRAPH PICTURES.

[4TH JUNE, 1930.]

BE IT ENACTED BY THE OIREACHTAS OF SAORSTÁT EIREANN AS FOLLOWS:

The Principal and Amending Acts

1.—In this Act—

the expression "the Principal Act" means the Censorship of Films Act, 1923 (No. 23 of 1923); and

the expression "the Amending Act" means the Censorship of Films (Amendment) Act, 1925 (No. 21 of 1925).

Extension of existing legislation to sounds accompanying pictures

2.—(1) Where a picture within the meaning of The Principal Act is accompanied by vocal or other sounds produced by mechanical means in synchronisation with the optical effect constituting such picture, then for the purposes of the application and construction of The Principal Act and the Amending Act respectively to and in relation to such picture the following provisions shall have effect, that is to say:—

(a) the said vocal or other sounds shall be deemed to be included in and to form part of such picture;

(b) the mechanical means by which such sounds are produced shall be deemed to be part of the cinematograph or similar apparatus by means of which such picture is exhibited;

(c) the exhibition of such picture shall include the production of the said sounds; and

(d) references to a film and to a negative shall be construed as including respectively references to a record from which such sounds are produced and to a matrix from which such record is made.

Excision of part of a picture

3.—Regulations made under section 12 of the Principal Act may make such provision as the Minister for Justice shall think proper in relation to the separation, surrender and retention under paragraph (a) of sub-section (4) of section 7 of the Principal Act of parts of pictures which include sounds produced by mechanical means and may in lieu of such separation, surrender and retention authorise any specified procedure which in the opinion of the Minister for Justice is a satisfactory and efficient substitute for such separation, surrender and retention.

Short title, construction and citation

4.—(1) This Act may be cited as the Censorship of Films (Amendment) Act, 1930.

(2) This Act shall be construed as one with The Principal Act and the Amending Act, and those Acts and this Act may be cited together as the Censorship of Films Acts, 1923 to 1930.

CENSORSHIP OF FILMS (AMENDMENT) ACT 1970

(No. 7 of 1970)

ARRANGEMENT OF SECTIONS

AN ACT TO AMEND AND EXTEND THE CENSORSHIP OF FILMS ACTS, 1923 TO 1930.

[9TH JUNE, 1970.]

BE IT ENACTED BY THE OIREACHTAS AS FOLLOWS:

Interpretation

1.—In this Act—
"the Acts" means the Censorship of Films Acts, 1923 to 1930;
"the Principal Act" means the Censorship of Films Act, 1923.

Application of Acts to pictures previously considered by Official Censor

2.—(1) Where an application is made under section 7 of the Principal Act in respect of a picture which was the subject of a decision of the Official Censor under that section or, if there was an appeal from that decision, a decision of the Appeal Board under section 8 of that Act and the decision, or, if there was more than one decision, the latest decision, was made before the 18th day of January, 1965, or not less than seven years before the date of the application—

(a) the application shall be entertained and decided by the Official Censor,

(b) any appeal to the Appeal Board from the decision of the Official Censor shall be entertained and decided by the Appeal Board, and

(c) a certificate under the Principal Act shall, if the person who brought the application so requests, be granted or withheld or the grant thereof shall be refused, in accordance with the decision of the Official Censor or the Appeal Board, as the case may be, as if the picture had not been the subject of a decision under the said section 7 or the said section 8 before the date of the application, and the Acts shall apply and have effect accordingly.

(2) Where a certificate under the Principal Act is granted or withheld or the grant thereof is refused in respect of a picture, any previous such certificate or refusal or withholding in respect of the picture shall cease to have effect.

Short title, construction and collective citation

3.—(1) This Act may be cited as the Censorship of Films (Amendment) Act, 1970.

(2) This Act shall be construed as one with the Acts and may be cited together therewith as the Censorship of Films Acts, 1923 to 1970.

CENSORSHIP OF FILMS (AMENDMENT) ACT 1992

ARRANGEMENT OF SECTIONS

(No. 35 of 1992)

ACTS REFERRED TO

Censorship of Films Act, 1923	1923, No. 23
Censorship of Films (Amendment) Act, 1970	1970, No. 7
Censorship of Films Acts, 1923 to 1970	
Video Recordings Act, 1989	1989, No. 22

AN ACT TO ENABLE THE MINISTER FOR JUSTICE TO APPOINT PERSONS TO BE KNOWN AS ASSISTANT CENSORS TO ASSIST THE OFFICIAL CENSOR OF FILMS IN THE PERFORMANCE OF HIS FUNCTIONS AND TO AMEND THE CENSORSHIP OF FILMS ACTS, 1923 TO 1970, AND THE VIDEO RECORDINGS ACT, 1989.

[21st December, 1992]

BE IT ENACTED BY THE OIREACHTAS AS FOLLOWS:

Definitions

1.—In this Act—

"the Act of 1923" means the Censorship of Films Act, 1923;

"the Act of 1989" means the Video Recordings Act, 1989;

"the Appeal Board" means the Censorship of Films Appeal Board established by the Act of 1923;

"functions" includes powers and duties and references to the performance of functions include, as respects powers and duties, references to the exercise of the powers and the carrying out of the duties;

"the Minister" means the Minister for Justice;

"the Official Censor" means the Official Censor of Films appointed under the Act of 1923 and includes a person appointed under section 2 (3) of that Act.

Appointment of Assistant Censors

2.—(1)(a) The Minister may as occasion requires appoint such, and such number of, persons (who shall be known as Assistant Censors) as he may determine to assist the Official Censor in the performance of his functions and for that purpose to perform, or to perform to such extent as the Official Censor may, subject to any directions that may be given to him by the Minister, determine, the functions (or such of them as the Official Censor may, subject as aforesaid, determine) of the Official Censor.

(b) The references in paragraph (a) of this subsection to the functions of the Official Censor do not include references to his functions under section 2 of the Censorship of Films (Amendment) Act, 1970, or section 4 (3), 7 (3) or 29 of the Act of 1989.

(2) An Assistant Censor shall perform his functions subject to the general superintendence of the Official Censor and shall consult with him from time to time in relation to such performance, and a function of the Official Censor performed pursuant to this Act by an Assistant Censor shall be deemed for the purposes of the Censorship of Films Acts, 1923 to 1992, and the Act of 1989 to have been performed by the Official Censor and those Acts shall be construed and have effect accordingly.

(3) If an Assistant Censor is appointed under section 2 (3) of the Act of 1923 to perform the duties of the Official Censor, he shall cease during the period of his appointment under that section to be an Assistant Censor.

(4) An Assistant Censor shall be paid, out of moneys provided by the Oireachtas, such remuneration and such (if any) allowances for expenses as the Minister, with the consent of the Minister for Finance, may from time to time determine.

(5) An Assistant Censor shall hold office for such period and upon and subject to such terms and conditions as the Minister may determine.

Amendment of section 11 of Act of 1923

3.—Section 11 of the Act of 1923 is hereby amended by the insertion of the following subsection after subsection (3):

"(4) Where, pursuant to section 8 (1) of this Act, the Appeal Board either reverses a decision of the Official Censor or varies such a decision by relaxing or removing a restriction or condition attached to a limited certificate, the fee paid in respect of the appeal pursuant to subsection (2) of this section shall be refunded to the appellant concerned."

Amendment of section 10 of Act of 1989

4.—Section 10 of the Act of 1989 is hereby amended by the insertion of the following subsection after subsection (6):

"(7) Where the Appeal Board revokes a prohibition order pursuant to subsection (1) of this section or directs that the video work concerned be given a higher classification pursuant to subsection (2) of this section, the fee paid in respect of the appeal pursuant to subsection (6) of this section shall be refunded to the appellant concerned."

Repeal

5.—Subsection (4) of section 12 of the Act of 1923 is hereby repealed.

Short title, collective citation and commencement

6.—(1) This Act may be cited as the Censorship of Films (Amendment) Act, 1992.

(2) The Censorship of Films Acts, 1923 to 1970, and this Act, in so far as it relates to those Acts, may be cited together as the Censorship of Films Acts, 1923 to 1992, and the Act of 1989 and this Act, in so far as it relates to that Act, may be cited together as the Video Recordings Acts, 1989 and 1992.

(3) This Act shall come into operation on such day or days as may be fixed therefor by order or orders of the Minister either generally or with reference to any particular purpose or provision and different days may be so fixed for different purposes and different provisions.

IRISH FILM BOARD ACT 1980

(No. 36 of 1980)

ARRANGEMENT OF SECTIONS

AN ACT TO PROVIDE FOR THE ESTABLISHMENT OF A BOARD (TO BE KNOWN AS THE IRISH FILM BOARD) TO ASSIST AND ENCOURAGE THE DEVELOPMENT OF A FILM INDUSTRY IN THE STATE, TO EMPOWER THE BOARD TO PROVIDE INVESTMENTS, GRANTS, LOANS AND GUARANTEES OF LOANS FOR THE MAKING OF FILMS IN THE STATE, TO DEFINE ITS OTHER POWERS AND FUNCTIONS AND TO PROVIDE FOR OTHER CONNECTED MATTERS.

[17TH DECEMBER, 1980]

BE IT ENACTED BY THE OIREACHTAS AS FOLLOWS:

Interpretation

1.—(1) In this Act—

"the Board" means the Irish Film Board established by section 3 of this Act;

"the establishment day" means the day appointed to be the establishment day for the purposes of this Act by order of the Minister under section 2 of this Act;

"film" means a motion picture;

"functions" includes powers and duties;

"the Minister" means the Minister for Industry, Commerce and Tourism.

(2) A reference in this Act to performance of functions includes, in relation to powers, a reference to exercise of those powers.

Establishment day

2.—The Minister may by order appoint a day to be the establishment day for the purposes of this Act.

Establishment of Board

3.—(1) There shall by virtue of this section be establised on the establishment day a board to be known as the Irish Film Board.

(2) The Board shall be a body corporate with perpetual succession and power to sue and be sued in its corporate name.

Amendment History

Section 3 name change amended by s.1 of the Irish Film Board (Amendment) Act 1997.

General functions of Board

4.—(1) In addition and without prejudice to any specific functions given to it by this Act, the Board shall assist and encourage by any means it considers appropriate the making of films in the State and the development of an industry in the State for the making of films, and may engage in any other activity (including the establishment of a national film archive) which it is empowered by this Act to engage in.

(2) In so far as it considers it appropriate, the Board shall have regard to the need for the expression of national culture through the medium of film-making.

(3) The Board shall have all such powers as are necessary for or incidental to the performance of its functions.

(4) Without prejudice to the generality of subsections (1) and (3) of this section, the Board shall have power to participate and promote participation in international collaborative projects in accordance with any of its functions under this Act and, where appropriate, to enter into agreements with comparable bodies outside the State, subject to the consent of the Minister and the Minister for Finance and, where appropriate, to consultation with the Minister for Foreign Affairs.

Grants to Board

5.—The Minister, with the consent of the Minister for Finance, may from time to time make, out of moneys provided by the Oireachtas, grants to the Board to enable it to perform its functions and to meet its administrative and general expenses.

Assistance by Board for making of films in the State

6.—(1) The Board may invest in, or make a loan or a grant to defray in whole or in part the cost of the making of, a film wholly or partly made in the State.

(2) The making of an investment, loan or grant under this section shall be subject to such terms and conditions as the Board may think proper, including terms and conditions relating to the repayment to the Board of any moneys paid by it and payment of interest on any such money.

Guarantees by Board regarding films made in the State

7.—(1) The Board may guarantee the due repayment of the principal of any moneys borrowed for the making of a film wholly or partly made in the State or the repayment of interest on such moneys, or both the repayment of the principal and the payment of such interest, and may, in accordance with its general functions specified in section 4 of this Act, provide other financial guarantees in respect of the making of such a film.

(2) A guarantee under this section shall be in such form and manner and on such terms and conditions as may be specified in a general scheme governing the giving of such guarantees sanctioned by the Minister, with the consent of the Minister for Finance.

(3) Moneys required by the Board to meet sums which may become payable by the Board under a guarantee shall be paid out of the grants provided to the Board under section 5 of this Act.

Grants by Board for training and other activities

8.—(1) The Board may, subject to such terms as it thinks proper, make grants to be used to defray in whole or in part the cost of providing training for persons in all aspects of the making of films.

(2) The Board may provide moneys, subject to such terms as it thinks proper, for general activities in accordance with its general functions specified in section 4 of this Act.

Contravention of term or condition of investment, loan, grant or guarantee

9.—Where a term or condition subject to which an investment, grant, loan or guarantee made or given by the Board under this Act is contravened by the person to whom or on whose behalf the investment, grant, loan or guarantee is made or given, any amount owed to the Board in respect of the investment, grant, loan or guarantee (together with the interest payable on it) shall, if the Board requests repayment of the whole or part of the amount, be deemed, to the extent of the request, to be a debt payable forthwith to the Board and may, to that extent, be recovered by it as a simple contract debt in any court of competent jurisdiction.

Maximum amount of investments, loans grants, etc. by Board

10.—The aggregate amount of any investments, loans, grants or moneys provided by the Board under sections 6 and 8 of this Act, together with the aggregate amount of principal and interest which the Board may at any one time be liable to repay on foot of any guarantee under section 7 of this Act for the time being in force, together with the amount of principal and interest (if any) which the Board has previously paid on foot of any guarantees and which has not been repaid to the Board, shall not exceed [£80,000,000].

Amendment History

Section 10 amended by s.1 of the Irish Film Board (Amendment) Act 2000.

Temporary borrowing by Board

11.—The Board may, with the consent of the Minister, given with the approval of the Minister for Finance, borrow temporarily, either by arrangement with bankers or otherwise, such sums as it may require for the purpose of providing for current expenditure.

Members of Board

12.—(1) The members of the Board shall be appointed by the Minister, with the consent of the Minister for Finance, for such period not exceeding four years as the Minister may determine, and shall not be more than seven in number.

(2) A member of the Board whose term expires by effluxion of time shall be eligible for re-appointment.

(3) A member of the Board may resign his office by letter sent to the Minister and the resignation shall, unless previously withdrawn in writing, take effect at the commencement of the meeting of the Board held next after the Board has been informed by the Minister of the resignation.

(4) A member of the Board shall be paid, out of funds at the disposal of the Board, such remuneration and allowances for expenses as the Minister, with the approval of the Minister for the Public Service, may determine.

(5) A member of the Board shall be disqualified from holding and shall cease to hold office if he is adjudicated a bankrupt or makes a composition or arrangement with creditors or is sentenced by a court of competent jurisdiction.

(6) The Minister, with the consent of the Minister for Finance, may at any time remove a member of the Board from office.

Chairman of Board

13.—(1) The Minister may, from time to time as occasion requires, with the consent of the Minister for Finance, appoint a member of the Board to be chairman of the Board.

(2) The chairman of the Board may at any time resign his office as chairman by letter sent to the Minister, and the resignation shall, unless previously withdrawn in writing, take effect at the commencement of the meeting of the Board held next after the Board has been informed by the Minister of the resignation.

(3) Where the chairman of the Board ceases during his term of office as chairman to be a member of the Board, he shall also cease to be its chairman.

Seal of Board

14.—(1) The Board shall as soon as practicable after its establishment provide itself with a seal.

(2) The seal of the Board shall, when applied to a document, be attested by the signature of two members or by the signature of a member and an officer or servant of the Board authorised by it to act in that behalf.

(3) Judicial notice shall be taken of the seal of the Board, and every document purporting to be an instrument made by the Board and to be sealed with the seal (purporting to be authenticated in accordance with this section) of the Board shall be received in evidence and be deemed to be such instrument without further proof unless the contrary is shown.

Meetings and procedure of Board

15.—(1) The Board shall hold such and so many meetings as may be necessary for the due fulfilment of its functions.

(2) The first meeting of the Board shall be held on or as soon as practicable after the establishment day.

(3) At a meeting of the Board—

(a) the chairman of the Board shall, if present, be chairman of the meeting;

(b) if and so long as the chairman of the Board is not present or if the office of chairman is vacant, the members of the Board present shall choose one of their number to be chairman of the meeting.

(4) Every question at a meeting of the Board shall be determined by a majority of the votes of the members present and voting on the question, and in the case of an equal division of votes, the chairman of the meeting shall have a second or casting vote.

(5) The Board may act notwithstanding one or more vacancies among its members.

(6) Subject to this Act, the Board shall regulate its procedure by rules or otherwise.

(7) The quorum for a meeting of the Board shall, unless the Minister directs otherwise, be three.

Committees of Board

16.—(1) The Board may from time to time establish committees to advise it in relation to the performance of its functions and to perform any functions of the Board which, in the opinion of the Board, may be better or more conveniently performed by a committee and are assigned to a committee by the Board.

(2) A committee established under this section may, if the Board thinks fit, include in its membership persons who are not members of the Board.

(3) The appointment of a person to act as a member of a committee established under this section shall be subject to such conditions (including conditions in relation to the term and tenure of office of the member) as the Board may think fit to impose when making the appointment.

(4) A member of a committee established under this section may be removed from office at any time by the Board.

(5) The Board may at any time dissolve a committee appointed under this section.

(6) The acts of a committee established under this section shall be subject to confirmation by the Board unless the Board dispenses with the necessity for confirmation.

(7) The Board may regulate the procedure of committees established under this section, but, subject to any such regulation, committees established under this section may regulate their own procedure.

Disclosure by member of Board or committee of interest

17.—(1) A member of the Board whose interests may be affected directly or indirectly by a decision of the Board in relation to any matter before the Board, shall, before the matter is discussed by the Board, disclose to it the fact and the nature of the interest, and the disclosure shall be recorded in the minutes of the Board.

(2) A member of a committee established by the Board whose interests may be affected directly or indirectly by a decision of the committee in relation to any matter

before the committee, shall, before the matter is discussed by the committee, disclose to it the fact and the nature of the interest, and the disclosure shall be recorded in the minutes of the committee.

Non-disclosure of information

18.—A member or officer or servant of the Board or a member of a committee established by the Board shall not disclose any information obtained by him in the performance of his functions except in so far as may be necessary for the performance of those functions.

Amendment History

Section 18 is saved from disclosure by s.32 and Sched.3 to the Freedom of Information Act 1997.

Making of contracts on behalf of Board by authorised persons

19.—Any contract or instrument which, if entered into or executed by an individual, would not require to be under seal may be entered into or executed on behalf of the Board by any person generally or specially authorised by the Board for that purpose.

Accounts and audits

20.—(1) The Board shall keep, in such form as may be approved of by the Minister, with the consent of the Minister for Finance, all proper and usual accounts of all moneys received or expended by it and, in particular, shall keep in such form all such special accounts as the Minister with such consent may from time to time direct.

(2) Accounts kept in pursuance of this section shall be submitted by the Board to the Comptroller and Auditor General annually for audit at such times as the Minister, with the concurrence of the Minister for Finance, directs and shall be the subject of a report by the Comptroller and Auditor General.

(3) As soon as practicable after audit under this section of the accounts of the Board the accounts as so audited and a copy of the Comptroller and Auditor General's report on the accounts shall be presented to the Minister, who shall cause a copy of the accounts as so audited and of the report to be laid before each House of the Oireachtas.

Annual report and information for Minister

21.—(1) The Board shall, in each year at such date as the Minister may direct, make a report of its proceedings during the preceding twelve months ending on that date, and the Board shall, within 90 days after such date or such longer period at the Minister shall in any particular case allow furnish the report to the Minister, who shall cause copies of the report to be laid before each House of the Oireachtas.

(2) The Board shall supply the Minister with such information as he may from time to time require.

Power to engage consultants and advisers

22.—The Board may engage the services of such consultants and advisers as it may think proper for the purpose of discharging its functions under this Act.

Donations

23.—(1) The Board may accept gifts of money, land or other property, on such trusts and conditions (if any) as may be specified by the person making the gift.

(2) The Board shall not accept any gift if the conditions attached by the donor to the acceptance of the gift are inconsistent with the functions of the Board.

(3) Any funds of the Board which are a gift or the proceeds of a gift to it may subject to any terms or conditions of the gift, be invested by the Board in any manner in which a trustee is empowered by law to invest trust funds.

Investment by Board

24.—The Board may invest any of its funds (other than funds referred to in section 23 of this Act) in any manner in which a trustee is empowered by law to invest trust funds.

Disposal of profits etc by Board

25.—Any profits or other moneys received by the Board in the exercise of its functions shall be disposed of in such manner (including application for the benefit of the Exchequer) as the Minister, with the consent of the Minister for Finance, may direct.

Acquisition and disposal of land and provision of offices

26.—For the purpose of the performance of its functions the Board may—

(a) acquire by agreement any land or any easement, wayleave or other right in respect of land,

(b) dispose of any land vested in it which it no longer requires, and

(c) provide, equip and maintain offices or other premises.

Officers and servants

[27.—(1) The Board may appoint such and such number of persons to be officers and servants of the Board as it may, with the consent of the Minister and the Minister for Finance, determine.

(2) An officer or servant of the Board shall be paid, out of moneys at the disposal of the Board, such remuneration and allowances for expenses incurred by such officer or servant as the Board may, with the consent of the Minister and the Minister for Finance, determine.

(3) An officer or servant of the Board shall hold office or employment on such terms and conditions as the Board may, with the consent of the Minister and the Minister for Finance, determine.

(4) The grades of the officers and servants of the Board and the numbers in each grade shall be determined by the Board with the consent of the Minister and the Minister for Finance.

(5) The Board may at any time remove an officer or servant of the Board from being its officer or servant.

Remuneration, etc., of officers and servants

27A.—(1). Without prejudice to section 27 of this Act, in determining the remuneration or allowances for expenses to be paid to its officers and servants or the other terms or conditions subject to which such officers and servants hold or are to hold their employment, the Board shall have regard to any nationally agreed guidelines and Government policy concerning remuneration and conditions of employment for the time being in existence.

(2) The Board shall comply with any directives with regard to the remuneration or allowances for expenses to be paid to its officers and servants or the other terms or conditions subject to which they hold or are to hold their employment as the Minister, with the consent of the Minister for Finance, may give.]

Amendment History

Section 27 substituted and s.27A inserted by s.3 of the Irish Film Board (Amendment) Act 1997.

Superannuation of officers and servants of Board

28.—(1) The Board shall prepare and submit to the Minister a contributory scheme or schemes for the granting of pensions, gratuities and other allowances on retirement or death to or in respect of such wholetime officers or servants of the Board as it may think fit.

(2) Every such scheme shall fix the time and conditions of retirement for all persons to or in respect of whom pensions, gratuities or allowances on retirement are payable under the scheme, and different times and conditions may be fixed in respect of different classes of persons.

(3) The Board may at any time prepare and submit to the Minister a scheme amending a scheme previously submitted and approved of under this section.

(4) A scheme submitted to the Minister under this section shall, if approved of by the Minister with the concurrence of the Minister for the Public Service, be carried out by the Board in accordance with its terms.

(5) If any dispute arises as to the claim of any person to, or the amount of, any pension, gratuity or allowance payable in pursuance of a scheme under this section, the dispute shall be submitted to the Minister, who shall refer it to the Minister for the Public Service, whose decision shall be final.

(6) Every scheme submitted and approved of under this section shall be laid before each House of the Oireachtas as soon as may be after it is approved of and if either House, within the next 21 days on which that House has sat after the scheme is

laid before it, passes a resolution annulling the scheme, the scheme shall be annulled accordingly, but without prejudice to the validity of anything done under it.

(7) No pension, gratuity or other allowance shall be granted to officers or servants of the Board, nor shall any other arrangement be entered into for the provision of a pension, gratuity or other allowance to such persons on ceasing to hold office, other than in accordance with a scheme or schemes submitted and approved of under this section.

Membership of either House of the Oireachtas

29.—(1) Where a member of the Board is nominated either as a candidate for election to either House of the Oireachtas or as a member of Seanad Éireann he shall on nomination cease to be a member of the Board.

(2) A person who is for the time being entitled under the Standing Orders of either House of the Oireachtas to sit in that House shall, while so entitled, be disqualified from becoming a member of the Board.

(3) Where a person who is either an officer or servant of the Board is nominated as a member of Seanad Éireann or for election to either House of the Oireachtas, he shall stand seconded from employment by the Board and shall not be paid by, or be entitled to receive from, the Board any remuneration or allowances—

(a) in case he is nominated as a member of Seanad Éireann, in respect of the period commencing on his acceptance of the nomination and ending when he ceases to be a member of that House;

(b) in case he is nominated for election to either such House, in respect of the period commencing on his nomination and ending when he ceases to be a member of that House or fails to be elected or withdraws his candidature, as may be appropriate.

(4) A person who is for the time being entitled under the Standing Orders of either House of the Oireachtas to sit therein shall, while so entitled, be disqualified from becoming an officer or servant of the Board.

(5) If a person who is or was an officer or servant of the Board becomes a member of either House of the Oireachtas or becomes entitled under the Standing Orders of either House of the Oireachtas to sit therein, he shall while he is such a member or while so entitled be disqualified from reckoning the period of membership or entitlement for any superannuation benefits payable under a scheme or schemes made in accordance with section 28 of this Act.

Membership of Assembly of European Communities

30.—(1) Where a member of the Board is nominated as a candidate for election to, or appointed to be a member of, the Assembly of the European Communities, he shall on such nomination or appointment, as may be appropriate, cease to be a member of the Board.

(2) A person who is for the time being a member of the Assembly of the European Communities shall be disqualified from becoming a member of the Board.

(3) Where a person who is either an officer or servant of the Board is nominated as a candidate for election to, or appointed to be a member of, the Assembly of the European Communities, he shall stand seconded from employment by the Board and shall not be paid by, or be entitled to receive from, the Board any remuneration and allowances—

(a) in case he is nominated as a candidate for election to that Assembly, in respect of the period commencing on his acceptance of the nomination and ending when he ceases to be a member of that Assembly or fails to be elected or withdraws his candidature, as may be appropriate;

(b) in case he is appointed to be a member of that Assembly, in respect of the period commencing on his appointment and ending when he ceases to be such a member.

(4) A person who is for the time being a member of the Assembly of the European Communities shall be disqualified from becoming an officer or servant of the Board.

(5) If a person who is or was an officer or servant of the Board becomes a member of the Assembly of the European Communities he shall while he is such a member be disqualified from reckoning the period of membership for any superannuation benefits payable under a scheme or schemes made in accordance with section 28 of this Act.

Directives to Board by Minister

31.—(1) The Minister may from time to time give to the Board such general directives concerning the performance of its functions as he considers appropriate, and the Board shall comply with the directives.
(2) A directive under this section shall not relate to any artistic aspect of a film.

Performance of functions of Board by officers or servants

32.—The Board may perform any of its functions through or by any of its officers or servants duly authorised by the Board in that behalf.

Exemption from stamp duty

33.—Stamp duty shall not be chargeable on any conveyance, transfer or other instrument executed for the purposes of vesting property or any interest in property in the Board.

Expenses

34.—Any expenses incurred by the Minister in the administration of this Act shall, to such extent as may be sanctioned by the Minister for Finance, be paid out of moneys provided by the Oireachtas.

Short title

35.—This Act may be cited as the Irish Film Board Act, 1980.

IRISH FILM BOARD (AMENDMENT) ACT 1993

(No. 36 of 1993)

ARRANGEMENT OF SECTIONS

AN ACT TO AMEND AND EXTEND THE IRISH FILM BOARD ACT 1980

[22ND DECEMBER 1993]

BE IT ENACTED BY THE OIREACHTAS AS FOLLOWS:

Amendment of section 10 of Irish Film Board Act 1980

1.—Section 10 of the Irish Film Board Act, 1980, is hereby amended by the substitution of "£15,000,000" for "£4,100,000" and the said section 10, as so amended, is set out in the Table to this section.

TABLE

The aggregate amount of any investments, loans, grants or moneys provided by the Board under sections 6 and 8 of this Act, together with the aggregate amount of principal and interest which the Board may at any one time be liable to repay on foot of any guarantee under section 7 of this Act for the time being in force, together with the amount of principal and interest (if any) which the Board has previously paid on foot of any guarantees and which has not been repaid to the Board, shall not exceed £15,000,000.

Short title and collective citation

2.—This Act may be cited as the Irish Film Board (Amendment) Act, 1993.

(2) The Irish Film Board Act, 1980, and this Act may be cited together as the Irish Film Board Acts, 1980 and 1993.

IRISH FILM BOARD (AMENDMENT) ACT 1997

(No. 44 of 1997)

ARRANGEMENT OF SECTIONS

ACTS REFERRED TO

Irish Film Board Act, 1980	1980 No. 36
Irish Film Board Acts, 1980 and 1993	
Irish Film Board (Amendment) Act, 1993	1993 No. 36

AN ACT TO AMEND AND EXTEND THE IRISH FILM BOARD ACT, 1980.

[18TH DECEMBER, 1997]

BE IT ENACTED BY THE OIREACHTAS AS FOLLOWS:

Bord Scannán na hÉireann

1.—(1) The Board established by section 3 of the Irish Film Board Act, 1980, shall, on and after the passing of this Act, be known as Bord Scannán na hÉireann or, in the English language, by the name specified in that section.

(2) The Board referred to in subsection (1) of this section may provide itself with a new seal under section 14 of the Irish Film Board Act, 1980.

Amendment of section 10 of Irish Film Board Act, 1980

2.—(*note: amendment applied to s.10 of Irish Film Board Act 1980*).

Officers and servants of Board and their remuneration, etc

3.—The Irish Film Board Act, 1980, is hereby amended by the substitution for section 27 of the following:
(*note: amendment applied to s.27 of the Irish Film Board Act 1980*).

Short title and collective citation

4.—(1) This Act may be cited as the Irish Film Board (Amendment) Act, 1997.

(2) The Irish Film Board Acts, 1980 and 1993, and this Act may be cited together as the Irish Film Board Acts, 1980 to 1997.

IRISH FILM BOARD (AMENDMENT) ACT 2000

(No. 35 of 2000)

ARRANGEMENT OF SECTIONS

ACTS REFERRED TO

Irish Film Board Act, 1980	No. 36 of 1980
Irish Film Board Acts, 1980 to 1997	
Irish Film Board (Amendment) Act, 1997	No. 44 of 1997

AN ACT TO AMEND AND EXTEND THE IRISH FILM BOARD ACT, 1980.

[15TH DECEMBER, 2000]

BE IT ENACTED BY THE OIREACHTAS AS FOLLOWS:

Amendment of section 10 of Irish Film Board Act, 1980

1.—(*note: Amendment applied to s.10 of Irish Film Board Act 1980*).

Short title and collective citation

2.—(1) This Act may be cited as the Irish Film Board (Amendment) Act, 2000.

(2) The Irish Film Board Acts, 1980 to 1997, and this Act may be cited together as the Irish Film Board Acts, 1980 to 2000.

NATIONAL FILM STUDIOS OF IRELAND LIMITED ACT 1980

(No. 37 of 1980)

ARRANGEMENT OF SECTIONS

AN ACT TO AUTHORISE THE MINISTER FOR FINANCE TO TAKE UP SHARES IN NATIONAL FILM STUDIOS OF IRELAND LIMITED, TO PROVIDE FOR THE GUARANTEEING OF BORROWINGS BY THE COMPANY AND TO PROVIDE FOR OTHER CONNECTED MATTERS.

[17th December, 1980]

BE IT ENACTED BY THE OIREACHTAS AS FOLLOWS:

Definitions

1.—In this Act—
"the Company" means National Film Studios of Ireland Limited;
"the Minister" means the Minister for Industry, Commerce and Tourism.

Share capital of Company

2.—Notwithstanding anything contained in the Companies Acts, 1963 and 1977, or in the memorandum or articles of association of the Company, the share capital of the Company shall be £2,000,000 divided into shares of £1 each, and the Company shall have power, with the consent of the Minister for Finance, to divide the shares in the capital of the Company into several classes and to attach thereto respectively any preferential, deferred, qualified or special rights, privileges or conditions.

Power of Minister for Finance to take up shares of Company

3.—(1) The Minister for Finance may, after consultation with the Minister, from time to time take up by subscription or purchase from the holder shares of the Company of any class or classes to an amount not exceeding in the aggregate £2,000,000.

(2) All moneys from time to time required after the passing of this Act by the Minister for Finance to meet payments required to be made by him in respect of any shares taken up or otherwise acquired by him shall be advanced out of the Central Fund or the growing produce thereof.

Holding and sale by Minister for Finance of shares of Company

4.—(1) The Minister for Finance may hold for so long as he thinks fit any shares of the Company taken up or acquired by him under this Act and, after consultation with the Minister, may as and when he thinks fit, sell all or any of such shares.

(2) The net proceeds of a sale by the Minister for Finance of shares of the Company shall be paid into or disposed of for the benefit of the Exchequer.

Exercise by Minister for Finance of right or power exercisable by holder of shares of Company

5.—Where the Minister for Finance holds shares of the Company, he may exercise a right or power exercisable by the holder of the shares and, where the right or power is exercisable by attorney, he may, if he so thinks proper, exercise it by his attorney.

Disposition of dividends, etc. on shares of Company held by Minister for Finance

6.—All dividends, bonus and other moneys received by the Minister for Finance in respect of shares of the Company held by him shall be paid into or disposed of for the benefit of the Exchequer.

Alteration of memorandum and articles of association of Company

7.—The Company shall take such steps as may be necessary under the Companies

Acts, 1963 and 1977, to alter the memorandum and articles of association of the Company to make them consistent with this Act.

Guarantee by Minister of borrowings by Company

8.—(1) The Minister, with the consent of the Minister for Finance, may guarantee, in such form and manner and on such terms and conditions as the Minister for Finance may sanction, the due repayment by the Company of the principal of any moneys (including moneys in a currency other than the currency of the State) borrowed by the Company, or the payment of interest on such moneys or both the repayment of the principal and the payment of the interest, and any such guarantee may include a guarantee of the payment by the Company of commission and incidental expenses arising in connection with such borrowings.

(2) The Minister shall not so exercise the powers conferred on him by this section that the amount, or the aggregate amount, of principal which he may at any one time be liable to repay on foot of any guarantee or guarantees under this section for the time being in force, together with the amount of principal (if any) which the Minister has previously paid on foot of any guarantee under this section and which has not been repaid by the Company, exceeds £2,000,000.

(3) For the purposes of calculating the amount of borrowings guaranteed by the Minister under this section by reference to the limit on principal in subsection (2) of this section, the equivalent in the currency of the State of borrowings in a foreign currency shall be calculated at the exchange rate prevailing at the time of the giving of the guarantee.

(4) The Minister shall, as soon as may be after the expiration of every financial year, lay beforeeach House of the Oireachtas a statement setting out with respect to each guarantee under this section given during that year or given at any time before, and in force at, the commencement of that year,—

(a) particulars of the guarantee,

(b) in case any payment has been made by the Minister under the guarantee before the end of that year, the amount of the payment and the amount (if any) repaid to the Minister on foot of the payment,

(c) the amount of principal covered by the guarantee which was outstanding at the end of that year.

(5) All moneys from time to time required by the Minister to meet sums which may become payable by him under this section shall be advanced out of the Central Fund or the growing produce thereof.

(6) Moneys paid by the Minister under a guarantee under this section shall be repaid to him (with interest thereon at such rate or rates as the Minister for Finance appoints) by the Company within two years from the date of the advance of the moneys out of the Central Fund.

(7) Where the whole or any part of moneys required by subsection (6) of this section to be repaid to the Minister has not been paid in accordance with that subsection, the amount so remaining outstanding shall be repaid to the Central Fund out of moneys

provided by the Oireachtas.

(8) Notwithstanding the provision of moneys under subsection (7) of this section to repay the amount to the Central Fund, the Company shall remain liable to the Minister in respect of that amount and that amount (with interest thereon at such rate or rates as the Minister for Finance appoints) shall be repaid to the Minister by the Company at such times and in such instalments as the Minister for Finance appoints and, in default of repayment as aforesaid and without prejudice to any other method of recovery, shall be recoverable as a simple contract debt in any court of competent jurisdiction.

(9) Moneys paid by the Company under subsection (6) or (8) of this section shall be paid into or disposed of for the benefit of the Exchequer in such manner as the Minister for Finance thinks fit.

(10)In relation to guarantees given by the Minister in money in a currency other than the currency of the State—

(i) each of the references to principal, each of the references to interest and the reference to commission and incidental expenses in subsection (1) of this section shall be taken as referring to the equivalent in the currency of the State of the actual principal, the actual interest and the actual commission and incidental expenses, respectively, such equivalent being calculated according to the cost in the currency of the State of the actual principal, the actual interest or the actual commission and incidental expenses, as may be appropriate;

(ii) the reference to principal in subsection (4) of this section shall be taken as referring to the equivalent in the currency of the State of the actual principal, such equivalent being calculated according to the rate of exchange for the time being for that currency and the currency of the State;

(iii) each of the references to moneys in subsections (5) to (8) of this section shall be taken as referring to the cost in the currency of the State of the actual moneys.

Advance of moneys out of Central Fund

9.—(1) For the purpose of providing for advances out of the Central Fund under this Act, the Minister for Finance may borrow from any person any sum or sums, and for the purpose of such borrowing he may create and issue securities bearing such rate of interest and subject to such conditions as to repayment, redemption or any other matter as he thinks fit, and shall pay the moneys so borrowed into the Exchequer.

(2) The principal of and interest on any securities issued by the Minister for Finance under this Act and the expenses incurred in connection with the issue of such securities shall be charged on and payable out of the Central Fund or the growing produce thereof.

Remuneration etc. of chief officer of Company

10.—There shall be paid by the Company to its chief officer (whether so described or otherwise) such remuneration and allowances for expenses as the Company thinks fit, subject to the approval of the Minister given with the consent of the Minister for the Public Service.

Superannuation of staff of Company

11.—Any alteration in the terms in operation at the passing of this Act governing the grant of pensions, gratuities, allowances or other payments on resignation, retirement or death, to or in respect of a member of the permanent staff of the Company, including its chief officer, or any other arrangement to provide for benefits additional to those terms, shall take place only by way of a superannuation scheme or schemes submitted to the Minister and approved of by him with the consent of the Minister for the Public Service.

Restriction on alteration of memorandum or articles of association of Company

12.—Notwithstanding anything contained in the Companies Acts, 1963 and 1977, or in the memorandum or articles of association of the Company, an alteration in the memorandum or articles shall not be valid or effectual unless made with the previous approval of the Minister, given with the consent of the Minister for Finance.

Restriction on issue of shares

13.—An issue of shares of the Company shall not he made unless the Minister for Finance after consultation with the Minister, has authorised the issue.

Balance sheet, accounts and directors' report of Company

14.—(1) The Company shall, as soon as may be after the end of each accounting year, furnish to the Minister—

(a) a balance sheet as at the end of the accounting year duly audited by the auditor of the Company,

(b) a profit and loss account for the accounting year so audited, and

(c) a copy of the report of the directors to the shareholders for the accounting year.

(2) The balance sheet and profit and loss account required by subsection (1) of this section shall be drawn up in such form as the Minister, with the consent of the Minister for Finance, shall direct.

(3) The Company shall, if so required by the Minister, furnish any information he may require in respect of any balance sheet, profit and loss account or report required by subsection (1) of this section, or in relation to the policy and operations of the Company.

(4) A copy of every balance sheet, profit and loss account and report furnished under subsection (1) of this section to the Minister shall be laid by him before each House of the Oireachtas as soon as may be after such balance sheet, profit and loss account and report are so furnished to him, and in any event not later than six months following the end of the period to which they relate.

Membership of either House of the Oireachtas by directors, officers or servants of Company

15.—(1) Where a director of the Company is nominated either as a candidate for election to either House of the Oireachtas or as a member of Seanad Éireann, he shall thereupon cease to be a director of the Company.

(2) Where a person who is either an officer or servant of the Company is nominated as a member of Seanad Éireann or for election to either House of the Oireachtas, he shall stand seconded from employment by the Company and shall not be paid by, or be entitled to receive from the Company, any remuneration or allowances—

(a) in case he is nominated as a member of Seanad Éireann, in respect of the period commencing on his acceptance of the nomination and ending when he ceases to be a member of that House,

(b) in case he is nominated for election to either such House, in respect of the period commencing on his nomination and ending when he ceases to be a member of that House or fails to be elected or withdraws his candidature, as may be appropriate.

(3) A person who is for the time being entitled under the Standing Orders of either House of the Oireachtas to sit therein shall, while so entitled, be disqualified from becoming a director of the Company or an officer or servant of the Company.

(4) If a person who is or was an officer or servant of the Company becomes a member of either House of the Oireachtas or a member of the Assembly of the European Communities, or becomes entitled under the Standing Orders of either House of the Oireachtas to sit therein, he shall while he is such a member or while so entitled be disqualified from reckoning the period of membership or entitlement for any superannuation benefits payable under a scheme or schemes made in accordance with section 11 of this Act.

Provisions having effect in certain circumstances

16.—Sections 12 to 15 of this Act inclusive shall have effect so long as—

(a) the Minister for Finance holds any shares of the Company,

(b) any moneys borrowed by the Company, the due repayment of which is guaranteed by the Minister under this Act, have not been repaid, or

(c) any moneys borrowed by the Company, the due repayment of which is so guaranteed and the amount of which has been paid by the Minister under the guarantee, have not (together with the interest thereon at the rates appointed by the Minister for Finance) been repaid by the Company to him or recovered from the Company by him.

Exemption from stamp duty

17.—Stamp duty shall not be chargeable in respect of any conveyance, transfer or other instrument executed for the purpose of vesting property or any interest in property in the Company.

Expenses

18.—Any expenses incurred by the Minister in the administration of this Act shall, to such extent as may be sanctioned by the Minister for Finance, be paid out of moneys provided by the Oireachtas.

Short title

19.—This Act may be cited as the National Film Studios of Ireland Limited Act, 1980.

ACTS REFERRED TO

Companies Act, 1963	1963, No. 33
Companies (Amendment) Act, 1977	1977, No. 31

VIDEO RECORDINGS ACT 1989

(No. 22 of 1989)

ARRANGEMENT OF SECTIONS

ACTS REFERRED TO

Broadcasting Authority Acts, 1960 to 1979	
Censorship of Films Act, 1923	1923, No.23
Censorship of Films Acts, 1923 to 1970	
Custom Acts	
Finance Act, 1983	1983, No. 15
Health Acts, 1947 to 1987	
Nurses Act, 1985	1985, No. 18
Medical Practitioners Act, 1978	1978, No. 4
Public Offices Fees Act, 1879	1879, c. 58
Roads Act, 1920	1920, c. 72
Road Traffic Act, 1961	1961, No. 24
Wireless Telegraphy Acts, 1926 to 1988	

AN ACT TO MAKE PROVISION FOR THE CONTROL AND REGULATION OF THE SUPPLY AND IMPORTATION OF VIDEO RECORDINGS AND FOR RELATED MATTERS AND TO AMEND SECTION 3 of THE CENSORSHIP OF FILMS ACT, 1923.

[27TH DECEMBER, 1989]

BE IT ENACTED BY THE OIREACHTAS AS FOLLOWS:

Interpretation

1.—(1) In this Act—
"the Appeal Board" means the Censorship of Films Appeal Board, established by the Censorship of Films Act, 1923;
"business", except in subsections (1) (b) and (3) (a) of section 2 and section 19 (2) (c) of this Act, includes any activity carried on by a club;

"a classification" means a classification of a video work by the Official Censor under section 4 of this Act;
"exempted supply" has the meaning assigned to it by section 2 of this Act;
"exempted work" means a video work that, taken as a whole—

(a) is designed to inform, educate or instruct,

(b) is concerned with religion, music or sport, or

(c) is a video game,

and that does not fall within a description specified in paragraph (a) or (b) of section 3 (1) of this Act;
"licence" means a wholesale licence or a retail licence;
"the Minister" means the Minister for Justice;
"the Official Censor" means the Official Censor of Films appointed under the Censorship of Films Act, 1923, and includes a person appointed under section 2 (3) of that Act;
"premises" includes any vehicle, vessel or stall;
"prescribed" means prescribed by regulations made by the Minister;
"prohibition order" has the meaning assigned to it by section 7 of this Act;
"retail licence" has the meaning assigned to it by section 18 (2) of this Act;
"supply" means supply in any manner, whether or not for reward and, therefore, includes supply by way of sale, letting on hire, exchange or loan, and cognate words shall be construed accordingly;
"supply certificate" has the meaning assigned to it by section 3 of this Act;
"video recording" means any disc or magnetic tape containing information by the use of which the whole or a part of a video work may be produced;
"video work" means any series of visual images (whether with or without sound)-

(a) produced, whether electronically or by other means, by the use of information contained on any disc or magnetic tape, and

(b) shown as a moving picture;

"wholesale licence" has the meaning assigned to it by section 18 (1) of this Act.

(2) For the purposes of this Act, a video recording contains a video work if it contains information by the use of which the whole or a part of the work may be produced; but where a video work includes an extract from another video work, that extract shall not be regarded, for the purposes of this subsection, as part of that other work.

(3) Where an alteration (which expression includes an addition) is made to a video work in respect of which a supply certificate is in force for the time being, the certificate shall not be treated for the purposes of this Act as being in force in respect of the altered work.

(4) References in this Act to selling or to letting on hire include references to agreeing or offering to sell or to let on hire and to inviting offers to buy or to take on hire.

Exempted supplies

2.—(1) In this Act "exempted supply" means a supply of a video recording—

(a) that is neither a supply for reward nor a supply in the course or furtherance of a business, or

(b) by a person to another person (including a person acting on behalf of that other person) who, in the course of a business, makes video works or supplies video recordings, being a supply—

(i) that is not made with a view to any further supply of the recording, or

(ii) if it is so made, that is not made with a view to the eventual supply of the recording to the public or is made with a view to its eventual supply to the first-mentioned person, or

(c) where the recording contains a video work designed to provide a record of an event or occasion for those who took part in the event or occasion or are connected with those who did so and the work does not fall within a description specified in paragraph (a) or (b) of section 3 (1) of this Act, and the supply is to a person aforesaid, or

(d) that is a supply for the purpose only of enabling the video work concerned to be exhibited in public in accordance with a certificate under the Censorship of Films Acts, 1923 to 1970, or

(e) that is a supply with a view only to its use for or in connection with a service under the Broadcasting Authority Acts, 1960 to 1979, or a service provided pursuant to a licence under the Wireless Telegraphy Acts, 1926 to 1988, or

(f) that is a supply for the purpose only of submitting the video work concerned to the Official Censor in connection with an application for a supply certificate in respect of the work or for the purpose only of an appeal to the Appeal Board under section 10 of this Act, or

(g) that is a supply with a view only to its use—

(i) in training for or carrying on an occupation for the carrying on of which a person is required to be registered under the Medical Practitioners Act, 1978, or the Nurses Act, 1985, or

(ii) for the purpose of services provided in pursuance of the Health Acts, 1947 to 1987,

or

(h) that is a supply otherwise than for reward and is made for the purpose only of supplying the recording to a person who previously made an exempted supply of it.

(2) Where on any premises facilities for supplying video recordings are provided in the course or furtherance of a business, the supply by a person of a video recording on those premises is, for the purposes of subsection (1) (a) of this section, a supply in the course or furtherance of a business.

(3) For the purposes of subsection (1) (b) of this section, a supply is a supply to the public unless it is—

(a) a supply to a person who, in the course of a business, makes video works or supplies video recordings,

(b) an exempted supply by virtue of paragraph (a), (c), (d), (e), (f) or (g) of subsection (1) of this section, or

(c) a supply outside the State.

Certification of video works

3.—(1) The Official Censor shall, on application to him in relation to a video work, grant to the person making the application (referred to in this section as the applicant) a certificate (referred to in this Act as a supply certificate) declaring the work to be fit for viewing unless he is of opinion that the work is unfit for viewing because—

(a) the viewing of it—

(i) would be likely to cause persons to commit crimes, whether by inciting or encouraging them to do so or by indicating or suggesting ways of doing so or of avoiding detection, or

(ii) would be likely to stir up hatred against a group of persons in the State or elsewhere on account of their race, colour, nationality, religion, ethnic or national origins, membership of the travelling community or sexual orientation, or

(iii) would tend, by reason of the inclusion in it of obscene or indecent matter, to deprave or corrupt persons who might view it,

or

(b) it depicts acts of gross violence or cruelty (including mutilation and torture) towards humans or animals.

(2) The Official Censor shall not refuse to grant a supply certificate in respect of a video work in respect of which a general certificate or a limited certificate under the Censorship of Films Acts, 1923 to 1970, is in force.

(3) Where, pursuant to subsection (1) of this section, the Official Censor is of opinion that a supply certificate in respect of a video work should not be granted, he shall thereupon—

(a) make a prohibition order in respect of the work under section 7 of this Act, and

(b) send a notification in writing to the applicant of his refusal to grant a supply certificate in respect of the work and of the making of a prohibition order in respect thereof.

(4) The applicant shall submit to the Official Censor a video recording of the video work to which his application relates and such other information as may reasonably be required by the Official Censor and shall pay to the Official Censor in respect of the application such fee as may be prescribed with the consent of the Minister for Finance.

Classification of video works

4.—(1) When granting a supply certificate the Official Censor shall determine, and shall include in the certificate a statement indicating, to which of the following classes the video work concerned belongs:

(a) fit for viewing by persons generally,

(b) fit for viewing by persons generally but, in the case of a child under the age of 12 years, only [under parental guidance],

[(bb) fit for viewing by persons aged 12 years or more,]

(c) fit for viewing by persons aged 15 years or more,

(d) fit for viewing by persons aged 18 years or more,

and for the purposes of this Act the class specified in paragraph (a) of this subsection is the highest classification and that specified in paragraph (d) of this subsection is the lowest classification and that specified in paragraph (b) of this subsection is higher than [that specified in paragraph (bb) and that specified in paragraph (bb) is higher than] that specified in paragraph (c) of this subsection and references in this Act to classification or higher classification or lower classification shall be construed accordingly.

(2) A statement indicating a classification other than the highest classification shall not be given in a supply certificate unless the Official Censor has examined a video recording containing the video work to which the certificate relates.

(3) Where the classification of a video work is not the highest classification, the Official Censor may withdraw the classification and give the work a higher classification and, if he does so, he shall revoke the supply certificate concerned and grant another supply certificate in respect of the work in which is included a statement indicating the higher classification.

(4)(a) The Minister may by regulations amend (whether by the addition, deletion or alteration of classes) the classes specified in subsection (1) of this section:

Provided however that an amendment under this paragraph shall not have the effect of providing a classification indicating that a video work is fit for viewing only by persons aged more than 18 years.

(b) Where it is proposed to make regulations under this subsection, a draft of the regulations shall be laid before each House of the Oireachtas and the regulations shall not be made until a resolution approving of the draft shall have been passed by each such House.

Amendment History

Section 4(1)(b) amended and para (bb) inserted by reg.2 of Video Recordings Act 1989 (Classification of Video Works) Regulations 1996 (S.I. No.403 of 1996). Section 4(3) is exempt from the provisions of s.2(1)(a) of the Censorship of Films (Amendment) Act 1992.

Prohibition of supply of video recordings of uncertificated video works

5.—(1) A person who supplies or offers to supply a video recording containing a video work in respect of which a supply certificate is not in force for the time being shall be guilty of an offence unless—

(a) the supply is, or would if it took place be, an exempted supply, or

(b) the work is an exempted work.

(2) It shall be a defence to a charge of committing an offence under this section to prove that the accused believed on reasonable grounds—

(a) that the video work concerned or, if the video recording concerned contained more than one work to which the charge relates, each of the works was either an exempted work or a work in respect of which a supply certificate was in force at the time of the commission of the offence alleged, or

(b) that the supply concerned was, or would if it took place be, an exempted supply by virtue of paragraph (b) or (c) of section 2 (1) of this Act.

(3) A person guilty of an offence under this section shall be liable—

(a) on summary conviction, to a fine not exceeding £1,000 or to imprisonment for a term not exceeding 12 months or to both, or

(b) on conviction on indictment, to a fine or to imprisonment for a term not exceeding 3 years or to both.

Prohibition of possession of video recordings for supply contrary to section 5

6.—(1) A person who has in his possession for the purpose of supplying it a video recording containing a video work in respect of which a supply certificate is not in force for the time being shall be guilty of an offence unless—

(a) he has it in his possession for the purpose only of a supply that, if it took place, would be an exempted supply, or

(b) the work is an exempted work.

(2) It shall be a defence to a charge of committing an offence under this section to prove that the accused—

(a) believed on reasonable grounds that the video work concerned or, if the video recording concerned contained more than one work to which the charge relates, each of the works was either an exempted work or a work in respect of which a supply certificate was in force at the time of the commission of the offence alleged,

(b) had the video recording concerned in his possession for the purpose only of a supply that he believed on reasonable grounds would, if it took place, be an exempted supply by virtue of paragraph (b) or (c) of section 2 (1) of this Act, or

(c) did not intend to supply the video recording concerned until a supply certificate was granted in respect of the video work concerned.

(3) A person guilty of an offence under this section shall be liable—

(a) on summary conviction, to a fine not exceeding £1,000 or to imprisonment for a term not exceeding 12 months or to both, or

(b) on conviction on indictment, to a fine or to imprisonment for a term not exceeding 3 years or to both.

Prohibition orders respect of video works

7.—(1) If the Official Censor, having examined a video recording containing a video work (whether or not it is a video work in respect of which a supply certificate is in force for the time being), is of opinion that the work is unfit for viewing because—

(a) the viewing of it—

(i) would be likely to cause persons to commit crimes, whether by inciting or encouraging them to do so or by indicating or suggesting ways of doing so or of avoiding detection, or

(ii) would be likely to stir up hatred against a group of persons in the State or elsewhere on account of their race, colour, nationality, religion, ethnic or national origins, membership of the travelling community or sexual orientation, or

(iii) would tend, by reason of the inclusion in it of obscene or indecent matter, to deprave or corrupt persons who might view it,

or

(b) it depicts acts of gross violence or cruelty (including mutilation and torture) towards humans or animals, he may make an order (referred to in this Act as a prohibition order) prohibiting the supply of video recordings containing the work.

(2) If a prohibition order is made in respect of a video work and a supply certificate is in force in respect of the work, the supply certificate shall cease to have effect on the coming into operation of the order.

(3) The Official Censor may by order revoke a prohibition order and, if he does so, he shall grant a supply certificate in respect of the video work concerned on the date the revocation takes effect.

(4) The Official Censor shall cause a copy of a prohibition order and of an order revoking a prohibition order to be published in Iris Oifigiúil as soon as may be after its making, and such an order shall come into operation upon such publication.

Prohibition of supply of video recordings of prohibited video works

8.—(1) A person who supplies or offers to supply a video recording containing a video work in respect of which a prohibition order is in force for the time being shall be guilty of an offence unless the supply is, or would if it took place be, an exempted supply.

(2) It shall be a defence to a charge of committing an offence under this section to prove that the accused believed on reasonable grounds—

(a) that—

(i) the video work concerned was not a work in respect of which a prohibition order was in force at the time of the commission of the offence alleged, or

(ii) if the video recording concerned contained more than one video work to which the charge relates, none of the works was a work in respect of which a prohibition order was in force at the time aforesaid,

or

(b) that the supply concerned was, or would if it took place be, an exempted supply by virtue of paragraph (b) or (c) of section 2 (1) of this Act.

(3) A person guilty of an offence under this section shall be liable—

(a) on summary conviction, to a fine not exceeding £1,000 or to imprisonment for a term not exceeding 12 months or to both, or

(b) on conviction on indictment, to a fine or to imprisonment for a term not exceeding 3 years or to both.

Prohibition of possession of video recordings for supply contrary to section 8

9.—(1) A person who has in his possession for the purpose of supplying it a video recording containing a video work in respect of which a prohibition order is in force for the time being shall be guilty of an offence unless he has it in his possession for the purpose only of a supply that, if it took place, would be an exempted supply.

(2) It shall be a defence to a charge of committing an offence under this section to prove that the accused—

(a) believed on reasonable grounds that—

(i) the video work concerned was not a work in respect of which a prohibition order was in force at the time of the commission of the offence alleged, or

(ii) if the video recording concerned contained more than one video work to which the charge relates, none of the works was a work in respect of which a prohibition order was in force at the time aforesaid,

or

(b) had the video recording concerned in his possession for the purpose only of a supply that he believed on reasonable grounds would, if it took place, be an exempted supply by virtue of paragraph (b) or (c) of section 2 (1) of this Act.

(3) A person guilty of an offence under this section shall be liable—

(a) on summary conviction, to a fine not exceeding £1,000 or to imprisonment for a term not exceeding 12 months or to both, or

(b) on conviction on indictment, to a fine or to imprisonment for a term not exceeding 3 years or to both.

Appeal to Censorship of Films Appeal Board

10.—(1) A person who is aggrieved by a prohibition order may, not later than 3 months after the date of the publication of the order in Iris Oifigiúil, appeal in the prescribed manner to the Appeal Board against the order and the Appeal Board may affirm the decision of the Official Censor or revoke the order.

(2) A person who is aggrieved by a classification may, not later than 3 months after the grant of the supply certificate concerned, appeal in the prescribed manner to the Appeal Board against the classification and the Appeal Board may affirm the

classification or direct that the video work concerned be given a specified higher classification.

(3) Where an appeal is brought under this section, the Official Censor shall—

(a) if so requested by the Appeal Board, furnish to it a statement in writing of the reasons for the making of the prohibition order, or the giving of the classification, concerned, and

(b) on application to him in that behalf by any person and on payment to him in respect thereof of such fee as may be prescribed with the consent of the Minister for Finance, furnish a copy of the statement to the person.

(4) The Appeal Board shall, as soon as may be, notify the Official Censor of a decision by it on an appeal under this section and—

(a) if the decision is to revoke the prohibition order concerned, the Official Censor shall, as soon as may be, grant a supply certificate in respect of the video work concerned, and

(b) if the decision is to direct that the video work concerned be given a higher classification, the Official Censor shall, as soon as may be, revoke the supply certificate concerned and grant another supply certificate in respect of the work in which is included a statement indicating the classification specified by the Appeal Board.

(5) The Official Censor shall cause a copy of any order of the Appeal Board revoking a prohibition order to be published in Iris Oifigiúil as soon as may be after its making.

(6) A person bringing an appeal under this section shall pay to the Official Censor in respect of the appeal such fee as may be prescribed with the consent of the Minister for Finance.

[(7) Where the Appeal Board revokes a prohibition order pursuant to subsection (1) of this section or directs that the video work concerned be given a higher classification pursuant to subsection (2) of this section, the fee paid in respect of the appeal pursuant to subsection (6) of this section shall be refunded to the appellant concerned.]

Amendment History

Section 10(7) inserted by s.4 of the Censorship of Films (Amendment) Act 1992.

Prohibition of exhibition of certain video works

11.—(1) Subject to subsection (2) of this section, a person who causes or permits, or is concerned in causing or permitting, a video work in respect of which—

(a) a supply certificate is not in force for the time being, or

(b) a prohibition order is in force for the time being,

to be viewed—

(i) elsewhere than in a private dwelling,

(ii) in a private dwelling for reward, or

(iii) in a private dwelling by persons other than himself, the occupier of the private dwelling where it is viewed, members of the family or the household of himself or of such occupier or bona fide guests of himself or such occupier, shall be guilty of an offence unless, in a case to which paragraph (a) of this subsection applies, the video work is an exempted work.

(2) Subsection (1) of this section does not apply in relation to the viewing of a video work if the viewing is only—

(a) by persons to whom a supply of a video recording containing the work would be an exempted supply by virtue of paragraph (b), (c), (d), (e), (f) or (g) of section 2 (1) of this Act, or

(b) to such limited extent as is in accordance with a permit under section 16 of this Act authorising the importation into the State of a video recording containing the work.

(3) It shall be a defence to a charge of committing an offence under this section to prove that the accused believed on reasonable grounds—

(a) if the charge of the offence is one to which paragraph (a) of subsection (1) of this section applies, that the video work concerned was either an exempted work or a work in respect of which a supply certificate was in force at the time of the commission of the offence alleged,

(b) if the charge of the offence is one to which paragraph (b) of the said subsection (1) applies, that—

(i) the video work concerned was not a work in respect of which a prohibition order was in force at the time of the commission of the offence alleged, or

(ii) the viewing concerned was only to such limited extent as was in accordance with a permit under section 16 of this Act authorising the importation into the State of a video recording containing the video work concerned,

or

(c) that the persons viewing the video work concerned were persons to whom the supply of a video recording containing the work would be an exempted supply by virtue of paragraph (b) or (c) of section 2 (1) of this Act.

(4) A person guilty of an offence under this section shall be liable on summary conviction to a fine not exceeding £1,000.

Labelling, etc.

12.—(1) The following provisions shall have effect in relation to a video recording containing a video work in respect of which a supply certificate is in force for the time being:

(a) the spool or other thing on which the recording is kept shall have affixed to it a label in the prescribed form (which may be obtained from the Official Censor by persons of prescribed categories on payment to him of such fee as may be prescribed with the consent of the Minister for Finance),

(b) any case or other thing in which the recording is kept shall bear such indication of the contents of the label as may be prescribed, and

(c) such indication (if any) as may be prescribed in relation to the label shall be included in the recording.

(2)(a) A person who supplies, offers to supply or has in his possession for the purpose of supplying it a video recording, or a spool, case or other thing on or in which it is kept, that (whether by the inclusion of any false statement in the label or indication concerned or otherwise) is not in compliance with subsection (1) of this section shall be guilty of an offence unless the supply is, or would if it took place be, an exempted supply or the video work concerned is an exempted work.

(b) A video recording or a spool, case or other thing on or in which it is kept shall not be deemed to be otherwise than in compliance with subsection (1) of this section by reason only that the classification it indicates is a lower one than that in force at the relevant time.

(3) It shall be a defence to a charge of committing an offence under this section to prove that the accused—

(a) believed on reasonable grounds that—

(i) the video work concerned or, if the video recording concerned contained more than one work, each of the works was an exempted work, or

(ii) the supply concerned was, or would if it took place be, an exempted supply by virtue of paragraph (b) or (c) of section 2 (1) of this Act,

or

(b) neither knew nor had reasonable cause to believe that the recording, spool, case or other thing, as the case may be, concerned was not in compliance with subsection (1) of this section.

(4) In this section "spool', in the case of a case or other article from which a video recording need not be removed in order that the video work contained in the recording can be produced, means that case or other article.

(5) A person guilty of an offence under this section shall be liable on summary conviction to a fine not exceeding £500.

Prohibition of supplying video recordings containing false indication as to supply certificate

13.—(1) A person who supplies, offers to supply or has in his possession for the purpose of supplying it a video recording containing a video work in respect of which a supply certificate is not in force for the time being shall be guilty of an offence if the recording, or any spool, case or other thing on or in which it is kept, contains an indication that such a certificate is in force for the time being.

(2) A person who supplies, offers to supply or has in his possession for the purpose of supplying it a video recording containing a video work shall be guilty of an offence if the recording, or any spool, case or other thing on or in which it is kept, contains an indication that the classification of the work is a higher classification than that in

force for the time being.

(3) It shall be a defence to a charge of committing an offence under this section to prove that the accused—

(a) in case the offence is under subsection (1) of this section, believed on reasonable grounds that the video work concerned was a work in respect of which a supply certificate was in force at the time of the commission of the offence alleged, or

(b) in case the offence is under subsection (2) of this section, believed on reasonable grounds that the classification specified in the indication concerned or a higher classification was in force in relation to the video work concerned at the time of the commission of the offence alleged, or

(c) neither knew nor had reasonable cause to believe that the recording, spool, case or other thing, as the case may be, concerned contained the indication to which the offence relates.

(4) A person guilty of an offence under this section shall be liable on summary conviction to a fine not exceeding £1,000.

Register of Certified Video Works

14.—(1) The Official Censor shall establish and maintain a register in the prescribed form (which shall be known as the Register of Certified Video Works and is referred to in this section as the register) of video works in respect of which a supply certificate is for the time being in force.

(2) The Official Censor may, as occasion requires, amend or delete an entry in the register.

(3)(a) Members of the public may inspect the register free of charge at all reasonable times and may take copies of, or of extracts from, entries in the register.

(b) In any proceedings a certificate signed by the Official Censor or by a person authorised by him and stating—

(i) that he has examined the register and a video work (or part of a video work) contained in a video recording identified by the certificate, and

(ii) that the register shows that on the date or during the period specified in the certificate a supply certificate was not in force in respect of the work,

shall be admissible as evidence of the fact that a supply certificate was not in force in respect of the work on the date or, as the case may be, during the period aforesaid.

(c) A certificate under paragraph (b) of this subsection may also state—

(i) that the video work concerned differs in such respects as may be specified in the certificate from another video work examined by the person signing the certificate and identified by the certificate, and

(ii) that the register shows that, on a date specified in the certificate under the said paragraph (b), a supply certificate was granted in respect of that other work,

and, if it does so, shall be admissible as evidence of the fact that the work concerned differs in those respects from that other work.

(d) In any proceedings a certificate signed by the Official Censor or by a person authorised by him and stating—

(i) that he has examined the register and a video work contained in a video recording identified by the certificate, and

(ii) that the register shows that on the date or during the period specified in the certificate a supply certificate was in force in respect of the work, and

(iii) that a document identified by and attached to the certificate is a copy of the supply certificate in force as aforesaid, shall be admissible as evidence of the fact that a supply certificate was in force in respect of the work on the date or, as the case may be, during the period aforesaid and of the terms of the supply certificate.

(e) A document purporting to be a certificate under paragraph (b) or (d) of this subsection shall be deemed to be such a certificate, and to have been signed by the person purporting to have signed it (and, in the case of such a document purporting to have been signed by a person authorised by the Official Censor, to have been signed in accordance with the authorisation), unless the contrary is shown.

Register of Prohibited Video Works

15.—(1) The Official Censor shall establish and maintain a register in the prescribed form (which shall be known as the Register of Prohibited Video Works and is referred to in this section as the register) of video works in respect of which a prohibition order is for the time being in force.

(2) The Official Censor may, as occasion requires, amend or delete an entry in the register.

(3)(a) Members of the public may inspect the register free of charge at all reasonable times and may take copies of, or of extracts from, entries in the register.

(b) In any proceedings a certificate signed by the Official Censor or by a person authorised by him and stating—

(i) that he has examined the register and a video work (or part of a video work) contained in a video recording identified by the certificate, and

(ii) that the register shows that on the date or during the period specified in the certificate a prohibition order was in force in respect of the work, and

(iii) that a document identified by and attached to the certificate is a copy of the prohibition order in force as aforesaid, shall be admissible as evidence of the fact that a prohibition order was in force in respect of the work on the date or, as the case may be, during the period aforesaid and of the terms of the order.

(c) In any proceedings a certificate signed by the Official Censor or by a person authorised by him and stating—

(i) that he has examined the register and a video work contained in a video recording identified by the certificate, and

(ii) that the register shows that on the date or during the period specified in the certificate a prohibition order was not in force in respect of the work, shall be admissible as evidence of the fact that a prohibition order was not in force in respect of the work on the date or, as the case may be, during the period aforesaid.

(d) A document purporting to be a certificate under paragraph (b) or (c) of this subsection shall be deemed to be such a certificate, and to have been signed by the person purporting to have signed it (and, in the case of such a document purporting to have been signed by a person authorised by the Official Censor, to have been signed in accordance with the authorisation), unless the contrary is shown.

(4)(a) The Official Censor shall from time to time cause a list of the video works entered in the register to be published in such manner as he thinks fit.

(b) The Official Censor shall keep the Revenue Commissioners informed of the video works entered for the time being in the register, and an officer of customs and excise shall, if so requested by a person when entering the State, furnish to him for examination a list of the video works entered for the time being in the register.

Restriction of importation of certain video recordings

16.—(1) A person shall not, except under and in accordance with a permit under this section, import into the State a video recording containing a video work in respect of which a prohibition order is in force for the time being.

(2) Without prejudice to the powers as to forfeiture and disposal of video recordings imported into the State in contravention of subsection (1) of this section conferred on the Revenue Commissioners by the Customs Acts, it shall be a defence to a charge of committing an offence against the Customs Acts in relation to the importation into the State of a video recording containing a video work in respect of which a prohibition order is in force for the time being to prove that the accused believed on reasonable grounds—

(a) that the work was not a work in respect of which a prohibition order was in force at the time of the commission of the offence alleged, or

(b) if the recording contained more than one work to which the charge relates, none of the works was a work in respect of which a prohibition order was in force at the time aforesaid.

(3)(a) Where the Minister is satisfied that the proposed importation concerned would not be for the purpose—

(i) of a supply, or of a supply other than to such limited extent as may be specified in the permit under this subsection, of the video recording concerned, or

(ii) of enabling the video work concerned to be viewed otherwise than to such limited extent as may be specified as aforesaid, the Minister may, on application in writing therefor, grant a permit in writing authorising a specified person to import into the State a specified number of video recordings containing a specified video work in respect of which a prohibition order is in force for the time being and may specify in the permit conditions to which it is subject; and the holder of a permit under this subsection shall comply with any conditions to which it is subject.

(b) A person who contravenes a condition of a permit under this subsection shall be guilty of an offence.

(c) A person guilty of an offence under this subsection shall be liable on summary conviction to a fine not exceeding £1,000.

Reference of certain video recording to Official Censor of Films by officers of customs and excise

17.—(1) An officer of customs and excise may detain on importation into the State any video recording that, in his opinion, ought to be examined by the Official Censor under this Act and refer it to him for the purpose of such examination.

(2) Where a video recording is detained pursuant to subsection (1) of this section, the officer of customs and excise concerned shall, as soon as may be—

(a) send the recording to the Official Censor, and

(b)(i) in case the recording was at the time of its detention in the custody of a person entering the State, notify him in writing, and

(ii) in any other case, notify in writing the person to whom the recording is consigned, or his duly authorised agent, that he proposes to send or has sent the recording to the Official Censor in pursuance of this section.

(3) Nothing in this section shall affect the operation of the Customs Acts.

Wholesale licences and retail licences for the sale, etc of video recordings

18.—(1) Subject to the provisions of this section, the Official Censor shall, on the application in writing of a person therefor and on payment to the Official Censor of such fee as may be prescribed with the consent of the Minister for Finance, grant to the person a licence (referred to in this Act as a wholesale licence) authorising the person to sell video recordings by wholesale or to let them on hire.

(2) Subject to the provisions of this section, the Official Censor shall, on the application in writing of a person therefor and on payment to the Official Censor of such fee as may be prescribed with the consent of the Minister for Finance, grant to the person a licence (referred to in this Act as a retail licence) authorising the person to sell video recordings by retail or to let them on hire.

(3)(a) A licence in relation to any premises (other than a vehicle that is not a mechanically propelled vehicle (within the meaning of the Road Traffic Act, 1961) or a vessel or stall) shall—

(i) authorise, and be expressed to authorise, the sale and the letting on hire of video recordings at or from those premises only,

(ii) if it relates to premises other than a mechanically propelled vehicle (within the meaning aforesaid) specify the premises, and

(iii) if it relates to a mechanically propelled vehicle (within the meaning aforesaid), specify the identification mark fixed to the vehicle pursuant to the Roads Act, 1920.

(b) A licence, other than a licence in relation to premise to which paragraph (a) of this subsection applies, shall authorise, and be expressed to authorise, the sale and the letting on hire of video recordings at one place only.

(4) The Official Censor shall not grant a licence to a person in respect of a period for which he is disqualified under section 24 of this Act for holding a licence.

(5) A licence, if not previously surrendered or forfeited, shall remain in force for a period of 12 months and shall then expire.

(6)(a) A person who applies to the Official Censor for a licence shall furnish to the Official Censor such information as he may reasonably require for the purpose of the performance of his functions under this Act including the tax reference number or, if he has more than one, one of the tax reference numbers of the person.

(b) In paragraph (a) of this subsection "tax reference number" means a number specified in the definition of "tax reference number" in section 22 of the Finance Act, 1983.

Prohibition of sale or letting on hire of video recordings by unlicensed persons

19.—(1) Subject to the provisions of this section, a person shall not sell, or let on hire, a video recording except in accordance with a licence for the time being in force.

(2) This section does not apply to—

(a) a sale or letting of a video recording containing only exempted works,

(b) a sale or letting for the purpose of an exempted supply,

(c) a sale by a person who, in the course of a business, makes video recordings to a person who holds a wholesale licence for the time being in force,

(d) a sale that is part of a transaction relating to the disposal of property generally of any person,

(e) a sale in respect of which it is shown by the seller—

(i) that any profits therefrom are for use for charitable purposes or for other purposes from which no private profit is derived, and

(ii) that no remuneration, emolument, gain or profit will accrue to the seller or his servants or agents there-from,

(f) a sale by an individual, other than in the course or furtherance of a business, to another individual, or

(g) a sale by wholesale for or in connection with the exportation from the State of the video recording concerned.

(3) It shall be a defence to a charge of committing an offence under this section to prove that the accused believed on reasonable grounds that the sale or letting on hire concerned was not one to which this section applies or that it was in accordance with a licence for the time being in force.

(4) A person who contravenes subsection (1) of this section shall be guilty of an offence.

(5) A person guilty of an offence under this section shall be liable on summary conviction to a fine not exceeding £1,000 or to imprisonment for a term not exceeding 12 months or to both.

Prohibition of possession of video recordings for sale or letting on hire contrary to section 19

20.—(1) A person who has in his possession a video recording for the purpose of selling it or letting it on hire contrary to section 19 of this Act shall be guilty of an offence.

(2) It shall be a defence to a charge of committing an offence under this section to prove that the accused had the video recording concerned in his possession for the purpose only of a sale or letting on hire in respect of which he believed on reasonable grounds that, if it took place, it either would not be a sale or letting on hire to which section 19 of this Act applies or would be in accordance with a licence for the time being in force.

(3) A person guilty of an offence under this section shall be liable on summary conviction to a fine not exceeding £1,000 or to imprisonment for a term not exceeding 12 months or to both.

Prohibition of false information and alteration of licences

21.—(1) A person shall not knowingly give false information to the Official Censor in relation to an application for a licence.

(2) A person shall not forge a document purporting to be a licence, or use any such document, with intent to deceive.

(3) A person shall not alter or use a licence, or use an altered licence, with intent to deceive.

(4) A person who contravenes this section shall be guilty of an offence and shall be liable on summary conviction to a fine not exceeding £1,000 or to imprisonment for a term not exceeding 12 months or to both.

Display of licences

22.—(1)(a) A person selling or letting on hire video recordings at or from any premises shall display the licence authorising the sales or lettings in such a position in the part of the premises where the sales or lettings are taking place as to be clearly visible to and easily legible by members of the public.

(b) Where the sales or lettings aforesaid are taking place in more than one part of the premises concerned, the licence concerned shall be displayed as aforesaid in a part where a substantial proportion of the sales or lettings are taking place.

(2) A person selling or letting on hire video recordings elsewhere than at premises shall produce the licence concerned on demand to any person at the place where the sales or lettings are taking place.

(3) A person who contravenes this section shall be guilty of an offence and shall be liable on summary conviction to a fine not exceeding £500.

Registers of licences

23.—(1) The Official Censor shall establish and maintain a register in the prescribed form of the wholesale licences for the time being in force and a register of the retail licences for the time being in force (which shall be known, respectively, as the Register of Video Recording Wholesale Licences and the Register of Video Recording Retail Licences).

(2) The Official Censor may, as occasion requires, amend or delete entries in the registers.

(3)(a) Members of the public may inspect the registers free of charge at all reasonable times and may take copies of, or of extracts from, entries in the registers.

(b) In any proceedings a certificate signed by the Official Censor or by a person authorised by him and stating—

(i) that he has examined one of the registers, and

(ii) that that register shows that on the date or during the period specified in the certificate a wholesale licence, or, as the case may be, a retail licence, in favour of a specified person was not in force or was not in force in relation to specified premises, shall be admissible as evidence of the fact that a wholesale licence, or, as the case may be, a retail licence, in favour of the specified person was not in force or, as the case may be, was not in force in relation to the specified premises on the date or, as the case may be, during the period aforesaid.

(c) In any proceedings a certificate signed by the Official Censor or by a person authorised by him and stating—

(i) that he has examined one of the registers, and

(ii) that that register shows that on the date or during the period specified in the certificate a wholesale licence, or, as the case may be, a retail licence, in favour of a specified person was in force or was in force in relation to specified premises, and

(iii) that a document identified by and attached to the certificate is a copy of the licence in force as aforesaid, shall be admissible as evidence of the fact that a wholesale licence, or, as the case may be, a retail licence, in favour of the specified person was in force or, as the case may be, was in force in relation to the specified premises on the date or, as the case may be, during the period aforesaid and of the terms of the licence.

(d) A document purporting to be a certificate under paragraph (b) or (c) of this subsection shall be deemed to be such a certificate, and to have been signed by the person purporting to have signed it (and, in the case of such a document purporting to have been signed by a person authorised by the Official Censor, to have been signed in accordance with the authorisation), unless the contrary is shown.

Forfeiture of licences and disqualification

24.—(1) If—

(a) a person is convicted of an offence under section 5, 6, 8, 9, 12, 13, 19, 20 or 21 of this Act, an offence referred to in section 16 (2) of this Act committed after the commencement of this section or an offence under the laws relating to copyright committed in relation to a video recording after such commencement,

(b) he has previously been convicted of any of those offences, and

(c) the offence or offences referred to in paragraph (b) of this subsection of which he has previously been convicted was or were committed at any time not earlier than 5 years before the commission of the offence referred to in paragraph (a) of this subsection,

the court shall—

(i) in case the person is the holder of a licence for the time being in force in relation to premises where any of the offences aforesaid was committed, order that the licence or licences be forfeited, and

(ii) order that the person be disqualified for a period of 5 years from the date on which the order takes effect for holding a licence in relation to any premises where any of the offences referred to in paragraphs (a) and (b) of this subsection was committed or any premises in relation to which he is not the holder of a licence on that date.

(2) An order under this section shall not take effect until the ordinary time for instituting an appeal against the conviction or order concerned has expired or, where such an appeal is instituted, until it or any further appeal is finally decided or abandoned or the ordinary time for instituting any further appeal has expired.

Search and seizure

25.—(1) If a justice of the District Court or a Peace Commissioner is satisfied on the sworn information of a member of the Garda Síochána not below the rank of sergeant that there are reasonable grounds for suspecting that—

(a) an offence under this Act or an offence referred to in section 16 (2) of this Act has been or is being committed on or at any premises or other place, and

(b) evidence that the offence has been or is being committed is on or at those premises or that place,

he may issue a warrant under his hand authorising any member of the Garda Síochána, accompanied by any other members of the Garda Síochána, at any time or times within one month from the date of the issue of the warrant, on production if so requested of the warrant, to enter, if need be by force, and search the premises or other place specified in the warrant and—

(i) to seize anything found there that he believes on reasonable grounds may be required to be used in evidence in any proceedings for an offence under this Act or an offence referred to in section 16 (2) of this Act, and

(ii) to require any person found there to give him his name and address.

(2) A person who—

(a) obstructs or interferes with a member of the Garda Síochána acting under the authority of a warrant under this section, or

(b) is found on or at the premises or place specified in the warrant by a member of the Garda Síochána acting as aforesaid and who fails or refuses to give the member his name and address when required by the member to do so or gives him a name or address that is false or misleading,

shall be guilty of an offence and shall be liable on summary conviction—

(i) if the offence is under paragraph (a) of this subsection, to a fine not exceeding £1,000 or to imprisonment for a term not exceeding 6 months or to both, or

(ii) if the offence is under paragraph (b) of this subsection, to a fine not exceeding £500.

Powers of arrest

26.—(1) If a member of the Garda Síochána reasonably suspects that a person has committed an offence under this Act (other than an offence under subsection (2) (b) of section 25), he may require him to give him his name and address and, if the person fails or refuses to do so or gives a name or address that the member reasonably suspects to be false or misleading, the member may arrest him without warrant.

(2) A member of the Garda Síochána acting under the authority of a warrant under the said section 25 may arrest without warrant a person whom the member reasonably suspects of having committed an offence under the said subsection (2) (b).

Offences by bodies corporate

27.—(1) Where an offence under this Act has been committed by a body corporate and is proved to have been committed with the consent or connivance of or to be attributable to any neglect on the part of a person being a director, manager, secretary or other officer of the body corporate, or a person who was purporting to act in any such capacity, that person as well as the body corporate shall be guilty of the offence and be liable to be proceeded against and punished accordingly.

(2) Where the affairs of a body corporate are managed by its members, subsection (1) of this section shall apply in relation to the acts and defaults of a member in connection with his functions of management as if he were a director or manager of the body corporate.

Forfeiture of video recordings

28.—(1) If a person is convicted of an offence under this Act (other than an offence under section 21 or 22 of this Act) or an offence referred to in section 16 (2) of this Act committed after the commencement of this section, the court may order a video recording that is shown to the satisfaction of the court to relate to the offence to be forfeited and either destroyed or otherwise disposed of in such manner as the court may determine.

(2) A court shall not order a video recording to be forfeited under this section if

a person claiming to be the owner of it or otherwise interested in it applies to be heard by the court, unless an opportunity has been given to him to show cause why the order should not be made.

(3) An order under this section shall not take effect until the ordinary time for instituting an appeal against the conviction or order concerned has expired or, where such an appeal is instituted, until it or any further appeal is finally decided or abandoned or the ordinary time for instituting any further appeal has expired.

(4) References in this section to a video recording include references to any spool, case or other thing on or in which the recording is kept.

Annual reports

29.—(1)(a) The Official Censor shall, in each year beginning with the year 1990, prepare a report on his activities in the preceding year under this Act and the Censorship of Films Acts, 1923 to 1970, and shall submit it to the Minister, who shall cause copies thereof to be laid before each House of the Oireachtas.

(b) The Appeal Board shall, in each year beginning with the year 1990, prepare a report on its activities in the preceding year under this Act and the Censorship of Films Acts, 1923 to 1970, and shall submit it to the Minister, who shall cause copies thereof to be laid before each House of the Oireachtas.

(2) Whenever he or, as the case may be, it considers it desirable to do so or is so requested by the Minister, the Official Censor or the Appeal Board, as the case may be, shall make a special report to the Minister in relation to any matter arising in connection with his or, as the case may be, its functions under this Act or the Censorship of Films Acts, 1923 to 1970.

Amendment History

Section 29 is exempt from the provisions of s.2(1)(a) of the Censorship of Films (Amendment) Act 1992.

Composition of Censorship of Films Appeal Board

30.—(1) Section 3 of the Censorship of Films Act, 1923, is hereby amended by the insertion in subsection (1) after "Chairman" of one at least shall be a man and one at least shall be a woman".

(2) Subsection (1) of this section shall come into operation upon the expiration of the term of office of the Commissioners holding office as members of the Appeal Board upon the passing of this Act.

Regulations

31.—(1) The Minister may make regulations for the purpose of enabling this Act to have full effect and, in particular, but without prejudice to the generality of the foregoing, regulations under this section may make provision in relation to—

(a) applications for supply certificates and licences and the procedure for and in relation to such applications,

(b) appeals under this Act to the Appeal Board and the procedure for and in relation to such appeals, and

(c) the Register of Certificated Video Works, the Register of Prohibited Video Works, the Register of Video Recording Wholesale Licences and the Register of Video Recording Retail Licences.

(2) Regulations under this Act may make different provisions for different kinds of video works and licences and for different circumstances.

Laying of regulations before Houses of Oireachtas

32.—Every regulation made under this Act (other than section 4) shall be laid before each House of the Oireachtas as soon as may be after it is made and, if a resolution annulling the regulation is passed by either such House within the next 21 days on which that House has sat after the regulation is laid before it, the regulation shall be annulled accordingly, but without prejudice to the validity of anything previously done thereunder.

Fees

33.—(1) Fees received by the Official Censor under this Act shall be paid into or disposed of for the benefit of the Exchequer in such manner as the Minister for Finance directs.

(2) The total amount of the fees charged annually under this Act shall, as nearly as may be, taking one year with another, be equal to the total expenditure incurred annually in the administration of this Act.

(3) The Public Offices Fees Act, 1879, shall not apply to any fees charged under this Act.

Expenses of Minister

34.—The expenses incurred by the Minister in the administration of this Act shall, to such extent as may be sanctioned by the Minister for Finance, be paid out of moneys provided by the Oireachtas.

Short title and commencement

35.—(1) This Act may be cited as the Video Recordings Act, 1989.

(2) This Act (other than sections 29 and 30) shall come into operation on such day or days as may be fixed therefor by order or orders of the Minister either generally or with reference to any particular purpose or provision and different days may be so fixed for different purposes and different provisions.

Index